Cardinal Duca d'Yorck Vice-Cancelliere della S.Rom.ª Chiesa, Sotto Decano del Sagro Collegio
Basilica Vaticana &c &c
in Vaticano, e Palazzo Pontificio Presenta, e Dedica
Cavaliere dell' Aula Lateranensi, dal medesimo disegnato ed inciso l'anno 1774.

Saint Peter's

JAMES LEES-MILNE

SAINT PETER'S

The Story of
Saint Peter's Basilica
in Rome

LITTLE, BROWN AND COMPANY
BOSTON

Library of Congress Catalog Card No. 67–16263
First published in the United States of America in 1967 by
Little, Brown and Company
34 Beacon Street, Boston, Massachusetts

This book was designed and produced by
George Rainbird Ltd,
2 Hyde Park Place, London w.2
House Editor: George Speaight
Designer: Anne Petrie
Index: Gladys Beck
Plans: John Flower

The text was phototypeset in 'Monophoto' Apollo by
Oliver Burridge Filmsetting Ltd, Crawley, Sussex, England
The text and colour plates were printed in Italy by
Amilcare Pizzi S.p.A., Milan
The book was bound by
S.A.G.D.O.S., Milan

PRINTED IN ITALY

Nihil obstat
Lionel Swain
S.T.L., L.S.S., Censor

Imprimatur
✠ Patrick Casey, Vic. Gen.
Westminster, 31st October 1966

The *Nihil obstat* and *Imprimatur* are a declaration that a book
or pamphlet is considered to be free from doctrinal or moral error.
It is not implied that those who have granted the
Nihil obstat and *Imprimatur* agree with the contents, opinions
or statements expressed.

Contents

Colour Plates

Preface

My greatest difficulty by far has been deciding what to leave out of this history of nineteen hundred years. Unfortunately a good many prosaic particulars are expected from the chronicler of a single building, even one of such diverse religious symbolism and romantic association as St Peter's, Rome. I found in the process of writing that facts, names and dates simply refused to be ignored. They swarmed around me like a cloud of gnats. The more I swatted them the more persistently they made themselves felt. At last I gave way to them in despair.

So there they remain, an abiding testimony of their victory and my defeat over several years' abortive effort to reduce them to a minimum. In consequence many picturesque incidents which came to light during my prolonged studies, have had to be sacrificed to drier data. I refer to those little kaleidoscopic scenes of the past, which bring constant delight and sometimes edification. There is, for example, that of King Theodoric staggering and sweating under the weight of two massive candelabra, which the engaging Ostrogoth insisted on personally handing to a cool and supercilious pope in old St Peter's. Or that of England's first royal pilgrim to Rome, King Caedwalla, who was so smitten with the city's beauty, that he refused to go home, abdicated, was baptized and ultimately buried in St Peter's in a snow white garment. I see too the horrified English pilgrims recovering pieces of the True Cross strewn in the mud after a Roman riot, and the good Pope St Nicholas I allowing them in reward to take a piece back to England for their king. Then I like to imagine the expression on the face of Pope Eugenius IV when on his return to Rome at the end of the Western Schism he came upon the wolves disinterring and eating corpses in the Vatican graveyard. Or the pleasure on that of Pope Leo X as he watched the Portuguese king's present of a white elephant bend the knee to him three times in the piazza. Or the expression on the faces of the cardinals who were obliged to witness Julius III bestowing the red hat upon the seventeen-year-old keeper of His Holiness's pet ape. I enjoy too dwelling upon the consternation of Pius IV's attendants as they desperately tried to keep pace with the sexagenarian pontiff, who would climb in midsummer, just for fun, to the top of the cupola with the agility of a squirrel.

These and countless other irrelevant incidents I may picture at leisure – now that my book is finished – while you, I like to suppose, will be grappling in the ensuing pages with matters of greater moment to the history of St Peter's, such as the number of pillars used in Constantine's basilica, or the vexed problem whether Michelangelo on his deathbed wanted the contour of his dome to be hemispherical or ovoid.

I am grateful to many friends for invaluable help – in particular, to Mr Geoffrey Houghton Brown for enlightening me on several questions of faith: Father Illtud Evans, O.P., for reading chapters 1 and 2: the late Mgr Guy Ferrari for directing my steps in the Vatican

Library: Mgr Pasquale Macchi of the Segretaria Pontificia for general permission, and Dott. Ing. Comm. Francesco Vacchini (Fattore Generale e Dirigente dell'Ufficio Technico of the Sacra Congregazione della Reverenda Fabbrica di S. Pietro) for indispensable assistance: to Sgr Mario Carrieri for taking such splendid photographs of the basilica: Mr Torgil Magnuson for the loan of his thesis on Roman fifteenth-century architecture: Miss Georgina Masson for numerous introductions in Rome and for her seemingly inexhaustible generosity to a fellow writer: Lord Methuen for allowing me to illustrate the Guido Reni portrait of Pope Paul V in his possession: Mr Peter Partner for putting me in touch with several abstruse works on Vatican history: Canon Ronald Pilkington for information on pontifical ceremonial: Sir Peter Scarlett, until 1965 H.M. Minister to the Holy See, for giving me special facilities in the Vatican City: and the Duke of Wellington for allowing me to look at various rare folios of St Peter's history in his library. Lastly, I am deeply indebted to my wife for her sound criticism and advice, and to Mr George Speaight, Managing Editor of George Rainbird Ltd, for his infinite pains in amending, improving and generally embellishing my text. No one but myself must be held responsible for its sentiments.

J. L-M
Alderley Grange
Wotton-under-Edge
1966

1 Peter Saint and Man

The most vehement anti-Catholic can hardly deny that St Peter's in Rome has become – I purposely emphasize the present tense, *has become* – a church with a unique position in the Christian world. The most fervent Anglican will not pretend that from Canterbury Cathedral, or the most complacent Mormon that from the Tabernacle of Salt Lake City, Utah, stems the immensely complicated genealogy, Catholic, Orthodox, schismatical and heretical, which makes up our strangely diverse Christian family tree. It is true that the Church of the Holy Sepulchre at Jerusalem and the great church at Antioch, both like St Peter's founded by the Emperor Constantine, could have advanced equally strong historical claims. The first was built over the site of Our Lord's burial, the second on the place where the term Christian originated. Yet neither has ever done so. St Peter's, on the other hand, was built more than a millenium and a half ago over what was believed to be the tomb of the first of the apostles, and on this account men have claimed that divine dispensation established it as the centre of the Christian world. Can these claims really be substantiated under the searching light of modern science and scepticism? Or are they preposterous and fraudulent? Are they based upon nothing more than a persistent determination (which for duration of purpose almost seems in itself to be of divine essence) of the oldest dynasty in the world to maintain sovereignty over the feeble will of credulous western humanity? The purpose of this book is to investigate these claims which inspire every stone of St Peter's church. They are the animating thread running through the building's long history. Dissipate them and the church will collapse like a pack of cards into the vastest ruin of misplaced beliefs that ever deluded mankind. Whether the investigation will strengthen or weaken the spiritual fabric of St Peter's is not within the unbiased historian's mandate to suggest. His job is only to record events as truthfully and objectively as his limited powers allow. The reader has the harder task in making up his own mind in the end.

The foundation of the proud and stupendous church is, needless to relate, the modest and uncouth fisherman from Galilee. The apparent incongruity between innovators of great ideals and those ideals' realization usually lies in a startling development from simplicity to complexity. 'Unlearned and ignorant' is the description of St Peter given in the Acts of the Apostles (4:13). Unlearned he certainly was, for his education must have been of the most rudimentary kind. Unlike the Greek- and Latin-speaking St Paul, he only knew – at least until Pentecost – his native Aramaic. He was merely ignorant, I suggest, in the niceties of diplomatic conduct during times of crisis – a failing he succeeded with time in overcoming. For he was naturally slow in understanding and hasty in action. Without pausing to consider whether the deed would help or hinder the cause of his master, he sliced off the ear of the high priest's servant at the moment of Christ's arrest.

The martyrdom of St Peter; detail from the Shrine of Sixtus IV

St Peter holding the roll of the law, a symbol with which he was often associated in early Christian iconography; an early fourth-century fresco

On other occasions he had been equally lacking in judgment and tact. He dared to remonstrate with Jesus for prognosticating his own Passion and was snubbed forthright: 'Get thee behind me Satan . . . for thou savourest not the things that be of God, but those that be of man.'[1] He fell asleep when he should have been keeping watch. He refused to let his master wash his feet. He gave vent to jealousy of favours promised to a fellow apostle, and received another rebuke in the words, 'What is that to thee?' His weaknesses are constantly apparent. Impulsive, demonstrative, he plunged without forethought into the Sea of Tiberias and started walking towards Christ, then, realizing the fearful danger, began to sink. He was easily downcast. The humanity of Peter is unfailing and touching, down to the terrible occasion of the denial of the being whom he worshipped more than life. 'To whom shall we go?' he had pleaded earnestly and piteously, when the other disciples, nonplussed by Jesus's difficult teaching, were drifting away and he was being asked whether he wished to leave as well. 'Thou hast the words of eternal life. And we believe, and are sure that thou art that Christ the son of the living God.'

Everything we know about Peter speaks of his humanity. In the first place he had a wife and, we are credibly informed, a daughter. Petronilla, after whom a catacomb was named, was according to tradition paralysed in youth but cured by her father. We may

[1] Throughout this book I shall take all biblical quotations from King James I's Authorised Version, because it is the most beautiful of the English translations.

Throughout the centuries artists have adopted a traditional style for portraying Peter that may well be based upon an authentic likeness. Perhaps the earliest surviving portrait of Peter; a mid third-century fresco *top left*. The call of Peter and Andrew; a sixth-century mosaic *top right*. Christ washing Peter's feet; a thirteenth-century fresco *bottom left*. Peter in prayer, by El Greco *bottom right*

Christ foretells Peter's denial of him; a relief on a sarcophagus, probably of the third century *above*.
An angel delivers Peter from prison, by Guido Reni *below*

discount the legend that when she announced her betrothal to a Roman patrician the saint, to make certain that her virginity would be preserved inviolate, struck her with a palsy, only curing her when all likelihood of marriage had passed. It is more typical of him that when Cornelius the centurion fell on his knees to worship him Peter put a stop to such nonsense. 'Stand up,' he ordered, 'I myself also am a man.' It is very fitting that the first representative of Christ's Church on earth should be that apostle whose personality is the most sympathetic and the most clearly defined. He is the one of the Twelve about whom we know the most. St Paul, who was not one of the Twelve and had never seen the incarnate Jesus, is equally distinctive. But his is a less endearing personality. Paul, almost by virtue of his sudden conversion, seems a fanatic. He was by nature an intellectual, and by temperament a revolutionary. Reading between the lines of the Acts one deduces that his pragmatical mind was irritated by Peter's irrational, but conservative response to ethical problems. Paul's philosophy outstripped the old Judaic law for which he substituted a burning faith. Peter on the contrary continued to observe, simple pious Jew that he was, the old laws in which he had been brought up. Just as the voice from heaven rebuked him for refusing to eat 'unclean' food when invited to do so in a dream on the roof of the tanner at Joppa – 'What God hath cleansed, that call not thou common' – so Paul upbraided him for acceding to the Christian Jews' demand to dissociate himself from the Gentiles. The sequel to both incidents proves merely that the bewildered fisherman was far more open to persuasion than the dogmatic little tent-maker from Tarsus. He capitulated immediately to the voice and to his friend without demur. 'Of a truth I see that God is no respecter of persons.' In baptizing the Roman Cornelius and in preaching afterwards to the pagans he accepted the astonishingly unconventional view in the eyes of an Israelite that in God's eye all men, whether Gentile or Jew, were equal. At the Jerusalem Council of A.D. 49 he promulgated it in a powerful speech. It is highly doubtful, however, whether he would have formulated such a policy on his own. According to St Paul, God originally intended St Peter to be dedicated to the Jews and himself to the Gentiles. At any rate Peter was always ready to be convinced. His humility was as genuine as his humanity. He made mistakes and his learning came the hard way. He was frequently subjected to the rebukes of his contemporaries as well as of his God. Invariably he accepted them with the grace of a docile child.

Peter's movements after Pentecost are not easily traced. In Galatians 1:18 Paul tells us that three years after his conversion, namely about A.D. 35, he went to Jerusalem in search of Peter, and stayed with him a fortnight. The only other apostle he met was James, the Lord's brother. This provides fairly clear, though not positive, evidence that Peter was at the time leader of the Christians, or head of the Church in Jerusalem. From there he went on occasional missions to Samaria, Joppa and Caesarea. He may have remained in the capital until Herod's persecution and his imprisonment in 42. After his miraculous delivery and escape he possibly fled direct to Antioch, where Paul's rebuke of him took place. That city too claims him as the first bishop of its Church. Corinth likewise makes a similar claim which cannot be substantiated. Henceforward Peter's movements become more than ever uncertain. The weight, if not evidence, of tradition is that he passed to Rome. He may have travelled by way of Pontus on the southern shore of the Black Sea, meeting and making a fast friendship with another tent-maker, Aquila, 'a Jew born in Pontus', whom he converted to the Christian faith. Here the two churches of Amasea and

Sinope claim to have been founded by him. Did he on the way land at Naples, where there is likewise a tradition of his apostolic foundation? Arrived in Rome, he is said to have lodged in the house of his friend Aquila and his wife Priscilla, who had preceded him, presumably on the husband's business. They are supposed to have lived on the Aventine Hill where St Prisca's church now stands. Most of Peter's Roman sojourn is thus speculative.

According to Eusebius (260–c. 340), the first great historian of the Christian Church, and to St Jerome (342–420), Peter arrived in Rome at the beginning of the reign of the Emperor Claudius. Since the former authority attributes his death in Rome to Nero's major pogrom of the Christians and the latter authority ascribes to him an episcopacy there of twenty-five years (a duration of time by which subsequent generations set much store) the date of arrival can be calculated at little later than A.D. 42. These two writers are the first to be absolutely categorical. We do not know of course on what data they based their premises so positively. But there are earlier written implications – not assertions – of Peter's presence in Rome. One is that of the theologian Tertullian who in a dissertation on baptism about the year 198 said: 'there is no difference between those whom John baptized in the Jordan and those whom Peter baptized in the Tiber', a statement which takes the Apostle's ministry in Rome for granted. Going further back still, we find some suggestive passages in the writings of a near contemporary and an exact contemporary. St Ignatius, the old bishop of Antioch, having been condemned to death in 107, was brought by slow stages to Rome for execution. On the way he was allowed to compose an epistle to the brethren in Rome announcing his coming. In the course of it he wrote these words: 'I do not command you as Peter and Paul did; they were apostles, I am only a condemned criminal.' In reading this passage we would be foolish to dismiss altogether Ignatius's implication that both apostles had exercised some very special authority over the Roman brethren. Then the Epistle of St Paul to the Romans, written in A.D. 58, contains an oblique reference to Peter's presence in the capital of the Roman world. Paul was expressing a desire to visit the community one day (in fact he did so three years later). He more or less explained why he had not come to them before. In chapter 15 verse 20 he said: 'Yea, so have I strived to preach the Gospel, not where Christ was named, lest I should build upon another man's foundation.' It seems probable that by the place 'where Christ was named' Paul meant Rome, and by 'another man' Peter.

The crowning implication of all these allusions comes in the famous penultimate verse of St Peter's own Epistle I to the communities of Asia Minor. 'The Church', he writes by way of farewell, 'The Church that is at Babylon, elected together with you, saluteth you, and so doth Marcus my son.' Nowhere in the Epistle, it is true, is the name Rome mentioned. Did however Peter mean Rome by his cryptic use of the word Babylon? The preponderating number of past and contemporary theologians, both Catholic and Protestant, affirm that he did. In early Semitic writings and in Christian apocryphal books the name Babylon is frequently substituted for that of Rome as a sort of chastening memorial, never to be forgotten, of the terrible Jewish sufferings in the Euphrates city at the hands of Nebuchadrezzar. Neither the ancient Babylon in Chaldea nor the military fortress of that name near Cairo can possibly fit the context in Peter's Epistle. It is an interesting commentary that by no early Church writers, not even indeed by Luther nor the sixteenth-century reformers, is any serious objection raised against the claim of Peter to have ministered in Rome. In their detestation of the papacy the reformers never seemed to bother to contradict this tradition.

Peter. The head of a statue in the crypt of St Peter's, formerly in the old basilica; this was added, probably in the thirteenth century, to a classical statue of a Roman philosopher

Peter then may well have governed the embryo church of Christ worshippers in Rome from about A.D. 42 until his death some twenty-five years later. There was most probably a temporary break in the ministry when he found it politic to leave the city. Chapter 18 verse 2 of the Acts mentions how Paul in Corinth met Aquila 'lately come from Italy, with his wife Priscilla (because that Claudius had commanded all Jews to depart from Rome)'. Here we are given the first approximate date assignable in the Acts. Roman historians likewise confirm this expulsion. Tacitus hints that in the year 47 the Emperor Claudius was beginning to murmur in the Senate against 'strange superstitions' in Rome. Suetonius states definitely that in 49 Claudius, angered by the Jews' disturbances at the instigation of one Christ – *impulsore Chresto assidue* were his words, mistakenly supposing the little sect's leader still to be alive – had them expelled. Claudius's action indicated no sympathy towards the Christians, but merely a determination not to brook the dangerous dissensions of a tiresome race of immigrants lest they spread among the other foreigners in the capital. Practising Jews and Christian Jews all had to leave, bag and baggage. Peter must have been among them. Not until 56 were they officially allowed to return. With them, presumably, came back the Christian leader. Where exactly he established the headquarters of the primitive Church in Rome at this date is quite unknown. It may have been in the house of St Prudence on the site of the church of S. Pudenziana. It may have been by the Ostrian cemetery on the Via Nomentana just outside the walls, where tradition has it that he set up his chair; or, less probably, in the catacomb of St Callixtus off the Via Appia, where the remains of the third-century popes repose. Such speculations are quite unavailing, and the question scarcely affects this history.

On the whole, the early Christian community did not fare too badly in Rome until the accession as emperor of a criminal psychopath in the person of Nero. He was handsome, unscrupulous, passionate and brutal, and in the absolute power that he wielded and the evil he caused may be compared with Hitler in our century. Not till the end of his reign however did Nero glut his jaded appetite for cruelty on the Christians. For nine days in July of 64 there had raged the great fire of Rome. Responsibility for this disaster, which was probably an accident, had to be harnessed to some innocent cause. The emperor, in order to divert attention from his extreme unpopularity and also for the ghastly fun of the thing, immediately blamed the Christians. They accordingly became the victims of a systematic persecution. They were submitted to every sort of refined torment in order to amuse the Roman citizens and take their minds off their grievances. The victims were clothed in the skins of wild beasts and torn to pieces by wolves, immersed in tar and turned into torches to illuminate the night, or merely crucified. Tacitus (*Annals* 15:44) records that 'a vast multitude was convicted, not so much of the crime of firing the city, as of hatred against mankind'. This indictment by an objective Roman observer of the Christians' apparent malevolence is interesting. We have to remember that in these early days the Christian community in Rome was composed almost entirely of Jews. Their community was numerous, ever on the increase, rich and powerful. The Jews were feared by the Romans because of their astuteness and courted by the State with an eye to their wealth. They were nevertheless despised for their exclusiveness, their strange and arrogant beliefs, and their apparent self-righteousness. Nor was the ostensible hatred between orthodox Jews and those Jews who had embraced the eccentric doctrines of Christ, at all attractive to the ordinary pagan. No wonder that a generally tolerant man like Tacitus implied that these people were disliked. They were doubtless dislikeable. Their faults at any rate did not merit the terrible retributions that they were made to endure. In the Neronian persecution both Peter and Paul almost certainly met their death.

What documentary evidence is there for this belief, which has become one of the most precious tenets of the Catholic Church? In the first place the only reference in the Gospels to St Peter's death is a forecast by Our Lord himself, recorded by St John (21:18–19) during the late nineties of the first century, that is to say some thirty-five years after the event had happened. 'When thou wast young,' Christ is made to say to Peter, 'thou girdedst thyself, and walkedst whither thou wouldest: but when thou shalt be old, thou shalt stretch forth thy hands, and another shall gird thee, and carry thee whither thou wouldest not. This spake he, signifying by what death he should glorify God.' The mysterious metaphor of stretching forth the hands is used by several heathen writers, including Seneca, in the phrase *brachia patibulo explicuerunt*, for the act of crucifixion. In the second place, about the same time as the aged St John was composing his Gospel at Ephesus three other persons were making cursory references to St Peter's martyrdom. They are the authors of The Ascension of Isaiah, and of the Apocalypse, and St Clement in his Epistle to the Corinthians. The Ascension of Isaiah (3 and 4) refers in unmistakable terms to Nero as Beliar the spirit of evil, ruler of the world, murderer of his mother, and persecutor of the Twelve, of whom *one* was delivered into his hands. The Apocalypse (11:7) calls Nero 'the Beast that ascendeth out of the bottomless pit', that made war against the saints after they had 'finished their testimony' and killed them, and then exposed their bodies 'in the street of the great city which spiritually is called Sodom and Egypt'.

Clement is a little less cryptic. He was the third bishop of Rome who had, according to St Irenaeus, actually met some of the apostles and possibly Peter himself. In his first Epistle written from Rome about 96 to the Corinthians and before he can possibly have read St John's Gospel containing Christ's prognostication, he refers (3:12) to the 'martyrdom among us' of Peter and Paul. Was not Clement assuming that his readers knew without need of reminder that the place of martyrdom was Rome where at the time he was inditing these very words?

Moreover St Clement introduces, albeit guardedly, a reason why Peter did not escape death in Nero's pogrom as he had escaped it on previous occasions of peril. It was 'because of unrighteous jealousy' and envy, he declares, that Peter 'had to bear not one or two but many torments' before his execution. Professor Oscar Cullmann in his book *Peter: Disciple, Apostle and Martyr* deduces that the Saint's martyrdom was due to Christian informers, a story so unedifying to the embryo Church that Clement thought fit to draw a discreet veil across it. It was as though the terrible prophecy of the day of reckoning in Matthew (10:21) had come to pass. 'And the brother shall deliver up the brother to death, and the father the child: and the children shall rise up against their parents, and cause them to be put to death.' Tacitus in the *Annals* and St Paul in his Epistle to the Philippians (1:14–15) let fall hints that such betrayals did indeed take place. Even the most stalwart early Christian hearts may have weakened under the ingenious tortures of Nero's henchmen. Racial loyalty alone would not have protected Peter and his followers from betrayal by weaker brethren, though we may be sure he would have accepted any fate as a just return for his own denial in the high priest's palace. Perhaps some orthodox Jews of the Roman colony took the opportunity of ridding themselves of a detested group of backsliders from the law and the prophets.

A leaf of an early fourth-century manuscript of the Acts of Peter *left*. Among the incidents described in this apocryphal work is the Fall of Simon Magus, depicted in the fifteenth-century Shrine of Sixtus IV, formerly in the old basilica and now in the crypt of St Peter's *right*

Lastly, we should not quite overlook what the so-called Acts of Peter has to say about the Apostle's martyrdom. These apocryphal fragments were composed in Greek between A.D. 150 and 200. They are not altogether reliable nor wholly untrustworthy. In addition to the questionable legend of St Peter's treatment of his daughter at the time of her engagement, the story of the Saint's introduction to the magician Simon Magus bears few signs of unmistakable truth. Simon Magus was living in the house of a rich Roman senator. Peter called on him one day but was not admitted. Then he sent a dog which delivered his message while standing on its hind legs. The magician was so impressed by this canine feat that he relented. But very shortly afterwards his presumption brought about a desperate fall. To display his magic, he took to the air in a chariot of fire from the Forum in the presence of Nero and a vast concourse. The emperor was delighted. The populace amazed by the performance straightway started to worship Simon, which was of course just what the magician wanted. But he had not reckoned on the Apostle being present among the spectators. Peter instantly uttered a prayer which brought the magician crashing to the ground. He broke a leg in three places.[1] This fable may be taken with a pinch of salt. The Acts of Peter on the other hand includes the Quo Vadis legend which, although not accepted as part of Catholic dogma, bears the stamp of probability and has ever proved popular. Warned of the imminent danger to his life, Peter fled from Rome. After all, had not Jesus advised, 'When they persecute you in this city flee ye into another' (Matthew 10:23)? On the outskirts of the city of Rome he suddenly appeared before Peter. 'Where are you going, Lord?' he asked breathlessly, to receive the reply, 'I am going to Rome to be crucified a second time.' The Acts then recounts Peter's return, his imprisonment for nine months in the pitch dark and stifling Mamertine dungeon with

[1] Curiously enough Suetonius, Dion and Juvenal all relate that during Nero's reign a magician attempted unsuccessfully to fly in Rome.

St Paul, and at his special request crucifixion upside down because he was unworthy to meet death in the same manner as his master. This request was wholly characteristic of St Peter's instantaneous repentance and ever-recurring humility.

So much for the historical and traditional evidence that St Peter went to Rome, the great capital of the ancient pagan world, and that he met his death there. In the words of Cardinal Newman: 'He who made us has so willed, that in mathematics indeed we should arrive at certitude by rigid demonstration, but in religious enquiry we should arrive at certitude by accumulated probabilities.' The probabilities exist in abundance. It is enough to say that already in the second century it never occurred to any of the several rival Churches of Christendom to contest Rome's claim that Peter was martyred in the city.

The divine primacy of St Peter over all the other apostles including St Paul who was likewise martyred in Rome, traditionally at the same time, and the consequent spiritual succession of this primacy in the person of individual popes, are factors less easily explainable and ones which the non-Catholic world has resolutely refused to countenance. They are on the contrary rigidly maintained by the Catholic Church which will not permit the slightest question of the dogma lest the whole papal constitution should dissolve like a dream. What, apart from faith – and the dogma is an article of faith – is the stuff of which it is composed?

Although nowhere in the New Testament is Peter specifically entitled leader of the apostles he clearly takes the lead on several occasions and is regarded by them as their spokesman. His name is mentioned in the Gospels and Acts 195 times, whereas those of all the rest of the apostles added together occur only 130 times. St John's Gospel alludes to him more than to any of the others and accepts his pre-eminence as a fact. This is a notable and generous acknowledgment when we recall that the author claimed to be

Nero, a classic bust *left*. It was under this emperor that Peter was arrested and imprisoned in Rome; a detail from a fourth-century sarcophogus *right* (see also p. 30)

Jesus's favourite, of whom Peter was apparently jealous. St Matthew's Gospel (10:2) emphatically puts Peter at the head of the list of apostles. 'The first' it calls him. St Luke's (22:31–2) clearly implies his supremacy. It states that Peter was present upon all the critical occasions of Jesus's earthly life and taking a foremost rôle – during the Transfiguration (with James and John), the Last Supper, the Arrest. Even at the empty sepulchre the angel tells the holy women to go and inform the disciples *and* Peter, the only one named, that the risen Lord has gone to Galilee. Mary Magdalene finds Peter and John before daybreak. Both of them run to the sepulchre but the younger man, being faster, gets there first, looks in and sees nothing but the discarded clothes. Nevertheless he waits respectfully for Peter who as a matter of right goes in ahead and confirms that the body of the Lord has vanished. Again, Peter is the first apostle to whom the resurrected Christ reveals himself (I Corinthians 15:4–8). Only then the Lord appears to the remainder of the Twelve, and later still to more than five hundred of the brethren. In spite of Peter's reprehensible human failings his strong personality seems to have set him apart as destined leader ever since the day when, having rashly expostulated with Jesus, he recognized that his passion and crucifixion were to be the atonement for the human race.

Of course the Catholic Church advances a higher claim than these to Peter's primacy. It cites the famous passage in St Matthew (16:13–20) where Jesus asks the disciples whom they think he is, and Peter answers for them: 'Thou art the Christ, the Son of the living

According to tradition, Peter was, at his own request, crucified upside down; a relief on the Shrine of Sixtus IV *left*. Peter was regarded as the leader of the apostles, as represented in this twelfth-century mosaic of the Entry into Jerusalem *bottom left*. Christ spoke of giving him the keys of the kingdom of heaven; from the Shrine of Sixtus IV *bottom right*

God.' On which response Jesus pronounces Peter specially blessed for being the recipient from God of this knowledge. He then proceeds: 'Thou art Peter, and upon this rock I will build my church: and the gates of hell shall not prevail against it. And I will give unto thee the keys of the kingdom of heaven: and whatsoever thou shalt bind on earth, shall be bound in heaven, and whatsoever thou shalt loose on earth shall be loosed in heaven.' The injunction contained in these sentences is pretty specific, at least in regard to Peter's status, if not that of his successors. The story is moreover confirmed in principle by Mark, Luke and John.

There is much significance in the name and meaning of Peter, which, it is necessary to bear in mind, was on this solemn occasion first given to the Saint, hitherto known as Simon Bar-Jona. No one before had ever been called by this name. In the original Aramaic text *kepha* is the identical word for Peter and rock, just as in Greek and Latin *petros* and *petra* are the synonymous terms. Peter the rock is to be the foundation of the Christian Church. To him are given the keys which admit to or exclude from the kingdom of heaven, which kingdom, Christ says at another time, 'is not of this world'. Whomsoever and whatsoever Peter approves or condemns in this world shall be approved or condemned in the next. Can Christ therefore have possibly meant, the Catholic Church argues, that this tremendous authority and power should be granted to one middle-aged man to be exercised solely during his comparatively short mortal life? In the Church's opinion such a limited delegation would have little point or sense. Clearly therefore if Peter was to become the Christ's delegate on earth, Peter must in due course be followed by a succession of others with the same authority until the day of judgment. And so in the eyes of Catholics it has come about. It is upon what she believes to be this divine revelation that the Catholic Church has built the towering fabric of the apostolic succession and the doctrine that the inheritance of St Peter's authority is of divine origin traceable from Pope Paul VI back without a break in the chain to Jesus Christ.

The incident of the rock and the keys is the basic authority for St Peter's primacy. There are others which suggest that Christ vested this fallible but most loveable man with the responsibilities of leadership. Luke recounts (22:32) that after chastising Peter for jealousy he prayed that his faith might not fail, and then exhorted him to strengthen that of his brethren. John relates how the Lord, having three times asked Peter if he loved him, repeated the command 'Feed my sheep'. To no other of the disciples were these express injunctions given. Nor did Jesus ever identify himself with another of the Twelve as he did with Peter, when he instructed him to pay the Temple tax collectors at Capernaum tribute 'for me and thee' (Matthew 17:27).

After the Ascension Peter was the first to address the disciples assembled in a state of bewilderment and muddle. Their master, for whose sake they had neglected their livelihoods in order to carry out his extremely exacting and idealistic commandments, had after a cruel death reappeared for a short while, only to disappear before their very eyes into a cloud. This time it really seemed that he had left them for good. How were they to begin to set up the ministry he had with incredible persuasiveness ordained for them? How were they to interpret the rôle each one of them was to fulfil? Peter without anyone disputing his right to do so first comforted, and then directed them. He organized the election of Mathias in place of Judas whose murky end in the field of Aceldama he described. At the feast of Pentecost, which soon followed, it was Peter again who rose and confronted the multitude assembled to mock the twelve Galileans so suddenly and

The Christ-Helios; a late second-century mosaic in the tomb of the Julii, in the Vatican cemetery (see text p. 69). *Overleaf* The mausoleum of the Caetennii, in the Vatican cemetery (see text p. 68)

strangely blessed with the gift of languages. In a downright manner he explained that they were not drunk, as the people supposed, adding with a touch of humour that anyway it was only nine o'clock in the morning. With great courage he turned the tables on them by accusing them of responsibility for Jesus's death and exhorting them, if they valued their souls, to be baptized without more ado. As a result three thousand were converted that very day. Next we read of the miracles and healings performed by the apostles. It is significant that the first to be invested with these supernatural powers was Peter, who was at pains to explain that they emanated not from himself but from God. The Acts of the Apostles puts his deeds in the forefront down to the Council of Jerusalem, which he opened with the address on the necessity for admitting Gentiles to the Church. Naturally and unassumingly Peter became the acknowledged leader of the earliest Christian community, as St Luke clearly narrates and St Paul confirms. There is absolutely no contradicting this perfectly apparent development.

It is arguable how far St Clement, to judge by his letter of admonishment to the Corinthians of A.D. 95, acknowledged the primacy of St Peter over St Paul when he bracketed them together. The inference is that he did because his letter was very authoritative in tone as though he – the inheritor of Peter's sovereignty – expected his abjurations to be obeyed. These were that the Corinthian Church should compose its differences and amend its morals at once. 'It is shameful, dearly beloved, yes utterly shameful and unworthy of your conduct in Christ, that it should be reported that the very steadfast and ancient Church of the Corinthians, for the sake of one or two persons, makes sedition against its presbyters.' And he concluded: 'For ye will give us great joy and gladness, if ye render obedience unto the things written by us through the Holy Spirit, and root out the unrighteous anger of your jealousy, according to the entreaty which we have made for peace and concord in this letter.' Clement was at the time bishop of Rome in succession, as he full well knew, to Peter after an interlude during which at most two other occupants had held the see. In his Epistle he said that the apostles foresaw 'that there would be strife over the name of the bishop's office and accordingly appointed persons to succeed them after their death'.[1]

By the end of the second century, it was fully believed that Peter's authority had been transmitted through Clement and a line of Roman pontiffs. St Irenaeus (c. 130–200) is the first man categorically to state in writing[2] that Peter had founded the Church and instituted an episcopal succession. He added that the office was after the Apostle's death entrusted to Linus who was succeeded by Anacletus, an Athenian, then by Clement. Linus gets a single mention in St Paul's last letter to Timothy as being one of his companions who sends greetings. According to the *Liber Pontificalis*[3] he was ordained by Peter; and after becoming pope ruled that women must veil themselves on entering a church. Of Anacletus nothing whatever is known.

The story of the Rock has only comparatively lately assumed importance. During the Middle Ages the words of Jesus to Peter were not heeded more than other Gospel passages. They were brought into great prominence at the Reformation by Catholic

[1] Clement Epistle I 19:16–17.

[2] *Adv. Haer.* III 1:2; III 3:1. Previously St Justin, who died in 165, had recognized that Christ revealed his divinity to St Peter.

[3] The *Liber Pontificalis* purports to be the official biographies of the popes from earliest times down to the

Christ between Saints Peter and Paul; a relief from the fourth-century sarcophagus of Giunio Basso, in the crypt of St Peter's

apologists in their compelling need to re-establish absolute papal claims. Even today they are not interpreted by the Protestant Churches as conveying rights of primacy to successors of Peter in the see of Rome. On the contrary Protestant theologians are satisfied that Jesus's words give no hint of a spiritual Petrine dynasty and make no mention whatever of transmittable virtues or powers. Professor Cullmann, a remarkably unbiased Protestant, who fully accepts the Catholic traditions regarding the manner and place of Peter's death, sees no reason for acknowledging Peter's primacy over Paul. He believes moreover that Christ intended not the persons of bishops but the apostolic scriptures to be the historic links between his ministry on earth and the living Church. The professor denies that there are any grounds for supposing Peter to have ruled all Christendom from Rome, which in his day was never regarded as its mainspring. To Protestants Rome is on the contrary the rock of dissension, upon which in the sixteenth century the ship of Christ foundered and split into two distinctive and hitherto irreconcilable halves.

I have already pointed out that the tone of Clement's famous letter to the Corinthians was throughout that of a superior directing his subordinates in a distant part of the Mediterranean. Towards them he nevertheless expressed the solicitude and affection of a father. Nowhere, it is true, does he lay down Rome's superior right positively to interfere with Corinthian church government, but he does imply its right to tender advice. The distinction is important. At the time Rome was the only bishopric in Italy, and Rome was still the capital of the civilized world. When, ten or eleven years after Clement's Epistle, another was sitting on his throne, St Ignatius during his slow journey to martyrdom addressed the Roman Church as 'president of the brotherhood of the faithful'. He made no mention of a bishop or pope, but referred to the elders who occupied the principal ecclesiastical seats in Rome. Rather his theme was that the gospel and the apostolate were the forces constituting the early Church and filling it with the Holy Spirit. He spoke of the stability of the Church of Rome, which in his eyes clearly gave the other Churches guidance as well as example. The fact that the early popes after Clement made themselves so little known was no bad thing. In a sense their obscurity contributed to the strength of the Roman see. They were all, as far as we know, good priests who did not embroil the growing community in controversies political or dynastic. At the same time, they quietly controlled their own immediate flock and evidently exercised an authority over the Churches abroad. Already in the Emperor Hadrian's reign the Roman Church was rich enough to distribute funds to other Churches in need or distress. This it regarded as a duty. By A.D. 150 Hegesippus, a Christian from Syria, compiled a list of the successive bishops of Rome, with their length of office, while vouching that they could all establish their apostolic succession from Peter. Before the end of the second century Irenaeus deliberately stated that the truth as preached by the apostles had descended through the line of the bishops of Rome.

Renaissance (Pius II). It was begun a little after 514 under Pope Hormisdas and continued by a nameless Vatican clerk *c.* 530. Information about the immediate successors of St Peter was taken from the Liberian Catalogue which was compiled in 354 and has little historical significance. Throughout the Middle Ages the *Liber Pontificalis*, kept entered fairly regularly, was considered an unimpeachable authority. In fact up to the seventh century the entries are often partisan, naively devout and over-credulous. Thereafter the book is reliable. It is always useful.

After his resurrection, Christ commanded Peter to 'feed my sheep'; a detail from the cartoon for the Vatican tapestries by Raphael

It is hardly surprising to find in 340 Pope Julius I making the earliest written affirmation of Rome's supremacy over all other Churches. In a letter to the Eastern bishops in
defence of St Athanasius and his stand against Arianism he claimed the right to judge even
the bishops of Antioch and Alexandria. 'Men write first to us,' the pope declared, 'and
it is here that justice is dispensed.' It is remarkable how the four great Eastern Churches
never had the will or the wish to dispute Rome's superior claims. The see of Antioch,
reputedly founded by St Peter, had consistently been contested by rival claimants and
its line vitiated by heretical bishops. Alexandria, which by the time of Julius I ranked
immediately after Rome as the second patriarchal see, was then a seat of Arianism.
Constantinople, because only newly founded on the site of the Greek Byzantium where
certainly there had been a Christian community since the second century, could advance
no pretensions. Lastly Jerusalem, which of the four cities boasted the greatest antiquity
in that it was the scene of Christ's ministry, crucifixion and resurrection, the disciples'
first teaching, and so was the virtual nursery of Christianity, yet put forward no right
to pre-eminence. That the heresies which flourished like weeds in the fourth century
were eradicated one by one or rendered innocuous, was without question owing to
Rome's firmness in denouncing them. By the fifth century the Pope in Rome was invariably consulted by overseas bishops for rulings in matters of faith and policy. He
responded in what are known as decretal letters having the force of law within his
supreme jurisdiction. The first was issued in 385. All bishops throughout Christendom
were ostensibly nominated by the Pope. Leo the Great (440–61) became the first true Pope
in the modern sense because he was the unquestioned supreme head of Christendom. He
raised himself to this dignity through staunchly upholding not only the primacy of Peter
over the other apostles, but that of his successors in Rome over other bishops. By a
process of gradual evolution, the primacy of Rome had become firmly established. For
a thousand years it did not occur to anyone in Christendom to question it.

The Catholic Church interpreted Christ's words as granting a supreme authority upon earth not
only to Peter but to his successors as bishops of Rome, the popes; a twelfth-century sculpture of
Peter carrying the keys as a symbol of his primacy

2 Christianity in the Making

We can be fairly certain that during the lifetime of Jesus Christ none of his disciples committed his sayings or actions to writing. The first person to do so was probably too young to have known him intimately, although as a boy he witnessed the arrest in the Garden of Gethsemane and when the disciples fled followed him, out of curiosity, to the high priest's palace. This boy, who in a tussle with the bystanders lost his linen garment so that he ran away stark naked, was St Mark. He was not one of the Twelve but closely connected with them. His widowed mother Mary was a friend of Jesus and in her house in Jerusalem the Last Supper was held. There too the disciples first assembled after the Ascension and thither St Peter hurried after his release by the angel from prison to find the household at prayer.

The next we hear of Mark is that he was accompanying St Paul and Barnabas on the apostle's first mission to the Gentiles. For some reason or other he parted from them in Pamphylia, and went home to Jerusalem. The desertion, as Paul interpreted it, so vexed him that it brought about a quarrel with Barnabas, who was Mark's cousin and friend. For when a second mission was proposed Barnabas wanted to take Mark with them, but Paul refused to agree and went off in a pique. This happened in the autumn of 49. Paul's resentment must have evaporated because twelve years afterwards he wrote about a complete reconciliation while warmly praising Mark's cooperation. But it is Mark's closer association with St Peter at a later stage which brings him into the very limelight of history. He became at some unknown date the Apostle's indispensable companion and confidential secretary until the terrible martyrdom under Nero. The Acts relates that Peter stayed with Mark in Jerusalem. In the only authentic writing of Peter, namely the first Epistle, he refers to him as 'Marcus my son'. Clearly the older man was devoted to and dependent upon the younger. The earliest Christian writers confirm it. Eusebius in his great *Ecclesiastical History* relates that Papias, bishop of Hierapolis, (c. 60–130) recorded in some fragmentary jottings – now lost – anecdotes of persons who had known Jesus. Papias was, Eusebius states, although learned, a man of limited intelligence. Nevertheless he was probably accurate enough in transcribing testimonies. Papias's story was that a certain elder of the Church once told him that Mark wrote exactly what Peter remembered the Lord did and said, but not in any orderly fashion. Mark assured the elder that, although he had not known Jesus, he made no mistakes in recording Peter's quotations; and that since Peter's native tongue was Aramaic he, Mark, was his Greek interpreter. Later authorities, namely Irenaeus, Tertullian and Clement of Alexandria, repeat Papias's testimony in only slightly different words. The last adds that Peter even commended what Mark had written and approved that it should be read in the churches.

One and all of these men are agreed that Mark was St Peter's 'interpreter'. Peter may

The Gospel of St Mark is generally believed to have been based by Mark upon Peter's preaching in Rome; an eleventh-century south Italian ivory

have acquired with the years a rudimentary understanding of the official and liturgical language in Rome which in his day was Greek: but not enough to speak or write fluently. He was almost certainly ignorant of Latin. Mark then will have been, as well as Peter's scribe in the official Greek tongue, his interpreter into the language of the people which was Latin. Since Peter was essentially the people's pastor, a simple working man like themselves whom they both understood and respected, Mark's services must have been indispensable.

There is every reason for assuming that St Mark's Gospel was compiled in Rome for the benefit of the Roman Church about the year 65, or shortly afterwards. It was written in Greek but abounds in Latinisms. It is discursive and frequently lacks sequence, as though the author merely jotted down the material as it fell from the old fisherman's lips, or recurred to him later, without really bothering to assemble it properly. In fact St Mark's Gospel is without literary style. Whether Clement of Alexandria had any grounds for asserting that the Apostle lived to approve Mark's writing is more doubtful. Modern scholars incline to the opinion that immediately after Peter's martyrdom the conscientious secretary decided to put on paper his recollections of the Apostle's words while they were still fresh in his memory. It is quite possible that he had notified Peter of his intention to do this and received his blessing on the enterprise, even his approval of the book being made known to the faithful after his death. At all events, Mark's Gospel bears the stamp of St Peter's bluff and straightforward character. It is not a work of literature and, as Mark's friend confided to Papias, the events contained in it are strung together haphazardly. Matthew's and Luke's Gospels are by comparison far more polished, so as to be at times over refined. For example, where Mark writes 'Master' as the term in which Christ was sometimes addressed, the other two evangelists substitute the word 'Lord' as being in their eyes more reverent and fitting. Mark's vivid narrative is that of a person who might easily have participated in it. We know that Mark had not done so but that the principal figure in his Gospel played a prominent part throughout. Furthermore, and this is an important point, Mark's is the one Gospel which contains most of the disparaging stories about St Peter, stories which we may be sure the Apostle insisted must be included, but which any other contemporary Christian chronicler would have omitted out of respect for his subject.

In addition to St Mark's Gospel, there is that first Epistle of St Peter which claims to come directly from the Apostle's own pen, or, to be more accurate, mouth.[1] Modern scholars accept Epistle I as written either by Peter himself, or by a close disciple immediately after his death, in order to encourage Gentile converts in Asia Minor. If it were not to the Apostle's actual dictation, then it may surely have been compiled from his own words by St Mark, who is so affectionately mentioned at the end. It does not vouchsafe a great deal of biographical material, apart from the famous reference to Babylon. It is very allegorical in its mention of stones and shepherds and somewhat repetitive of Gospel injunctions. Epistle II is generally regarded as a posthumous exercise of the mid-second century and is accordingly pretty valueless as history.

You may think it is all very fine to refer, as I have been glibly doing, to the Gospels, the Acts of the Apostles and the First Epistle of Peter as furnishing the basic life story of the Saint. For where, you will pertinently ask at this stage, are the original manuscripts of

[1] Peter's Epistle I is accepted among the Muratorian fragments (second century) as part of the New Testament.

Mosaics from the old basilica. A swan, symbol of purity and love, pecks at a pineapple, symbol of the works of justice; from the Constantinian apse, fourth-century restored *c.* 1200 *top.* Peter preaching to the Romans; from the oratory of St John VII, *c.* 700 *bottom* (see text p. 95)

these works? Can they be produced as evidence that these sacred writings are in fact genuine history? The answer to your questions must unfortunately be a succinct – no. The original manuscripts do not exist. No one knows what has happened to them, and the genuineness of all the writings which make up the Old and New Testaments must either be rejected out of hand, or accepted on the claims and evidence which the theologians and scholars advance. After all, because no manuscripts of Shakespeare's plays and poems survive, it does not mean that they were not composed by an Englishman in the late Elizabethan and early Jacobean age; nor, which is more important still, that they do not constitute the greatest poetry of the world. The early folios declare these obvious truths in Shakespeare's case. The same argument may hold good for the authenticity of the inspired writings that comprise the Testaments. The earliest complete Testament manuscript to survive is probably the so-called Codex Sinaiticus (now in the British Museum) which dates from the end of the fourth century. It is written in Greek uncials, a cursive form of majuscule script, on vellum made from stretched sheepskin, four columns to a page, in quires of eight leaves. Several hands or scribes took part in this beautifully clear and easily readable Codex. The complete Codex Vaticanus, written on antelopes' skin in three columns dates likewise from the fourth century. The original New Testament manuscripts (which do not exist) will have been written on papyrus sheets, like the Dead Sea scrolls, and subsequently bound together. In 1935 a minute fragment of such a manuscript, not indeed original but dating from about A.D. 130 and containing a passage from St John's Gospel chapter 18, was found in an Egyptian tomb. It is now in the John Rylands Library in Manchester.[1]

The approximate hundred years after the death of St Peter and the majority of Christ's disciples are admittedly a dark period in our knowledge of Christian history. During this period Christianity was gradually evolving. The oral traditions of Christ and the first generation of disciples were being kept alive and handed down by pious admirers, some reliable and others unreliable. Piety is not necessarily dissociated from well-intentioned fraud, and access of zeal will too often strain and bend the rod of reason into uncouth and awkward shapes to attract and convert the credulous. That a few oral traditions had become misleading by the second century needs no emphasizing. We may take one example which, incidentally, did little harm to anyone. It was universally believed by the faithful that Judas Iscariot after the Betrayal grew so inordinately fat that he could not possibly pass along a road. His eyes completely disappeared into mountains of rolling flesh. And after his death the stench from his remains poisoned the locality so that no one could approach it for years to come without dropping down dead, and no vegetation would grow upon it. Towards the latter half of the second century, however, oral tradition began to give way to the written word. With the advent of the Early Church Fathers like St Irenaeus, Tertullian and others, to whom I have already referred in chapter 1, all that constitutes the New Testament of today, and the anonymous Apocryphas besides, had been written down and codified.

By now there could scarcely be a person alive who had spoken with, far less known, any of Christ's Twelve or even the disciples of Peter and Paul. The last was probably the

---

[1] Both the Codex Sinaiticus and the Codex Vaticanus are in Greek. The Vulgate is the Latin translation of the Testaments by St Jerome done at the end of the fourth century. The Greek language was used for church liturgy throughout the first and second centuries. During the third century the Mass as we know it – or rather I should say as we knew it until 1965 – was emerging.

Peter; mosaic by Melozzo da Forli, c. 1480, from the choir of Sixtus IV in the old basilica. The surviving mosaics from the Constantinian basilica are now preserved in the crypt of St Peter's

sainted Polycarp martyred in extreme old age in A.D. 155. He had actually been a pupil of St John. His Epistle to the Philippians, in which he quotes John, is accordingly a very valuable corroboration of the authenticity of the fourth Gospel. His death marks the end of an era. Thereafter, oral tradition could not be accepted without question, and new legends must be investigated with deep suspicion. The Fathers of the Church were evidently aware of this fact because by the beginning of the third century nearly all the books in our present day New Testament were accepted by general consent of the various Churches throughout Christendom. Those books thought to be spurious, or in any way casting doubts upon the divinity of Christ, such as the Essene Apocalypses, had been discarded one by one. In the Codex Sinaiticus every book of our New Testament is included, with the addition of the Epistle of Barnabas and part of the Shepherd of Hermas. By the end of the fourth century these two were eliminated. In other words, a series of episcopal pronouncements confirmed what amounted to a gradual and cautious selection over the years. The scriptural canon was not therefore the result of an arbitrary decision made at one particular date by an individual bishop or even council. It was the fruit of several generations of church theologians and scholars acting with good sense and discernment.

Before we move away from the gestatory stage of Christianity, that is to say during St Peter's lifetime and the hundred years after his martyrdom, we may as well take a quick glance at the earliest Christians. It is questionable whether St Paul when he first came to Rome in A.D. 59 found anything like an organized Church there. The believers in the crucified Christ formed a fairly scattered community. They met regularly in the houses of well-to-do Roman citizens who had embraced the newly founded faith, where they performed their exclusive rites. These were in fact of the simplest nature. Peter in his lifetime would take the chair with the chief elders grouped around him in a semi-circle facing the congregation. A pious dissertation would be followed by discussion; sometimes passages from the Hebrew Testament were read. A common meal, the *agape*, would be eaten, at the end of which the Eucharist was celebrated reverently in memory of the Last Supper. Recent converts would be admitted by baptism with water. The service invariably ended with the holy kiss of peace.

No doubt for reasons of safety the meeting places varied. It was not in these very early days in the brethren's interest to attract the State's attention to their activities. As it happened, the Christians soon came to be regarded as a semi-political sect of the suspicious Jewish minority. They were revolutionaries who boasted that they owed their first allegiance not to the Emperor but to a mysterious leader – was he still alive or recently dead? At all events he was a criminal – exalted by them as the conqueror over sin and death and their rightful sovereign, a man who was about to return and claim his kingdom. Whatever that precisely meant it suggested sedition. As we have seen, Claudius had already expelled all Jews, including the Christians, from Rome in 49. By the date of Paul's visit to the city they had only been back again some three years. It behoved them therefore to behave with the utmost circumspection if they wished to avoid trouble. The truth is they did not always wish to avoid it.

It would be patently absurd and unjust to blame the early Christians for the revolting persecution under Nero which brought about the death of thousands of their number including Peter and Paul. Nevertheless there is no doubt that by their provocative

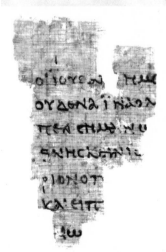

New Testament manuscripts. The opening of the First Epistle of St Peter, from the Codex Vaticanus, fourth century *left*. A passage from the Gospel of St Mark, chapter 14, containing the account of Peter's denial; from the Codex Sinaiticus, fourth century *top right*. The earliest known New Testament manuscript; a fragment of the Gospel of St John, second century *bottom right*

The offering of sacrifices to the pagan gods was regarded by the Romans as a civic duty *left*. It was the refusal of the Christians to make these sacrifices that led to their religion being proscribed by Trajan *right*

pietism they often attracted if they did not actually invite punishment upon themselves. The writings of Tacitus and Pliny show that the Jews and Christians, whom they confuse, were not understood by the educated Romans; nor did they set out to be. We should try to understand how this minority group of people appeared to the Romans of the second century after Christ. Tacitus complained that they were not content to ignore the pagan gods and goddesses. They positively and loudly reviled them and declined to sacrifice to them. As a result they were dubbed atheists by the Romans to whom the ritual exacted by their gods implied a recognition of the structure of society and State. Unlike Christian ritual, which is an expression of religious doctrine, theirs meant the observance of civil laws and customs. To refuse to perform ceremonial rites was therefore in Roman eyes extremely wrong and shocking. The strictest Jews and, of course, the Christians did resolutely refuse to make even token sacrifice to the gods. What was most galling about their refusal was their implicit denial of the Emperor's divinity notwithstanding the Christians' recognition of the Master's injunction to render unto Caesar the things that were Caesar's. Withholding this recognition was tantamount to treason. The uncompromising monotheism of the brethren caused them to be particularly suspect. It led to Christianity being made a proscribed religion by Trajan, so greatly did the emperor dread the existence of secret societies. The mere confession of Christianity henceforth became a capital offence for which, in fairness to this emperor, the punishment was only imposed upon suspected persons in times of national crisis. Often such occasions were deliberately incited by the vengeful orthodox Jews, who informed upon the Christians to the governors of cities.

Again, Jews insisted upon the practice of circumcision which to decent-minded Romans seemed a very revolting and barbaric operation. Their repeated daily washings too were considered ostentatious and offensive. Their acceptance of certain meats and rejection of others as unclean was deemed ridiculous. The Christians called themselves *Hagioi* or *Eklektoi*, the holy ones or the elect, which was considered presumptuous. In one way and another they created the very worst impression. Moreover, in spite of their supererogatory claims to virtue, their rites were thought to be obscene. At their meals, called by them love feasts, which were in fact perfectly innocuous, they were believed to murder and feast upon new born infants; afterwards, it was said, they extinguished the lights and indulged in promiscuous sexual intercourse under the pretence of holiness. The Romans were not squeamish about lust, whether hetero- or homo-sexual, but they liked it to be above board. The somewhat prudish Christians, instead of laughing at these accusations, pursed their lips, refused in a superior manner to contradict them and appeared more mysterious than ever. In short, they made it apparent that they welcomed persecution because it thereby opened to them the gateway to eternal bliss hereafter. No wonder then that the Romans who were cynics willingly helped them to enter it.

Had the Romans only known, the Christians far from enjoying indiscriminate sexual licence were inclined to cultivate celibacy to extravagant lengths. Some of them even tended to regard the body as irredeemably evil. A group, the Encratites, prohibited all sexual intercourse even in marriage. By the second century this unnatural doctrine became so popular among the overzealous that the Church, faced with the total extinction of the faithful, pronounced Encratitism to be a heresy. Few married Christians in fact went to such extreme lengths of abstention. Yet, according to Justin Martyr, many pious Christians who in youth took the oath of chastity observed it throughout life and in consequence were not deflected from a dedicated service to the things of the spirit. On the whole, the Christian sect was composed of virtuous, charitable men, if perhaps a trifle pietistical. The younger Pliny's well-known letter of A.D. 112 to the Emperor Trajan shows the Christians in the Asian provinces in a more favourable light than that usually viewed by the Romans. As imperial legate to Bithynia he is reporting on their activities. He is perplexed by these people. They are so numerous, he says, in the cities, villages and farms that at one moment he seriously feared lest the pagan temples might become deserted. Those who make themselves a nuisance are brought to trial. If they persist in as many as three confessions of faith they are condemned to death, 'for I am persuaded,' he writes, 'whatever the nature of their opinions may be, a contumacious and inflexible obstinacy certainly deserves correction' – a delicate understatement perhaps when the word 'correction' implies crucifixion. Then Pliny goes on to tell in an objective manner what from his experience were their customs. They would assemble together before sunrise to chant an antiphonal hymn of praise to Christ, as to a divinity. Next they bound themselves by solemn oath not to steal, cheat, commit adultery, nor to break their faith.

They were, he states, on the whole a harmless lot of people, only given to absurd and extravagant superstition. To this letter the emperor replied succinctly that it was not necessary to hunt the Christians out, but if when questioned they confessed, they must be punished. Anonymous delation, however, must not be accepted in any prosecution. That would be a horrid precedent quite foreign to the spirit of the age.

Notwithstanding the stringent measures against them, the Christians were, as Pliny ruefully observed, cropping up all over Asia Minor. Worst of all, they were making converts among the rich patrician families in Rome. There were several influential and virtuous ladies of the capital who shortly after St Peter's death embraced the new faith. At last they had come upon a religion which upheld the decencies of everyday domestic life, for which they looked in vain from paganism. The only pagan religion of the time with any pretension to a moral ethic was Mithraism. It at least acknowledged that the world was the battleground of good with evil, and promised that the champions of the first would be rewarded with a blessed immortality. But this tenet was offset by the revolting taurobolism, or bath of bull's blood, by which means alone purification from guilt and a rebirth into the immaculate life could be arrived at. Furthermore, it excluded women from its privileges, which meant that the Roman matron had to seek spiritual solaces elsewhere. By the middle of the second century, the new Christian faith had infiltrated through all the distant centres of the far-flung empire. The Emperor Hadrian was astute enough to realize that little could now be done to arrest its progress. He there-fore reiterated Trajan's command to Pliny that no malicious accusations against the Christians should be accepted by state officials on pain of severe penalties. His tolerance did not however mean that he was drawn to the new religion and he greatly shocked the Christians by deifying the beautiful and gracious boy, Antinous, after his tragic death from drowning, and by erecting temples to him. By A.D. 180 Christianity was established in Spain, Gaul, Germany, Africa, Egypt and the countries east of the Euphrates, as well as in Italy and Greece. Nevertheless, the unrepealed statutes ordained that self-confessed Christians, whose very name was still a capital charge, had to die.

The fortunes of the early Christian Church depended very largely upon the whims of individual emperors, and these when not prompted by personal vanity were often dictated by political vicissitudes. We have seen how the Jews of Rome, although disliked and despised by the Romans, were for periods courted by the emperors because of their money, and when this was no longer needed or forthcoming were persecuted. The Jews soon learned how and when to ingratiate themselves. For example, soon after the fall of Jerusalem in A.D. 70 when the Temple was burned to the ground and the holy vessels and the seven-branched candlestick were carried in triumph into the Roman Forum by the victorious Titus and his troops, the captive Jews through their superior intelligence and cunning made their services in court circles so necessary that they were soon raised to influential positions. The Christians, who were still identified with the Jewish colony and were indeed mostly of the same race, benefited and suffered to the same degree. Both enjoyed a comparative calm until the ten years (A.D. 85–95) of tyrannous persecution under Domitian, who demanded worship of himself as a divine being. The refusal of the Jews and Christians to comply excited violent resentment and retaliation. Domitian's successor, Trajan, as we have seen, discouraged persecution while making Christianity a proscribed religion. The motives of this wise ruler were purely political. Hadrian and

The Jewish revolt was suppressed under Titus, and the seven-branched candlestick from the Temple carried in triumph through Rome *above*. Under later emperors the fortunes of the Christians varied; they were persecuted under Domitian *below left* but tolerated under Hadrian *below right*

Marcus Aurelius, the philosopher emperor *left*, considered it his duty to suppress Christianity.
Commodus *right*, however, had no interest in religion and left the Christians in peace

Antoninus Pius (138–61), an excellent administrator, were naturally peace-loving and,
in the interests of the empire, averse to persecution. The saintly Polycarp's martyrdom in
distant Smyrna during Antoninus Pius's reign was not a result of the emperor's policy.
The old bishop fell victim to an isolated outburst of paganism. During a jolly carnival, he
was seized by intoxicated revellers and ordered to blaspheme Christ. His spirited retort,
repeated so often by the early Christian martyrs, has echoed down the ages and sounds as
nobly to our ears as it did to those of his faithful brethren in Smyrna in A.D. 155. 'These
eighty-six years I have served him; and he has never done me wrong. He is my king and
my saviour; how can I deny him?'

After many years of peace, the reign of Marcus Aurelius (161–80) saw a resumption of
Christian persecutions. This emperor was a great and religious man and his cruelty
sprang, not for the first or last time in history, from an access of piety. He firmly believed
in the Latin gods who had made the empire the power it was. He sincerely believed that
the Christians practised incest and cannibalism and ought in the moral interest of his
subjects to be exterminated. Wherever their malpractices were brought to his notice, he
set about the quickest way of getting rid of the offenders. Thus he organized at Lyons, to
the intense gratification of pagan sportsmen, a grand hunt of Christians just as though

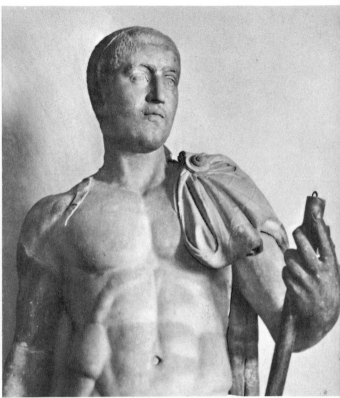

Septimus Severus *left* was unable to comprehend the monotheism of Christianity and forbade conversions. Alexander Severus *right* offered worship to Christ alongside the pagan gods

they were wild boars. Commodus, his successor (180–92), relaxed these persecutions. His reign brought relief to the Christians, not because he sympathized with their creed, but because his inordinate vanity demanded, instead of his subjects' worship, their ardent approval of his person. Indeed, his god-like looks and physical splendour invited unsolicited commendation. He would strut around the military camps with gold dust sprinkled on his hair, and assemble admiring crowds to watch him transfix with a spear ostriches running at full speed. His love of admiration was innocuous and rather endearing.

Septimius Severus (193–211) was of very different metal. A bluff honest soldier of little imagination he acknowledged a multiplicity of gods, and was genuinely puzzled and shocked by the Christians' monotheism. He employed many Christians in his household and was surprised and displeased when his second wife, the beautiful and accomplished Julia Domna, whom he had chosen by horoscope, was attracted by their belief. Septimius forbade Christian conversions and resumed persecution in violent but sporadic measures. A persistent and worse terror was only forestalled by the fearless fulminations of Tertullian, who convinced the bewildered emperor that the more the Christians were harried the more they were strengthened in their faith. On Septimius's death in 211, a

Under Gallienus *left* Christianity was allowed to flourish and many converts were made; but Diocletian *right* launched the last and most bitter of the persecutions against the Christians

long period of peace ensued broken only by the short and savage Decian persecution of 250–1, when Pope Fabian was martyred. It was brought about by the emperor's alarm at the apparently disruptive effect the Christians were having upon the imperial authority, and by his belated attempt to revive the state religion. Alexander Severus who came to the throne in 222 had been eclectic in his tastes. He built a chapel in which to set up the images of Orpheus, Abraham, Apollonius and Christ. To this curiously assorted quaternity he did homage and offered sacrifices. Gallienus (260–8) actually issued an edict of toleration of the Christians and restored to the Church those lands which had been confiscated. During his reign the imperial prestige was at a low ebb and Christian proselytism in full flood. The contingency was shrewdly assessed by one who was to be a near successor to the throne.

With Diocletian everything was changed. This low-born soldier from Dalmatia was the saviour of the Roman Empire after a century of gradual dissolution, and the re-founder of its greatness. He came to the conclusion that so large a territory and so complex a federation of nations could not be governed effectively by one man. So he divided the empire into two parts, appointing himself Augustus of the East with his capital at Nicomedia, and Maximian Augustus of the West, with a Caesar delegating under each. The reorganization led Diocletian to assume during his lifetime semi-divinity, which once more occasioned trouble from his Christian subjects. The emperor would not tolerate within the State the possible menace of an independent community over whose ordinations he had no control. To strengthen the empire he, like Decius, tried to revive the old religion by decreeing that no one was to resist the authority of the pagan gods. 'The old religion', he ruled, 'must not be criticized by a new one. It is a great crime to go back on anything which, having been established by our forefathers, is now in our possession and use.' Accordingly the Christians were soon obliged either to sacrifice to Diocletian, or die. Tens of thousands preferred to meet death rather than compromise with their principles. Eusebius, a contemporary, recorded the loathsome tortures inflicted upon and the heroism displayed by the Christians in this, of all persecutions up to date, the worst and most prolonged. Diocletian was the first emperor systematically to set about razing the Christians' assembly rooms to the ground and destroying their sacred writings. The persecutions were only relaxed when the government sensed that the people were finally sickened by the profitless brutalities and bloodshed.

No wonder that during the worst persecutions early Christian fugitives took to the catacombs, where it was safer to celebrate the rites of their faith than in private houses within the city. The catacombs had not been constructed for this purpose. They were merely cemeteries of the Christians, where, fully in accordance with Roman law, they were obliged to bury their dead beyond the city walls. There was nothing secretive in such burials, but during bad times the almost infinite underground passages provided temporary shelter for Christians under threat of capital punishment. Since the State regarded all cemeteries as sacrosanct, it was unlikely that the authorities would dare to abuse the observance by pursuing a victim beyond the entrance unless he was obviously venturing there for public worship. This was definitely proscribed in the second century. Catacombs provided infinite loopholes. The police had no means of telling what celebrations, apart from burial services, took place inside them. After a few days and nights underground the victim could usually slip away from one of several exits, known only to the constructors of the labyrinths. The greater number of the important Christian catacombs belong to the second and third centuries. With the sack of Rome by Alaric in 410 the custom of underground burial ceased entirely.

   In the catacombs no recognizably Christian inscriptions of a date before the last half of the second century have so far come to light. What there are of this century usually consist of the chalice, fish, and loaf of bread: occasionally of an anchor, and never the cross. By the third century the anchor and a simple cross are common; and the dove and olive branch make an appearance. On the other hand, pagan symbols were commonly adapted and on sarcophaguses, for example, conventional Roman decorations were freely applied. The very early Christians did not beget an art form. They were far too busy defending their newly formulated dogmas and eluding the state police to attend to such matters. They merely took over the motifs of a flourishing artistic era in the greater pagan world around them.

If the periodic persecutions to which the early Christian Church was submitted were in a sense one cause of its strength – kindling in the brethren a heightened faith and inducing often an unwonted charity and virtue – the divisions and heresies which beset it were

The early Christian art of the catacombs. A gallery in the catacomb of Priscilla *left*. Christ in the form of the Good Shepherd *above*; a wall painting in the cemetery of the Giordani; at this period Christ was sometimes depicted as a youthful figure, with the attributes of a Greek god. The sacrifice of Isaac by Abraham *top right*; a wall painting in the catacomb of Calixtus. The three children in the fiery furnace *bottom right*; a wall painting in the catacomb of Priscilla. Both these third-century paintings depict figures as Orantes, in the classic attitude of prayer with arms outstretched

an unmitigated evil. Attack from outside will always rally a community in proud defence of its principles, whereas civil discord invariably brings disintegration within the ranks. The divisions and heresies came early on and have continued ever since. They nearly brought complete disaster to the infant Church in days when it was not firmly rooted. The first two centuries saw the Church assailed from west to east by a succession of usually senseless arguments over matters of purely academic concern. As soon as one was disposed of another arose. It was as though the devil were determined to undermine the central foundation of the Faith. The heresies have consistently proved the Church's most poisonous bane. Yet by some miraculous grace the heritage of traditional Christian theology survived intact until the Reformation; this catastrophe caused the disruption of the Church which has never recovered its universal authority.

We well know from St Paul's writings that even in this saint's lifetime different opinions were upheld by different factions among the elders of the primitive Church. There was the sharp disagreement between Paul and Peter over treatment of the Gentile converts. There was at one moment threat of a rift among the brethren over the question whether the Gentile converts should submit to circumcision. If laceration of the foreskin was considered a disgusting operation by the Romans it was equally repugnant to all orthodox Jews to eat meals with uncircumcised persons. And the common meal was the most sacred rite of the new Christian community. The quick-wittedness and authoritativeness of Paul, who scented far-reaching consequences unless the issue was tackled courageously, put an end to the trouble by instant action. He pronounced circumcision an unnecessary accompaniment of baptism. There were other arguments among the apostles about foods and the observance of fasting on certain days. After the great martyrdoms at Nero's hands, the surviving apostles closed their ranks and reached unanimity. Mark, who had known Peter so intimately, was largely responsible for the improvement in their relations one with another. St Clement in obliquely referring to the tragic result of jealousy in the early Church, bore witness that the disciples had learned their lesson from disunity. He exhorted the Corinthians to take similar heed.

The third century drew to a close in a whirlwind of the most ruthless and extensive persecution of the Christian Church by the State so far experienced, and in a crescendo of disturbing heresies. It is a wonder that the Faith, which had been in existence only two hundred and sixty odd years since the death of its founder and a bare two hundred since that of the last of the Twelve, should have survived the deterrents of unspeakable pogroms from without and the insidious disturbances from within its ranks. On the contrary, it was during the third century, about which we have less factual knowledge than any other, that, tested by reverses and provoked by every sort of intellectual and ethical enquiry, the Faith established itself as something supremely unassailable and perdurable. Much credit for the ultimate triumph, which was to come about in the fourth century, can be given to a succession of remarkable popes in the third. Most of them were truly saintly men, and several were martyrs. This century coincided with the puberty of the Church, which survived its growing pains to blossom into adolescence in the next. Whereupon instead of being a harassed minority, victimized by the great Roman Empire it became the guiding principle of that empire. The most momentous change in its whole history was brought about by one man, astonishingly enough himself an emperor, Constantine the Great. In the year 306 Constantine, on the death of his father, was pro-

Despite differences of temperament and of emphasis, Peter and Paul are grouped together as the greatest personalities of the early Church; a twelfth-century mosaic of their meeting in Rome

S PAULO ROMIAM ADVENIEN
CUM PAUCIS CHRISTIANIS OCCURRI
AC TRES TABERNAS. QUOS C
GRATIAS AGENS. DEO A

S
PAU
LUS

S
PET
RUS

claimed Augustus by his troops while serving in York in distant Britain. In 312 he succeeded in establishing himself on the throne. The story of his march on Rome is one of the most notable traditions in Christian annals. While crossing the Alps to join issue with Maxentius, the imperial rival standing in his way, Constantine was confronted by a vision of the cross over the midday sun. At the same moment he clearly heard the encouraging words, 'Conquer by this!' The next day he had his standard marked with a monogram, representing the first two Greek letters of Christ's name, *Chi* and *Rho*, the symbol that goes by the name 'labarum'. Thus fortified by the divine will and protected, as he believed, by a miraculous sign, he marched towards the capital. At the famous battle of the Milvian Bridge over the Tiber he destroyed Maxentius, thus becoming undisputed master of Rome and the West.

Constantine was not merely one of the greatest Roman emperors. He was the first to make the core of his greatness the Christian religion. Historians have disagreed over the measure of the man's personal belief in Christianity. Some have found it impossible to impute sincerity to one capable of such un-Christianlike acts as murdering his wife and son and stuffing the mouths of adulterous priests with molten lead. But consistency of virtuous conduct has never been peculiar to Christian rulers in any age since the fourth century. The Romans were an abominably cruel people and Constantine was no exception. On the other hand, it is impossible to suppose that Constantine's favour of Christianity was not inspired by genuine respect and reverence. The tremendous services which he, a born pagan autocrat brought up in the belief that emperors were divinities, gratuitously rendered the Church, are surely good enough indication that he acknowledged, if he did not always follow, the commandments of a sovereign even superior to himself, namely Christ. Of course, in identifying himself with the Christian cause and Church, he benefited politically. He saw in the adoption of the victorious Christian religion the last chance of preserving unity within the tottering empire. But when he sent a letter to his rival, Sapor II King of Persia, urging him to become a Christian he cannot have been impelled by motives of imperial aggrandizement. Nor were there hidden motives in the confession of faith he made shortly before his death: 'I am absolutely persuaded that I owe my whole life, my every breath, and in a word my most secret thoughts to the supreme God.' He is described as by nature not a deeply religious man. True, he was impatient with metaphysical speculation, which he deplored as leading to dissensions. With sparring theologians and churchmen he was dictatorial and brusque. He ruled the bishops with severity in the same way as he drilled his troops. He expected them to submit to his discipline; and they did. Yet this ruthless conqueror and stern administrator, able to cope successfully with armies, governments and clerics, was also a dreamer. He brooded late into the night and tossed sleepless on his bed when other men were at rest, pondering the purposes of human existence. He stood for hours alone on the sea shore wrapt in meditation which none of his attendants dared to interrupt; or strode with a wild look in his eyes upon the open plains wrestling with his soul. He had many uncertainties to resolve and expiations to endure before the final acceptance of Christ's doctrine on his deathbed. Is it possible that such a man, who boasted that the brightest jewel in his diadem was one of the nails used upon Christ's cross, was the materialist and sceptic that he has been called? To be fascinated by the barbed dogmas of the Christian Faith is one thing; to be able to swallow them hook, line and sinker without question is another. Many more mystical persons than the Emperor Constantine have failed to do so after a lifetime's

St Bernard of Clairvaux; a fifteenth-century mosaic intended for the cupola above the altar of St Petronilla, now in the crypt of St Peter's

flirtation with the Church; he managed to overcome his scruples in the end and was baptized.

The Emperor Constantine, though a layman, was, as we are about to see, the re-founder in a sense of a religion only two centuries and a half old. It does not therefore strike me as odd that this serious man, tormented by dubieties and curiously unsure of himself, waited before accepting unreservedly a creed, to the re-drafting of which he himself had so largely contributed.

In whatever way we may care to interpret the effect the vision in the Alps had upon Constantine's soul, whether it meant to him no more than a magical portent to which military commanders are sometimes prone before momentous battles, or the true revelation of Christ's dominion over man, the emperor determined instantly to advance the Christian cause. After the golden victory over Maxentius which confirmed his favour towards the Church, he undertook two courses of action. The first was to bring the persecution of the Christians to an end; the second to overthrow the heresies.

After vesting himself with the imperial purple, Constantine issued from Milan an Edict of Toleration of all religions. In this far-reaching Edict he was joined by his brother-in-law Licinius, then Augustus in the East. It put an immediate stop to the hideous processes against the Christians throughout the whole empire. 'It is one thing', the enlightened emperor wrote, 'to enter voluntarily upon the struggle for immortality, another to compel others to do so from fear of punishment.' The phrase expresses absolute conviction that freedom of belief is an ethical principle, transcending all political expedients. It shows an extraordinary freedom from bigotry hitherto unknown to pagan rulers. It implies an understanding of that charity introduced to the Roman world by Christ's teaching. If only the Church had heeded these words addressed, as they were, to its own enemies! 'No person', the emperor went on, 'shall molest another; everyone shall keep in check the dictates of his heart . . . no one may, through his convictions, do harm to another.' Yet the Church never learned to digest these sentiments, derived as they were from the Sermon on the Mount, and, as soon as Christianity became the established state religion, turned the tables on its persecutors in an unwholesome coercion of dogmas.

Toleration had hardly been proclaimed before the emperor was obliged to adjudicate upon the Church's internal disorders. First he was asked to settle the Donatist controversy then raging among the bishops of North Africa. Donatism proclaimed that the sacraments administered by an unworthy priest were invalid. Constantine pronounced against this heresy. His decision did not exterminate the error, which persisted in an ever weakening degree until the eighth century; but it left the African clergy in no doubts that the Church condemned it. In 325 the emperor summoned the first ecumenical Council at Nicea, ostensibly to combat Arianism, which maintained that God the Son was not of the same substance as the Father. Constantine who had a year previously declared himself to be a Christian, although still not baptized, conducted the proceedings, disposed of Arianism as heresy, laid down twenty canons, instituted a number of reforms, such as the abolition of concubinage among the clergy, made Sunday a public holiday, may have fixed the celebration of Christmas Day on 25th December, and certainly drew up the Creed which takes the name of the city where the Council was held. The essence of the Nicene Creed was to settle once and for all the divinity of the second person of the Trinity. Having affirmed a strict and undeviating orthodoxy this statement of faith thereby established the absolute authority of the Church of Rome. It confirmed Christianity as the official

The Woebegone Madonna; a fresco by Lippo Memmi, 1486, from the old basilica, now in the crypt of St Peter's

The dream of Constantine *top left* and his victory at the Milvian Bridge *bottom left*; from a ninth-century manuscript. A twelfth-century fresco of Constantine and Pope Sylvester I *above*

religion of the empire in the West and, since Constantine had in 324 conquered and deposed Licinius so as to reunite the empire under his single rule, in the East also.

As head of the Emperor's religion, the Bishop of Rome became the first Christian in the first city of the reunited empire. The authority bestowed upon him by the Emperor seemed unassailable. At once the Church ceased to be a small subject community in an overwhelmingly hostile State. It ceased too to be the defender of the individual against that State's oppressive arm. Instead it was soon to associate itself with a totalitarian form of government and to be the intolerant exterminator of pagans. It had reached a stage in its history which demanded a concrete expression of its newly established greatness, its universality and might. Once again the Emperor Constantine by his munificence supplied this need. Already he had after the execution of his second wife, Faustina, in 312 given her palace called the Lateran to Pope Sylvester for a residence. At the instigation of the pope, and in expiation of the murder of Faustina, he caused to be built the two greatest basilicas of Christendom, those of St John Lateran on the Coelian, and St Peter on the Vatican Hill. Of the two, St Peter's Basilica soon became the first in size and magnificence. Clearly there were no doubts in Constantine's mind which of the apostles enjoyed the primacy over all others.

3 Constantine's Basilica

Constantine the Great brought about the triumph of Christianity in making it the religion of the State. The subversive, oppressed, underground creed had been raised out of obscurity to a height of authority of which no third-century pope could have dreamed. What the Faith owes to this extraordinary layman cannot be assessed in terms of ordinary human gratitude. Constantine was a soldier and dictator, a ruthless and ambitious ruler, whose worldly interests played a prominent, but not a predominant part in his determination to advance the banner of Jesus Christ. He was helped and exhorted in the rôle of supreme protagonist of Christianity by Pope Sylvester. The reigns of popes are not usually long. The longest in history has been that of Pius IX, which was thirty-two years. Before his death in 1878, no pope had covered more than twenty-five years, the presumed limit of St Peter's spiritual sovereignty in Rome; and until Pius reached his quarter of a century tradition always maintained that it would never be exceeded. Pope Sylvester did not reach twenty-five years, yet he reigned for twenty-two, which was a record not to be broken before the death in 795 of Adrian I who surpassed it by one year. Very little is known about Sylvester's character or life beyond the legend that he baptized Constantine and cured him of leprosy in the process. He clearly laboured diligently to promote the Faith and encouraged the emperor's pious reinstatement of martyrs' remains and erection of magnificent churches over their tombs. That he was a saintly, disinterested bishop we guess from his achievements. We may surmise that he was also a man of immense tact and diplomacy to have worked in partnership and apparent harmony from 314 until 335 with an autocrat of Constantine's passion, violence and unpredictability.

The munificent emperor founded, in addition to St Peter's and St John's Lateran,[1] the original basilicas of S. Croce in Gerusalemme (in which to deposit the sacred relic of the cross brought to Rome by St Helena his mother), S. Agnese,[2] St Paul and S. Lorenzo, (five of them over the remains of their titular saints and only St John's and S. Croce within the city walls,) the churches of the Nativity at Bethlehem and the Holy Sepulchre in Jerusalem, besides lesser churches outside Rome and in other parts of the ancient world of which no vestiges now remain. No pagan emperor before Constantine had raised so many temples to the old gods within so short a space of years; and it is exceedingly doubtful if before his reign a single Christian assembly room had ever been built speci-

[1] It was originally dedicated to Christ the Saviour, receiving in the sixth century its present title, but known as the Constantinian Basilica. Several times repaired, it fell down in 897. It was totally rebuilt by Pope Sergius III (904–11). St John's Lateran is the Cathedral Church of Rome.
[2] According to Georgina Masson's *The Companion Guide to Rome*, 1965, S. Croce was converted into a basilica any time between 313 and 361, whereas S. Agnese may have been founded by Constantine's daughter Constantia, or even granddaughter of the same name, between 337 and 350.

Constantine erected the greatest of his Roman basilicas over the spot where the body of Peter was believed to lie buried; a fourth-century bust

fically for a Christian congregation. That the Church had owned property in the third century we already know from the fact that the Emperor Gallienus, a tolerant predecessor, restored it after the Decian persecutions. And by property land, and not churches, is meant. There was no church architecture before Constantine's day, even if some private houses were used more or less exclusively for worship, and had been given decoration of a religious character. Architecturally, such places would be indistinguishable from dwellings, for which purpose they had been erected. From the earliest times the houses of rich Christians may have contained small oratories set aside for prayer, and nothing else.[1] With Constantine all was changed. There was no longer any need for the worshippers of Christ to assemble behind closed doors. Christianity was adopted as the state religion and came into the open. Artists appeared whose talents were in sudden demand. The emperor's churches glowed with rich decoration and treasure. An appreciative contemporary[2] describes the 'paints of every colour' of church exteriors, 'reflecting their gold, which the water blends with green reflections in the ornamental pools,' made for ablutions in the courtyards. He rhapsodizes over the interiors and their 'ceilings with gilded beams that make the whole chamber seem like a sunrise. And in the windows glowing stained glass, so that they look like fields studded with gorgeous flowers'.

We shall only be dealing with one of Constantine's basilicas, and that the greatest in the Christian world. In precisely which year St Peter's was begun is not known. Certainly not at the beginning of the emperor's reign. Whereas the endowments for the earlier Lateran basilica came from Italian sources, those for St Peter's were financed by the eastern provinces which only fell to the emperor in 324. The year 322 has been suggested for the foundation date by Toynbee and Perkins.[3] They believe that Constantine may have anticipated the colonial riches which were shortly to come to him. By his death in 337 at least the structure of St Peter's was completed.

The Site

The first questions which present themselves to us are these. Why was the particular site on the Vatican Hill chosen by the emperor for his church? And did a previous building associated with St Peter exist upon it? These questions, which have been examined and thrashed out by many eminent past and present-day scholars with the most scrupulous attention, I shall endeavour to summarize. For a start, let us consider the history of the site in ancient times.

The Mons Vaticanus, or Vatican Hill, derives its name from the worship of Cybele, whose fertility rites associated with her youthful lover Attis were performed here, *ex vaticinatione archigalli* – that is to say in accordance with the prophecies of the goddess' high priest. On this hill of prophecy the annual spring festival was held. A pine tree, the phallic symbol of Attis, was reared outside the temple in preparation for the Day of Blood. The events that took place on this occasion were to commemorate the self-castration of the youth at the instance of Cybele, whose motives were to prevent him marrying another. In Asia Minor, whence the Cybele cult was brought to Rome, Attis was called Papas, or Zeus Papas. By certain ancient writers his myth has been confused with that of Apollo

[1] At Herculaneum, which was destroyed in A.D. 79, a prie-dieu with an incised cross above it has survived.
[2] Prudentius, born 348, Latin poet and hymn writer.
[3] Jocelyn Toynbee and John Ward Perkins, *The Shrine of St Peter*, 1956.

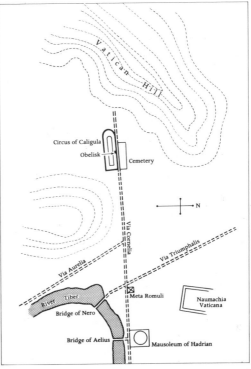

Peter was probably martyred in the Circus originally built by Caligula *left*. It was situated beyond the Tiber with a cemetery nearby; a conjectural sketch map of the Vatican area in the first century A.D. *right*

and, like the great god of perennial youth and beauty, he was supposed to have been slaughtered by a wild boar. But Attis was rather a god of vegetation and propagation, and the spring festival coincided with his death and resurrection. The hill to which the worshippers resorted at the festivals being outside the city walls was indeed until medieval times at the mercy of enemy assaults. This was a cogent reason why the earliest popes preferred not to reside in the Vatican but in the comparative safety of the Lateran Palace. The elder Pliny clearly thought the hill a barren and unattractive spot. He referred to it as *infamis Vaticanis locis*, an area infested with mosquitoes, which in the summer of 69 decimated the troops of Vitellius posted there. Few people lived on it apart from some fabricators of cooking utensils and wine jars. Worse still, the hill produced a horrible wine. 'If you drink Vatican wine', wrote the satirist poet Martial, 'you are drinking poison: if you like vinegar you will like Vatican wine: Vatican wine is perfidious.' From time to time members of the imperial family attempted to improve the soil. Agrippina senior, Nero's grandmother, drained it, digging channels to take the water down the sticky clay slopes, altering the contours and constructing terraced gardens, and even a covered way to the Tiber. When Nero inherited or appropriated the gardens after murdering his mother, Agrippina junior, in A.D. 59 they were flourishing. He built a bridge over the river near where the Santo Spirito hospital now stands. So whenever he wished to dally in his grandmother's pleasances or to disport himself in the circus which

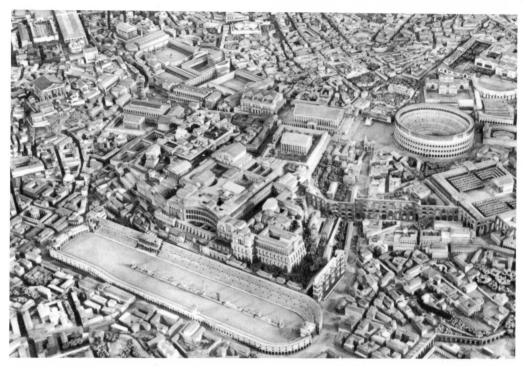

Caligula's Circus was probably similar in shape to the Circus Maximus, shown here (bottom left) in a reconstruction of fourth-century Rome

his predecessor Caligula had made on the lower ground, he could go there at a moment's notice.

The whereabouts of Caligula's Circus was until only a few years ago a puzzle. Most historians were of the opinion that the south wall of Constantine's basilica had been built on the foundations of the northern boundary of the circus. The misapprehension was caused by a belief that the famous Egyptian obelisk, which had been brought from Heliopolis by Caligula, was set up on the central point of the low wall, called the *spina*, dividing lengthwise the new circus around which the emperor raced his chariots; and that, until its re-erection by Pope Sixtus V in the present piazza in 1586 it had never been moved from its original setting. This was on a spot fairly close to the south side of the medieval St Peter's, and midway between the east and west ends. Yet the excavations which Pope Pius XII put in train in 1940 have proved conclusively that Constantine did not build his basilica over the northern boundary of Caligula's Circus. So contemporary historians now suggest that the great needle must have been shifted after Caligula's and before Sixtus's time. But when, and by whom? Did Constantine in discontinuing the use of the circus need the site for some buildings ancillary to his basilica, and finding the obelisk in his way move it closer to his new south wall? This question will be considered when we come to the story of Pope Sixtus V's removal of the obelisk in a later chapter.

At all events Nero made his predecessor's racecourse his favourite playground.

Here on every possible occasion of popular holiday he would take the reins and drive frenziedly round and round, his egregious vanity tickled by the obligatory plaudits of his embarrassed subjects. Here too after the Fire of Rome, in order to distract the minds of the miserable citizens from their plight and the whispered allegations of his reckless responsibility for the disaster, he organized in A.D. 67 spectacles of ineffable carnage and brutality at the expense of the Christians. We may therefore assume, until archaeological or literary evidence to the contrary is forthcoming, that St Peter met his death by crucifixion in the field of blood, Caligula's Circus. Why then did Constantine not select the circus terrain for the foundations of his huge basilica? As the presumed site of the Apostle's martyrdom and as a relatively level space at the foot of the Mons Vaticanus, it offered sentimental as well as physical advantages apparent to the least percipient builder.

On the contrary, Constantine did a very extraordinary thing. He chose to erect the great basilica in honour of the Apostle Peter on the steep slope of the Vatican Hill and right on top of an existing cemetery.[1] We shall come to the difficulties he encountered from geographical causes in due course. First of all, there were distinct legal and moral ones involved in the total destruction of a burial ground in full use. The profanation of a Roman cemetery (*violatio sepulchri*) was in Roman law a criminal offence. Not even the highest officials of the land dared do such a thing without risking prosecution and the direst penalties. And here was the emperor himself razing tombs and sepulchres in order to build over the rubble to which they were reduced. That he could flout public opinion and the law in this flagrant manner is an indication of the height of power the emperor had now attained. The Vatican cemetery was not a very old one. It had developed within a comparatively short period. The large majority of its tombs date from A.D. 125–200. Pope Pius XII's excavators have established that it was not a particularly high-class cemetery. Few persons belonging to the old Roman families were buried in it. Some of the deceased had been freeborn, many not. Most were of Greek-speaking origin. Nearly all came from the lower clerical and administrative grades of the civil service. As the place became a more and more popular burial ground – remember it was outside the city walls – speculators began buying up plots which they resold for the building of family tombs. The process continued on somewhat haphazard lines and showed little advanced planning. Several of the excavated tombs are, in spite of their middle-class ownership, objects of much beauty as well as interest. Those which escaped total pulverization by Constantine lie below the western half of the old basilica where the land slopes steeply away to the south. The emperor left their roofs intact, merely filling the interiors with rubble to make a firm foundation. The rubble has lately been dug away. The tombs below the eastern half of Constantine's church, which unlike the western half was not built over a crypt, were absolutely razed and cannot for reasons of safety to the present fabric be investigated.

The most notable of the surviving tombs are those facing south across a very narrow street. The fronts, which were of course originally above ground, are more finished than the side and back walls, which were thrust into the northern slope. They present a long line of carefully coursed and jointed brick, washed with thin coats of crimson. They have

---

[1] That Constantine's basilica was built over a pagan cemetery was suspected in renaissance times.

The street façade of the mausoleums in the Vatican cemetery *left*. A niche in a mausoleum *right* (see also pp. 28–9)

doorways of travertine and windows and relief panels of terra cotta. The surrounds and lintels of the windows are sharply cut. The perspective reliefs of receding arcades and the figures of quails and other birds are delicately moulded. The street façade is as functional and satisfying as that of a late Georgian London street – which it somewhat resembles only in miniature – where exceedingly plain surfaces are broken by an economy of classical detail in door and window features. The interiors on the other hand are exuberant and aglow with colour and decoration. The barrel-vaulted roofs are either panelled with stucco squares and hexagons, framing little rosettes, or painted with arabesques and figures. The walls which provided for the urns or sarcophagi are pierced with shell-headed niches stuccoed in allegorical reliefs, with recesses in lunettes and simple pigeon-hole boxes. In between are crude divisions framing birds and animals finely painted in tempera. The marble sarcophagi are sculptured. Some bear scenes in relief; others are strigilated (that is to say channelled in the familiar Roman S scrolls), flanking a single maenad, a naked Dionysus, or perhaps a bust of the deceased in relief. The second century saw a gradual supercession of cremation by burial, since the Christians favoured the latter way of disposal of their dead, regarding the former as essentially pagan. In the third-century tombs of the Vatican cemetery more definite proof of Christian burial is supplied by some of the inscriptions. Familiar phrases like *Dormit in pace* are taking the place of the old pagan ejaculations such as 'I am ash, ash is earth, earth is divine; therefore I am not dead', or that moving epitaph to a dead boy: 'I pray that his ashes may become violets and roses, and that the earth, whose child he now is, rest light upon him, as he in life weighed heavy on no man.' Paganism was obsessed by speculations on the hereafter.

There are even earlier hints of Christian burial in the mosaic decorations on vault and

A portrait bust of a woman, from the Vatican cemetery *left*. A graffito, believed to be of St Peter's head, in the tomb of the Valerii *right*

wall of at least one of the Vatican tombs, namely that of the Julii family. These fragments are the oldest Christian mosaics so far discovered. They date from the late second century. On the east wall Jonah is depicted falling feet foremost from board ship into the whale's jaws. A matrix, deprived of the tiny cubes, shows what looks like St Peter casting his net into the sea. On the west wall the Good Shepherd carries a sheep on his shoulders. Again, on the ceiling vault appears the earliest discovered representation of Christ. Surrounded by spreading vines, in three tones of vivid green, the beardless figure wearing a tunic, his cloak flying in the wind, stands driving a chariot of which one wheel and two white horses in scarlet harness are intact. From his head nimbus rays shoot upwards and sideways. In his left hand he carries a globe. The mosaic is known as the Christ-Helios and illustrates the syncretism of Christianity with the pagan sun-worship instituted at the winter solstice by the Emperor Marcus Aurelius at the end of the second century.

Lastly, in the tomb of the Valerii the excavators revealed what they believe to be the head of St Peter drawn in faded red lead, with an inscription, 'Peter, pray Christ Jesus for the holy Christian men buried near your body.' Several experts have claimed that the drawing and inscription date from before the basilica was built. Toynbee and Perkins on the other hand conclude that they were roughly daubed by one of Constantine's workmen at the start of the emperor's building operations. There is no reason to regret the later date. On the contrary, it affords striking corroboration of the motives which were behind the whole gigantic enterprise. The sketch and inscription are important evidence of the emperor's own belief. They go a long way to answer the question raised earlier why Constantine chose the awkward site of an existing cemetery on the slopes of a hill for the foundation of his great basilica. He was convinced that the remains of St Peter lay buried there. And he was determined, no matter what the cost, to raise the most central, sacred part of his basilica right above the Apostle's resting place.

Clearly then Constantine made a distinction between the site of St Peter's martyrdom and that of his burial. If, as all the records suggest, Peter met his death among hundreds, and perhaps thousands of other victims in the circus, it would have been difficult for his disciples, after the carnage was over, to identify the precise spot. Moreover, did it greatly matter? They will have had a delicate enough task secretly gathering together, probably by night, the cherished remains, of which a reverent interment was their chief concern.

Even the manner of the Apostle's death is conjectural. The first written reference to it comes in the Acts of Peter, supposedly compiled by the Gnostic Pseudo-Linus in the second or third century. He stated that the Apostle was crucified 'ad locum qui vocatur Naumachiae iuxta obeliscum Neronis in montem' – in the place called Naumachia [i.e. the artificial lake where sea battles amongst other diversions were staged] close to Nero's obelisk and on the hill. The artificial lake could only have been made on level ground, with the rising stone seats of the circus acting as a bank to the waters. Eusebius writing[1] a little later than the author of the Acts asserted that the crucifixion took place head downwards, and that the body was buried in the Vatican 'field'. Did he mean by 'field' the pagan cemetery nearby? And was this understood to be the case by all Christians in the centuries intervening between the martyrdom and the building of the first basilica? Eusebius evidently thought so, for he went on, ' . . . his memory among the Romans is still more alive than the memory of all those who had lived before him'.

It is true that men born Greeks and even slaves have their tombs in the Vatican cemetery, but before their death they had presumably become Roman citizens, who observed Roman customs and rites. St Paul, who suffered an ignominious death similar to St Peter's, was buried in a pagan cemetery. But unlike Peter he had from birth been a citizen in spite of his Jewish descent. There can be little doubt that during or just after the Neronian pogrom the less attention drawn to Peter's burial the better. The Acts of Peter maintains that the body was placed in the tomb of a senator, named Marcellus, presumably a Christian convert and follower, a kind of Joseph of Aramathea. But it does not state where the tomb was.

Constantine had absolutely no doubts in his mind where the Apostle lay buried. In order to get the centre of the apse of his basilica over what he believed to be the grave he was obliged to cut deeply into the rock of the Vatican Hill which rose in a northerly direction. To extend the level platform to the south, an equally formidable operation had to be undertaken. This was the raising of massive foundations by means of artificial terraces over the descending hillside to a height of thirty-five feet above the bottom of the southern slope. Into the space tons of earth and rock scooped from the northern slope and debris from the desecrated cemetery were shovelled, then packed with concrete and faced with brick and tufa stone.

What exactly the emperor found over the Apostle's grave before he began to build will be discussed shortly, and can in the light of the recent excavations be assessed fairly accurately. What, if anything, he found within it is still open to some conjecture. Let us deal first with the last query. This involves taking into account the claims of another

[1] About A.D. 333.

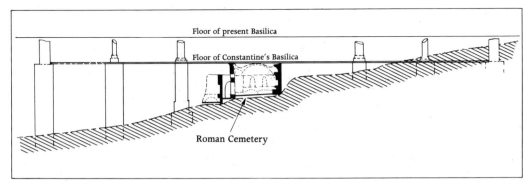

Floor of present Basilica

Floor of Constantine's Basilica

Roman Cemetery

In order to place the centre of the apse of St Peter's exactly over the Apostle's grave it was necessary to dig into the upper part of the Vatican Hill and to raise massive foundations on the lower
part

resting place, or grave of the Apostle Peter. Pope Damasus (366–84) left an inscription in
verse (long ago destroyed) to the effect that Peter and Paul 'once dwelt' on the site now
covered by the Church of St Sebastian, likewise built by Constantine, three miles outside
Rome along the Appian Way. Gregory the Great (590–604) recorded that the two saints'
remains were taken there immediately after their deaths and before their final resting
places were prepared for them. It is not impossible that during the lull that followed the
Neronian persecution Peter's body, after being hidden at St Sebastian's, was transported
to the Vatican cemetery, and Paul's to the Ostian Way. Be this as it may, early documents
and a plethora of tradition claim that for a second time the bodies returned to the catacomb of St Sebastian in the year 258 when the persecutions under Valerian were impending, and that they remained there until Constantine's basilicas were ready to receive
them. I see no reason to dispute the likelihood of these precautions having been taken.
After all, a similar situation arose more than thirteen hundred years later. When Sir
Francis Drake threatened to sack the tomb of St James at Santiago de Compostella, the
archbishop and three clerics hastily removed the body to a safe place. They died and when
the danger lifted no one knew where the body had been hidden. Not until 1879 was it
rediscovered. The St Sebastian tradition is given credence by the discovery under the
church of over two hundred graffiti scratched on plaster by pious pilgrims invoking the
intercession of Peter and Paul. The date of the graffiti is late third century. Why, if the
bodies were not in the locality, should these prayers have been addressed to the saints?

The Shrine

Whether the remains of St Peter were in the tomb on the Vatican Hill when Constantine
began to build, or whether the emperor brought them back again from St Sebastian's we
may never know. We can only be sure that a monument or shrine to Peter of some kind
already existed in the Roman cemetery. Apart from the recent archaeological discoveries,
there is written evidence. First of all, the *Liber Pontificalis* tells us that St Anacletus
(A.D. 79–91), the second pope after Peter, who had ordained him, erected a memorial 'in
the vicinity of the Neronian Circus beside the Vatican', to mark the spot where the
Apostle's remains were buried after his crucifixion; and that Linus, Peter's immediate
successor, had been 'buried there beside Peter's body'. Unfortunately, the *Liber Ponti-*

ficalis is not an invariably trustworthy guide and, as we are about to see, the recent excavations throw doubts upon this early claim. A more revealing quotation is the well-known extract from a letter by a certain Roman priest, named Gaius,[1] written some time between the years 199 and 217. This is what he, an eyewitness, tells his correspondent. 'If you go to the Vatican or to the Ostian Way [where St Paul's outside the Walls is] there you will find the trophies [*tropaia*, for he writes in Greek] of those who founded this church.' Now the meaning of the Greek word *tropaion* is neither place of martyrdom, nor indeed place of burial, but monument, to be exact triumphal monument, in this context signifying the victory of the winged soul over darkness. In early Christian years before the cult of relics and the morbid lamentation over death had become common, the glory rather than the suffering of martyrs was recorded. Shrines were erected over their graves where commemorative celebrations were held from time to time by jubilant – not mourning – friends and admirers. In the same spirit, early Christian art represented Christ by a variety of cheerful symbols, like the fish, loaf of bread and vine, but never depicted him hanging in agony on the cross.

The extract from the letter of the priest Gaius need not be questioned. It affords very important written evidence. The evidence of the *Liber Pontificalis* compiled several centuries later, although probably taken from earlier testimony, is, as I have suggested, less reliable. It is not, however, necessarily a fabrication. Pius XII's excavators incline, on the archaeological data revealed to them, to believe that the name Anacletus, the second pope after Peter, was a mistake made by the scribe of the *Liber Pontificalis* for Anicetus, a pope in office from A.D. 155–66. Tiles discovered by them in a drain close to the site are stamped with the name of the Emperor Marcus Aurelius whose reign coincided with that of Pope Anicetus. In their view, the remains of the shrine, or *tropaion*, which Gaius knew and saw are of the same date as the tiles, that is to say about A.D. 160, only four years after the death of Polycarp, who had been the pupil of St John!

The long and exciting story of the investigations of the Apostle's grave and monument beneath the basilica has been most skilfully and impartially recorded in Professor Jocelyn Toynbee and Mr John Ward Perkins's exciting book, *The Shrine of St Peter and the Vatican Excavations*, 1956. It would be redundant to go over their ground in detail. I will just summarize very briefly indeed what the excavators' discoveries amounted to. They found immediately below the central chord of the apse of Constantine's basilica sufficient remains of an aedicular shrine for a conjectural sketch to be made of what the structure looked like in A.D. 160. Somewhat similar aedicular shrines to this one have been found intact in other Roman cemeteries in Italy. The St Peter's shrine, a fairly straightforward and simple affair, was built against and into a wall of the same date, called by the excavators the Red Wall because it is lined with a red plaster – which runs from south to north. The so-called Red Wall was built in order to form a division in the cemetery between certain tombs on the west and an uncovered space, or court, on the east. The shrine within the court and facing east consisted of two superimposed niches, originally visible above ground. The upper niche was round headed and was contained within a little tabernacle under a pediment. The little tabernacle rested on a projecting ledge like a table – only slightly higher from the ground than an ordinary table would be – supported in its turn by two advanced columns. Under the ledge and in front of the lower niche were found the remains of a carefully fitted, moveable slab. The odd thing

[1] Quoted by Eusebius in *Historia Ecclesiastica*.

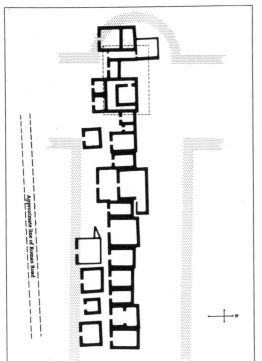
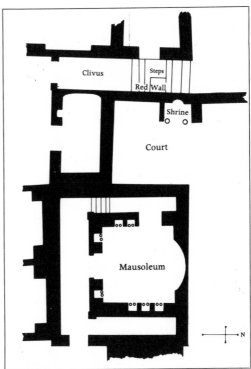

The excavated portion of the Vatican cemetery, with the existing foundations of the old basilica *left*. The area within the dotted line, shown in detail *right*, contained the shrine over Peter's grave

about the slab is that it was not set flush with the shrine and the Red Wall, but asymmetrically at an angle of ten degrees to the north. The irregular setting of the slab at first gave rise to much conjecture until it was found that two very deep graves on either side of the shrine were orientated at precisely the same angle. These graves have been dated from the first century, one of them, again owing to a sealed tile, from Vespasian's reign of A.D. 69–79. The inference to be drawn from the irregularly set slab and the first-century graves parallel to it is that a previous shrine existed on the site of the A.D. 160 one, but flush with the slab. Other graves dating from the next century were found grouped around the foundations of the shrine, not at the same angle but, as it were, radiating from them. A statement in the *Liber Pontificalis* that Linus, the first pope after Peter, who died in 79, and the next eleven popes were buried round the remains of St Peter may then be borne out by these first- and second-century graves. The fact that the graves are inhumation, not cremation, resting places and were all humble ones, compared with the richly decorated tombs in other parts of the cemetery, contributes to the likelihood that Christian bodies reposed in them.[1]

And what did the excavators find directly beneath the second-century shrine? Below

[1] In 1626 when the deep foundations for Bernini's baldacchino were being dug the workmen came upon a number of Christian corpses clad in linen, their heads turned towards a central point beneath the high altar. There is no means now of telling the date of the burials.

the lower niche, under the floor level, and hacked out of the foundations of the Red Wall, a third niche or arch, the purpose of which can only have been to avoid disturbing a grave below it. On the south side of the lowest niche, and below the foundations of the Red Wall were traces of a short projecting wall parallel with the first-century graves and the moveable slab already referred to. Clearly this deep wall had been built to form on the slope of the hillside a revetment to a grave above it. On examination, the grave proved to be shorter than it originally had been. One third, which lay on the west side of the Red Wall, had at the time of the wall's building been filled in. In the recess which the remainder of the grave formed, on the east side of the wall, was found a pile of human bones without a head. Heaped together the bones were obviously not in the position of their original burial, and the area showed distinct signs of subsequent looting and desecration. Scientific tests have certified that the bones are the remains of a person of the male sex, of advanced age and powerful physique. Tradition has always maintained that Peter's head was removed for safety in 846, when the threat of Saracen invasion reached Rome, to the Lateran church, where it still remains. Of the many sacks of Rome by barbarian tribes and Christian potentates, the only one which did not spare the tomb of Peter was the Saracens'. Whereas the Nordic invaders of Rome had all been Christians of a sort, the infidel Saracens alone were in no awe of the Faith's most sacred shrine in the west. Contemporary writers mention that they destroyed the altar over the grave, committing unmentionable wickednesses around it. The excavators are satisfied that they went further than this in smashing and looting what they found within the tomb itself. Toynbee and Perkins sum up their synopsis of the long official report made by Pope Pius's excavators with these words: 'Although it is not certain that the aedicula marks the site of an earlier grave, the hypothesis that it did so explains much that is otherwise obscure; and although there is nothing to prove that this grave was that of St Peter, nothing in the archaeological evidence is inconsistent with such an identification.' To which we may merely add that the second-century builders of the aedicula, or shrine, must have had sounder reasons for putting it where they did than any which we of the twentieth century are likely to discover.

The excavations carried out by a group of highly-trained and skilled archaeologists in most difficult circumstances, chief of which was the abiding threat of danger to the great fabric of the present-day St Peter's above ground, have not then established once and for all, as was so ardently hoped, that the Apostle's body rests beneath the heart of the basilica. On the other hand, they have enabled the experts to draw a picture of what Constantine the Great saw when he decided to raise a vast basilica in Peter's honour on the slopes of the Vatican Hill. After crossing the Tiber by Nero's bridge, the emperor would leave on his right hand the great drum of Hadrian's Mausoleum, (now the Castle of S. Angelo) which dominated the river where it loops sharply to the south. He would then ride, or be driven, along a narrow straight road to where the southern arm of the present colonnade now claws at the entrance of St Peter's Piazza. Ahead of him no sharp cliff of papal palace buildings so familiar to us today, but a steepish slope of poorly cultivated vine terraces. At this spot his road would incline to the west. On his left, on the low ground stretched the oval expanse of Caligula's Circus, punctuated in the centre perhaps by the sharp needle brought from Heliopolis and now gracing the piazza. On his right, reaching to the very edge of the road, the rows of the cemetery tombs, looking like little garden pavilions, spruce and compact and huddled closely together. Dis-

The Pigna fountain, a giant pine-cone of bronze, originally stood in the atrium of the old basilica and now stands in the Pigna Court of the Vatican (see text pp. 90, 232)

mounting, the emperor would walk through an entrance gate up a narrow path paved with rough concrete, the Red Wall of brick coated with washed plaster to his right, and some grandiose family mausoleums to his left. Skirting the Red Wall, he would emerge into the small courtyard by an entrance in either its northern or eastern enclosure. He then found himself in an altogether humbler quarter of the cemetery. Rising above the unpaved earthen floor a few headstones, or twin slabs of stone leaning together in the form of a tent marked the inhumation graves of St Peter's spiritual heirs. Only against the west wall of the court stood the more prominent aedicula, or shrine, which we have already described as open to the skies. This was the object which the emperor sought to make the central feature of the most ambitious church yet projected by a member of the new Christian faith. As he stopped to gaze upon it and then turned to survey the extremely awkward and steep contours of the surrounding land, which sloped to south and east, he must have pondered the immense task confronting him as well as the odium to be incurred in the total destruction of the cemetery crowded with sepulchres and graves of rich and poor alike.

The *Liber Pontificalis* states quite categorically that the emperor's first action was to put the Saint's remains, which he either found below the shrine or brought back from St Sebastian's, in a new coffin of cypress wood; this in turn he enclosed within a sarcophagus of bronze. Over the sarcophagus *fecit crucem ex auro purissimo* – he laid a cross made of purest gold, on which an inscription recorded that it was his and his mother, Helena's, gift. This statement has given rise to what in the light of the excavation discoveries must be a fable, namely that the gold cross was seen in 1594.[1]

The Church

Constantine's next move was the levelling of a great space at least 750 feet long and 400 feet broad to accommodate his projected basilica and atrium. That the emperor regarded the whole enterprise as an act of piety is suggested by the tradition that he carried on his imperial shoulders the first twelve basketfuls of earth for the foundations. Then came the orientation of the church. At St Peter's the setting is the reverse of the later, general custom of having the sanctuary at the east end of the axis. Here the entrance is at the east end and the sanctuary, upon which the body of the church is focussed, at the west. This arrangement, not unusual in Constantinian churches, was to enable the rays of the rising sun to fall on the celebrant as he stood before the high altar facing the congregation at Mass. In fact at the vernal equinox the great doors of the porch and those of the church were thrown open at dawn to allow the first beams to illuminate the Apostle's shrine, while the choir and congregation burst into a paean of thanksgiving. The setting is compatible with Constantine's youthful predilection for sun worship and the Roman Christians' tendency to identify Christ with the god of the rising sun.

Just as many pagan traditions of ritual were adapted to the requirements of the new Faith, so too was pagan architecture largely copied in the building of churches by the early Christians. The plan of Constantine's several churches deliberately followed the conventional plan of the Roman hall of justice, called the Basilica. This law court was habitually rectangular, divided by rows of columns into nave and aisles. At one end,

[1] For particulars of this story see page 225.

The Niche of the Pallia, immediately below the high altar of St Peter's, occupies the area of the niches in the shrine above Peter's grave (see text p. 81)

steps led to a platform within a semi-circular apse, in the middle of which sat the chief judge on an armed chair, or throne, made of marble. On either side of him assistant judges perched on curved benches of marble, or stone. A rail or low screen would separate the judges from the populace in the hall below. Before either end of the arc of the apse, and in the body of the hall, stood a box, called the 'ambo', from which counsel and witnesses could address the court. In the middle of the chord of the apse there was often an altar dedicated to Minerva, goddess of wisdom, to whom sacrifice might be made before the legal proceedings began.

Out of these various conventional features the Christian basilica derived. The chief judge's throne was turned into the bishop's throne. The assistant judges' benches became those of the presbyters. The two 'ambos' the pulpits from which the Gospel and Epistle were read. The altar of Minerva gave way to that of the Christian Lord. In execution the chief difference between old St Peter's and a basilica like that of Maxentius lay in the roofing. Whereas Maxentius's basilica had elaborate coffered vaults carried on stout piers in the classical manner admired and followed by the Renaissance, the Christian basilica was roofed in a simple wooden construction which was to be widely imitated by early church builders in Italy. The effect was less remarkable as architecture but more aspirant spiritually. The open timber roofs of most Gothic churches were filled in by later ages contemptuous of this primitive form of carpentry.[1] S. Sabina on the Aventine

---

[1] S. Apollinare in Classe at Ravenna (sixth century) is possibly the most glorious exception. Its roof has been left untouched.

A column of the shrine above Peter's grave remains in its original position *left*. A conjectural reconstruction of the appearance of the shrine *right*

 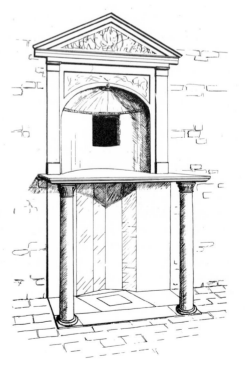

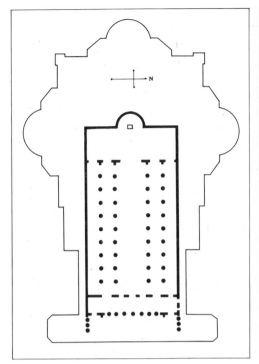

The probable plan of Constantine's basilica, shown in relation to the renaissance church *left*.
One of the original twisted columns that surrounded the shrine of St Peter in the old basilica *right*

Hill, dating from about 425 and owing much to St Peter's model, has a flat boarded ceiling inserted beneath the timbers. This church, of nave and two aisles separated by arcades in place of architrave, is in other respects the perfect example of an early medieval Roman basilica, its ample width savouring of serenity and peace.

When St Peter's Basilica was built, the second-century shrine was not buried beneath an altar. On the contrary, it was purposely allowed to stand above the pavement level, but encased in a lavish, contemporary framework befitting so precious a relic. Everything else formerly around it in the old pagan cemetery had been flattened. It alone was made the focal point to which all eyes in the church were to be turned. We may refer once again to the *Liber Pontificalis* to learn precisely what Constantine did. 'Et exornavit supra,' we read, 'ex columnis purphyreticis et alias columnas vitineas quas de Graecia perduxit.' The little, old-fashioned and rude shrine he enclosed with corner columns, or to be accurate, with pilasters of porphyry. The 'other vine-clad columns', specially brought from Greece, formed part of a new screen across the apse and the canopy over the shrine. This is the earliest reference to six of the strange barley sugar columns of translucent white marble, wreathed with vine tendrils, which still remain in the present St Peter's. Each column, capital, shaft and base is a single block, carved probably around the year 200. Their provenance is not known, and the legend that they came from Solomon's Temple is worth no more than the name of *solomónica*, which they have given

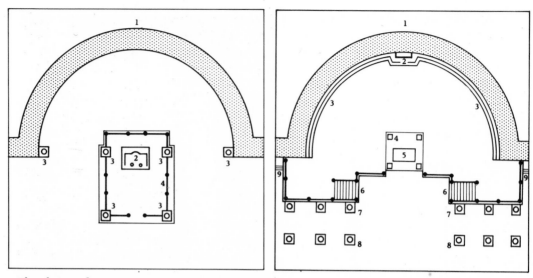

The shrine of St Peter in Constantine's basilica *left*; 1 apse, 2 original shrine encased in marble, 3 twisted columns, 4 low railings. The shrine as reconstructed by Gregory the Great *right*; 1 apse, 2 bishop's throne, 3 bench for presbyters, 4 columns of ciborium, 5 altar over shrine, 6 steps up to raised presbytery, 7 original twisted columns, 8 columns added later by Gregory III, 9 steps down to crypt and confession

to those ubiquitous twisted columns copied on altars and reredoses in innumerable Spanish renaissance churches. Presumably their pagan significance was Dionysiac, which conveniently became translated by the Christians into the vintage of the Lord. For two centuries and a half the Constantinian setting of the shrine survived. A fifth-century ivory casket, unearthed in 1906 at Samagher, bears in relief a faithful outline of what the canopy looked like. Curved ribs from the corners of four of the columns meet in a boss from which is suspended a lamp shaped like a crown, another gift to St Peter's from the emperor. Between each rear column of the canopy and a pair of separate columns placed at the corners of the apse curtains are hanging. Two priests officiate at the shrine while four more with hands upraised in blessing face the congregation from the sides. Shortly before the Constantinian arrangement was altered a certain deacon, called Agiulf, gave a description of the shrine and the strange antics that took place at it. For anyone wishing to pay particular reverence to the Apostle's tomb, the doors, probably at the rear of the shrine, were unlocked and a small window was opened. The pious person thrust his head inside and was sure to be granted whatever he asked for, provided of course that it was meritorious. Then, having weighed a piece of cloth he might have brought with him, he dropped it on the end of a string into the tomb below. After fervently praying, fasting and waiting, he drew up the cloth. If he was a person of worth, the cloth on being weighed again would prove to be appreciably heavier than before on account of the special virtue with which it had become impregnated while in contact with the holy remains. Agiulf spoke of the 'snow-white columns of wondrous elegance, four in number' of the canopy, as did his contemporary Gregory of Tours in almost the same phraseology – *mirae elegantiae, candore niveo*.

About 594, however, Gregory the Great thought fit to raise the presbytery some four and a half feet above the level of the rest of the church. The platform contrived was approached by steps leading to a central throne and benches fitted into the apse. In consequence of this alteration, the shrine was left below the presbytery pavement and must henceforth be looked at through a grill from the lower level. A new canopy with different supports was provided for an altar which was now built over the sunken shrine. The six twisted columns were advanced to form a screen to the sanctuary. By these means, a primitive sort of confession was formed. It was entered from the sides at the base of the platform and gave access to the shrine by a passage running round the apse. Thus was established a precedent to be widely followed in Italy and France in early medieval church building. The first purpose of St Gregory's alterations was to protect from barbarian incursions – alas, he did not forestall that of the Saracens! – the shrine now enriched with the treasure of successive donors. This had been accumulating for over two centuries. Emperors and popes competed with one another in making splendid gifts to the Apostle in earnest of their devotion. Pope Pelagius II, St Gregory's predecessor, had, according to the *Liber Pontificalis*, 'enclosed the body of Blessed Peter, the Apostle, in plates of gilded silver', which will mean that he had started to redecorate the shrine. Gregory's second purpose was to form out of the two upper of the three niches of the shrine – all now submerged below the raised presbytery level – one high and narrow niche to contain the historic pallia. The pallium is a circular band of white material,

Cross section, looking north, of the area below the high altar in the present basilica *left*. This incorporates part of the reconstruction carried out by Gregory the Great *right* (see also p. 76)

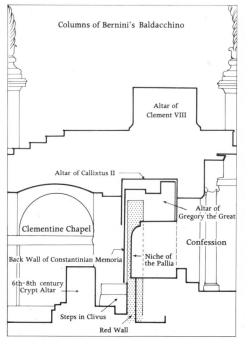

marked with six purple crosses, having pendants on the front and back, to be worn on the shoulders over the chasuble. It is solely the Pope's right to grant the pallium to archbishops in symbolism of the plenitude of the pontifical office. The coveted garment is made from the wool of lambs blessed on St Agnes's Day in the church of S. Agnese fuori le Mura, and before being despatched to each recipient rests for a night in front of St Peter's tomb. In the course of forming the single Niche of the Pallia, the axis of the shrine was shifted some ten to twelve centimetres to the south.

Renovations

I have mentioned that by the date of Constantine's death – A.D. 337 – the architecture of the old St Peter's was fairly complete. We do not know how long or closely the emperor followed the course of the building which he had initiated in a frenzy of enthusiasm. During the later part of his reign he was kept extremely busy establishing his authority in the Eastern Empire and raising the new capital called after him Constantinople. His main interests had undoubtedly veered from the Tiber to the Bosphorus. Nevertheless, from the precious gifts which he continued to bestow upon the Apostle Peter – gilded candelabra ten feet high, silver vessels, chalices encrusted with gems, and a gold paten with finialled lid, its stem inset with emeralds and amethysts – we may suppose that he still looked upon the adornment of the great basilica of the old western capital as a primary duty. St Sylvester, who had been pope when the emperor began to build, predeceased him by only one year. Sylvester shared, as may be supposed, Constantine's enthusiasm and just lived to consecrate St Peter's with much solemnity, granting generous remission for sins committed to all overseas visitors who came to venerate the great mother church of the Christian faith.

No contemporary descriptions in writing, no frescoes nor mosaics survive to give us a full and satisfactory picture of the basilica as built by the Emperor Constantine round the shrine of the Apostle to whom it was designed to bring honour. There is, curiously enough, nothing of consequence in the way of illustrations before the Renaissance began its long toll of destruction. Of the process of this destruction and the rebuilding, numerous frescoes, drawings and sketches bear record. Of the several descriptions given in late medieval times, hardly one agrees with another. This is not altogether surprising because in the twelve to thirteen hundred years of its existence the basilica underwent repeated restoration and alteration. Quite apart from frequent embellishments of detail, wide-scale renewal was from time to time found necessary. For instance, little more than a hundred years after the church was finished, Leo the Great was obliged to repair terrible damage caused by an earthquake. He had to renew large areas of the ceiling and replace quite sixteen of the forty columns of the nave. Honorius I (625–38) had to re-roof the whole building with tiles taken from the Basilica of Maxentius. This pope was incidentally responsible for adorning the principal entrance with silver. His pious benefaction tempted the Saracens in 846 to enter and bring unwonted havoc upon the shrine and tomb. Sergius I (687–701) in the course of restorations came upon a piece of the True Cross hidden in the sacristy and as a thanksgiving presented splendid vessels of gold and silver. To Adrian I (772–95) more than to any other medieval pope the basilica and campanile were indebted for expensive ornament. Gregory IV (827–44) largely rebuilt the atrium. Gregory VI in 1045 had to appeal to Christendom for money to avert total collapse of the fabric; the response was negligible, only one French duke subscribing to the fund. St Leo IX's first act on his accession in 1049 was to put work of restoration in hand, money or no money forthcoming from the European princes. Gregory IX (1227–41) actually had to issue a threat of excommunication against any persons caught treating the walls of the basilica as a quarry. Nicholas III (1277–80) resumed work of restoration, as well as presented to the Treasury magnificent copes of English needlework, then acknowledged to be the finest in the world. John XXII (1316–34) deprived himself of means of subsistence in order to launch repairs which his successor Benedict XII continued until the intervention of the Black Death and the Hundred Years' War. When Urban V (1362–70), urged by Petrarch, was persuaded to return to Rome from Avignon, he found St Peter's in decay and abandonment, the cattle grazing off weeds in the atrium and even wandering up to and nuzzling the altars within the church. On Martin V's reaching Rome in 1420, conditions were such that not a soul could be found to light a lamp before the confession, far less to pay for the oil required. The portico was tumbling into ruins and the Vatican walls, breached in several places, allowed wolves from the Campagna to forage at night time for dead bodies in the Campo Santo. With commendable zeal, Martin rebuilt and repainted the portico, repaired and largely re-roofed the fabric. No wonder then that the building which the renaissance popes decided to do away with barely resembled the one raised by Constantine the Great. The vicissitudes of centuries had altered its appearance in very many particulars.

As regards plan, it had not altered substantially. From the western end of the Borgo, where now the great piazza is, a flight of thirty-five steps led to an ample platform paved with marble before an irregular huddle of buildings. These did not form the front of the basilica, but the entrance to a vast court, or atrium, an early Christian arrangement which may still be seen at the rebuilt basilica of St Paul outside the Walls. To the left lay the square tower-like church of St Apollinaris, its base splaying out like a fortress over the valley; to the right, behind what was to become the balcony reserved for papal benediction, the campanile. The conspicuous tower was the largest in Rome. Emile Mâle[1] was satisfied that it had been built by Stephen III, and given three massive bells, after the coronation of Pepin in 745. It was square with finials at the four corners, and crowned with a dunce cap steeple, partly tiled in laminated gold and silver. In 1574 a small dome was substituted for the steeple. The sixteenth-century drawings are not in agreement whether all the pairs of Gothic openings on each face of the tower were of two lights, or some of three. Since the campanile was struck by lightning and seriously damaged three times during the fourteenth century alone, the openings probably varied in size and shape as they were frequently being renewed.

The thirty-five steps to the atrium were in five flights. They were greatly extended in width by Pope Symmachus (498–514). At their foot, visitors were pestered by the beggars who besieged the steps day and night. All the way up on either side, and even within the entrance to the atrium, were makeshift kiosks and stalls, mostly kept by Jews who did a thriving trade, selling cheap jewelry, rosaries and veronicas (handkerchiefs bearing the impression of Christ's head), figs and salt fish, and acting as quack doctors and dentists. At the top of the steps emperors and royal potentates were received by the

[1] *The Early Churches of Rome*, trs. 1960.

OLD·SAINT·PETERS·ROME.
ABOUT THE YEAR MCCCCL.
RESTORED FROM ANCIENT AUTHORITIES.
BY H.W. BREWER 1891

A conjectural reconstruction of the old basilica as it appeared shortly before its demolition

The earliest known illustration of the old basilica; a fresco map of Rome, 1413. The Castel S. Angelo, the pyramid of the Meta Romuli, and the campanile of St Peter's, with the façades of the atrium and the basilica, are at the bottom right

Pope, and on the level platform Charlemagne, having mounted on his knees, was raised to his feet and embraced by Adrian I. Here too heretical books were burnt with much solemnity, those of Photius, the deposed patriarch of Constantinople, emitting – so it used to be said – a noticeably offensive odour to the intense gratification of the righteous dignitaries present.

The entrance to the atrium was by a two-storeyed portico of three arches. These had great bronze doors which in 1167 were stolen and carried as trophies of war to Viterbo by the German troops of Frederick Barbarossa. On this terrible occasion, the emperor stormed the basilica, desecrated the altars with blood, and left heaps of slain weltering on the nave pavements. Above the portico doors, mosaics were introduced in the

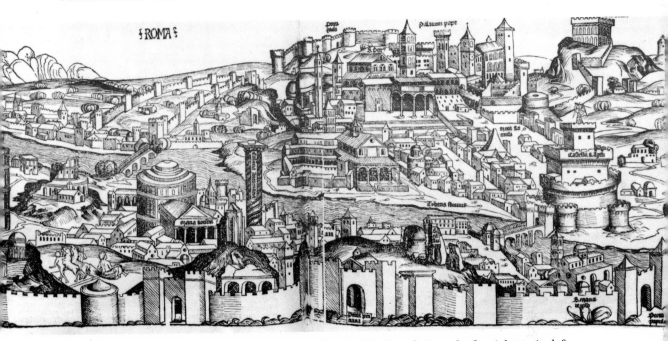

A view of Rome from an engraving of 1493 *top*; the Castel S. Angelo is at the far right, to its left lies the Borgo leading to St Peter's, with the steps to the atrium, the campanile and the basilica. A seventeenth-century engraving *bottom*, showing the entrance to the atrium in its final state

FACCIATA ESTERIORE, E LOGGIA DELLA BENEDITTIONE   DELL' ANTICHA BASILICA VATICANA
Descritta da Carlo Padredio   *Diß. et Intag. da Gio. Batta Falda.*

The inner court of the atrium. Seventeenth-century engravings looking towards the entrance *top* and the basilica *bottom*

The mosaic of the Navicella by Giotto, originally in the atrium, as it now appears in the portico of St Peter's. It is intended to symbolize the Church in the form of a ship

fourteenth century. On the inner wall of the portico facing the atrium was Giotto's famous mosaic, the Navicella. It was saved from the renaissance demolitioners and re-set, in a horribly over-restored condition it is true, within the portico of the present church. This mosaic depicts the tempestuous scene on the Lake of Galilee. St Peter, having left the ship to walk across the waves to Jesus, loses heart. From the sky, allegorical winds are blowing violently through conches. The huge sail billows. The other disciples on board pray, or merely wonder, and a man under a dead tree on dry land, which seems to be a handclasp distance from the tossing vessel, placidly fishes.

The vast atrium, 200 feet long and 180 feet broad, enclosed a level area from a line where the present piazza joins the ellipse of the colonnade to the junction of the first with the second bay of the renaissance nave. As the ground on which the atrium's eastern half, and indeed that on which its entrance and the platform as far as the steps stood, is now again sloping, and was then flat, some idea is given of Constantine's tremendous work of levelling. The atrium was surrounded on four sides by colonnades, called the quadriporticus, which were opened about the year 1500 on the north and south sides to lesser courtyards. The atrium was reserved for the penitents, who were not allowed admission to the church. Originally laid out as a garden decked with flowers and shrubs, it soon acquired the name of Paradise, which lost some significance when Pope Donus I (676–8) scrapped all vegetation and laid down paving instead. In the middle of the garth, where today are the steps in front of the present church, arose two fountains for the ablution of those passers-by privileged to enter the basilica. The one nearer to the entrance, known as the 'cantharus', which is Latin for a large holy water vessel, was according to the *Liber Pontificalis* finished and decorated by Pope Symmachus – 'beautified with marble work and with lambs and crosses and palms in mosaic'. This fifth-century pope did more than any other to finish the works begun by Constantine. Owing to an anti-pope being entrenched in the Lateran for much of his reign he was obliged to live at the Vatican on which he therefore concentrated improvements. Symmachus's cantharus took the form of a square tabernacle with dome of gilt bronze, supported by eight columns of red porphyry.[1] The cornice was adorned with four bronze dolphins to spout rain water from the roof, and four peacocks, symbols of eternity. Behind classical *plutei*, or solid marble panels carved with griffins holding candelabra in their paws, rose the giant pine-cone of bronze. All the bronze ornaments, except the peacocks and pine-cone, were melted down by Paul V in 1614. These last now embellish the great niche of the Belvedere Court of the Vatican Palace. The pine-cone on which the name of its bronze founder is incised was, according to the *Liber Pontificalis*, taken by Pope Symmachus from the summit of Hadrian's Mausoleum but, according to an English traveller to Rome in 1344–5, carried from the pagan monument by the devil on the night in which the Virgin Mary bore Christ into the world. The mosaics with which Pope Symmachus covered the west walls of the quadriporticus were removed in the late thirteenth century. Instead, the space was painted with ten frescoes of scenes in the lives of Saints Peter and Paul, including the Quo Vadis and the Fall of Simon Magus. They in turn were all destroyed by Paul V to make way for the present nave and façade. Fragments of copies taken before their destruction survive. One fresco of Constantine's Dream includes the head and shoulders of Peter and Paul. Against a green ground, Peter under a yellow halo is given the tradi-tional white hair and beard and wears a dark red mantle.

In this delectable court, sheltered on all sides, fragrant with the scent of blossom and aromatic herb, and enlivened by the dripping of water into the central cantharus and the splashing of a plume of spray into the second fountain, devout pilgrims and curious sight-seers would mingle with the wretched penitents before passing into the church. Until the sixth century, an odd custom was observed in the atrium in front of the basilica. Rich senators and members of the upper classes would hold banquets in the open air, at which they patronized the poor. They dispensed charity of all kinds, clothing, food and drink. It was a sort of prolongation of the very early Christian habit of commemorating the dead by pouring libations down a pipe into the coffins. The atrium banquets soon led to the wildest excesses. The fashionable revelled; the *hoi poloi* got drunk. Eventually, the clergy put a stop to this time-honoured procedure as incompatible with the reverence expected within the sacred precincts.

Above the atrium's west colonnade, which formed the portico to the church, loomed two stages of the façade. This was a straightforward affair much modified by Gregory IX (1227–41). He opened two rows of three great round-headed windows, each of three pointed lights. Over them in the tympanum he put a rose window like the all-seeing eye of God. The façade as altered by Gregory is partly shown in the Fire of the Borgo fresco in the Raphael Stanze. Gregory also inserted mosaics to take the place of Leo the Great's Twenty-four Elders offering Gifts to Christ between pairs of Evangelists. The substitute mosaics were of Our Lord enthroned with Peter and Paul on either side – clearly visible

[1] These adjuncts may date from Stephen III's reign (752–7).

Interior views of the old basilica. Looking west, sixteenth century *top left*. Looking east, seventeenth century *top right*. St Paul outside the Walls retained many of the features of old St Peter's; an engraving by Piranesi *bottom*

over the portico in renaissance drawings – and on his left Pope Gregory IX[1] suppliant on his knees. From the portico, under the floor of which more than forty medieval popes were buried (the three other colonnades were reserved for the coffins of emperors and kings), five doorways, silvered by Honorius I, opened into the basilica, the central three to the nave, the end ones to the aisles. The middle nave door was called 'Porta Mediana', 'Regia', or 'Argentea', because of the solid silver plates which, until they were plundered, enriched it. The first on the right, 'Porta Romana', for the use of Romans only. The second on the right, 'Porta Guidonea', because of the guides who conducted the tourists through it. The first on the left, 'Porta Ravenniana', for the use of those living in Trastevere, the west bank of the Tiber; and the second on the left, 'Porta del Giudizio', for the dead – an ominous reminder that enjoyment of the next world would be measured by the relative degree of man's sins in the present.

The unknown English pilgrim of 1344–5 was filled with suitable awe by the time he had crossed the atrium. 'And then,' he said, 'lie open the doors ['sumptuously constructed'] to the church, which is the largest of all churches in the world.' He went on to emphasize its alarming grandeur by remarking that, 'If one loses his companion in that church, he may seek for a whole day, because of its size and because of the multitudes who run from place to place, venerating shrines with kisses and prayers, since there is no altar at which indulgence is not granted.' By contrast, a stranger visiting St Peter's at the time of Pope Sylvester's dedication would not have been the least confused. There was then no likelihood of losing himself. The plan of the building as Constantine left it was very straightforward indeed. It was a perfect rectangle with only an apse at one end to break the uniformity. As the centuries advanced, the basilica became more and more cluttered with chapels, monuments and treasure of all sorts. Until the sixth century there were no side chapels at all. Thereafter, they cropped up literally by dozens, clinging like barnacles to the hull of a submerged man-of-war. At one time, there were over ninety projecting from the aisles or propped haphazard against open wall spaces, the piers, and columns of the nave. When there ceased to be room in the portico in which to bury popes, their corpses were deposited under the floor of the church and monuments raised as close to the remains as the restricted space allowed. Most of these monuments were destroyed with the old basilica. Some were re-erected in the crypt of the new building. Where altars and tombs had not been jammed together, those precious fabrics for which St Peter's was renowned were spread or hung. Rare oriental cloths of purple Tyrian dyes, the gifts of eastern potentates or the spoils of pious crusaders, Turkish and Persian tissues, and English embroideries in gold and silver thread on a ruby red background, dazzled the eye. Glass witchballs, silvered, gilded, or stained a sapphire blue, tinkled against ivory ostrich eggs, symbols of the world's mystery and the source of life, which were threaded on wire attached to chandeliers. And always the dark interior was brightened by the innumerable lamps kept burning before the shrines, and the thirteen hundred and seventy wax candles of Adrian I's great pharos in the shape of crowns and crosses suspended from a central beam on a glittering silver chain.

The size of the building was certainly impressive. The interior was divided by four rows of twenty-two Corinthian columns in each, so as to form a nave and four aisles. The height of the inner rows of columns, which were raised above the nave on five steps, was

[1] The mosaic head of Pope Gregory IX survives in the Cappella Conti at Poli. It is tilted at an angle, and the mouth a little drawn to one side, like the face of a Modigliani.

The dome of St Peter's as seen from the Vatican Gardens (see text p. 215)

from base to architrave nearly thirty feet. Since these columns had been taken from various pagan temples, their size and shape were not exactly uniform. They carried a straight, projecting entablature (on which one could walk, protected by a rail), broken in the middle of the church by two huge arches rising to the roof plate. The first two columns at the entrance to the nave, being of rare black African marble, were eventually spared and re-erected on either side of the central door of the renaissance church. The space immediately over the nave entablature had been decorated by Pope Liberius (352–66) with conjectural medallion portraits of all the popes since Peter. Above them were three tiers of compartments painted, the upper between the windows with patriarchs, prophets and apostles, and the two lower with forty-six scenes from the Old and New Testaments. They were restored for Popes Gregory IV and Formosus (891–6), and again by Giotto. The four aisles were separated by further rows of columns, nineteen to twenty feet high, forming arcades. In all, precisely one hundred columns made the interior into a closely packed forest – but for a wide central clearing – seemingly of great depth and distance. I have said that the roof, like those of all Constantine's churches, was of open timber. One very like it to survive, although subsequently renewed, is that of the Church of the Nativity at Bethlehem. Since the Romans had long ago perfected a form of brick arched vaulting, Constantine's comparatively primitive and economic method can only be explained by his desperate hurry in building so many basilicas. Here rafters laid from one wall plate to another, and clamped in the middle with iron stays, were painted in bright mosaic-like patterns. The floor of the nave was paved in squares and rectangles in two coloured marbles.

The sanctuary and apse were framed through a high arch supported at the end of the nave by two great detached columns of the Ionic order in granite. This very distinctive arrangement, shared only by St Paul's outside the Walls, allowed an uninterrupted view from one end of the church to the other. Over the triumphal arch, Constantine had inscribed in mosaic, in gratitude for the undeniable mercies bestowed upon him, these words:

'Quod duce te mundus surrexit in astra triumphans
Hanc Constantius victor tibi condidit aula(m).'[1]

Surely they are the final acknowledgment of the supreme Christian God by this level-headed ruler who was also an indefatigable seeker after religious truth.

The head of the apse too was long renowned for its beautiful mosaics. Leo the Great (440–61) first decorated it in this medium. But the mosaic which remained until the apse was finally destroyed only dated from the reign of the Conti Pope Innocent III (1198–1216). A fragment was removed to the chapel in the Conti Palace at Poli, and a painting of the whole was hung in the crypt of St Peter's. Christ sits enthroned between St Paul on his right hand and St Peter on his left, both standing. Behind each apostle a palm tree. There are figures of men in small and animals grouped round a fountain gushing at Our Lord's feet. Below, the Lamb of God, Pope Innocent III and a female figure, representing the Church.

And of course there stood conspicuously in the middle of the sanctuary the nucleus

---

[1] Because under your leadership the triumphant universe has reached to the furthest stars, victorious Constantine dedicates this church to you.

The Maderno fountain, reconstructed by Bernini, on the north side of St Peter's piazza (see text p. 232)

The twisted columns around St Peter's shrine had a wide influence upon European art. Detail from Raphael's cartoon of Peter healing the lame man in the Temple *left*. Jean Fouquet's miniature of Herod entering the Temple *right*

and very reason of Constantine's basilica, namely the shrine over St Peter's tomb. This most sacred object by no means escaped alteration throughout the centuries. I have already described how Gregory the Great raised the presbytery floor, built a new canopy over the shrine which he enriched with rare marbles, and formed the first sunk confession. The next pope to make notable changes was Gregory III (731–41). He duplicated the six vine-wreathed, twisted columns by six more, a present from the Exarch of Ravenna, which he placed in front of the others. In this formation the twelve columns stood throughout the Middle Ages, objects of wonder and admiration to pilgrims and artists alike. Their introduction into various fields of art during many different stylistic periods is proof of their extraordinary popular appeal. They gave rise to the Easter candle-

In Stuart England the barley sugar columns were copied in ecclesiastical architecture, as, somewhat vaguely, in the porch of St Mary's, Oxford *left*, and in domestic buildings, as in the fireplace at Ham House *right*

sticks of marble and mosaic fashioned by the Cosmati family in romanesque days. They appeared in Jean Fouquet's illuminations of Pompey and of King Herod entering the Holy of Holies in 'Les Antiquités Judaiques', as a consequence of the artist's visit to Rome in 1443. Raphael introduced them into his cartoon, 'The Healing of the Lame Man', which was reproduced in Flemish and Mortlake tapestries. Rubens and Rembrandt put them in the background of their pictures. Spain copied them upon countless gilded reredoses and tombs. England upon the Jacobean porch of St Mary's church at Oxford, and a Charles II fireplace in Ham House. In most European countries baroque architects of the seventeenth and eighteenth centuries seemed never to weary of reinterpreting a theme first invented by some unknown Greek carver of the third century after Christ.

Gregory III did not stop at duplicating the barley sugar columns. In defiant protest against the Iconoclasm raging in the East, he erected two magnificent monuments on either side of the Apostle's tomb. He also built a new canopy over the tomb itself. It had columns of onyx surmounted by a silver encrusted architrave, upon which were engraved images of the Saviour with the Twelve Disciples and the Mother of God accompanied by the Holy Virgins – the very kind of things which the Byzantine emperors were ruthlessly destroying. Close to the shrine Gregory built a chapel to contain various holy relics of such sort as were being dispersed in Constantinople. Did he by any chance also set up at the north-west corner of the crossing the seated figure of St Peter and institute the tradition of kissing that bronze toe? If so, Pope Gregory III could not have lit upon a scheme better calculated to confound the Iconoclasts of the eighth century and those of every subsequent century down to our own.

The experts have not yet reached agreement upon the date of the famous bronze statue. A long honoured tradition, almost certainly without foundation, claimed that St Leo the Great had it converted from an ancient statue of the Capitoline Jupiter. Until recent times it was believed to date from the fifth or sixth century. Antonio Muñoz and other scholars observing the seemingly Gothic rigidity of the draperies, attributed the figure not to pagan derivation, but to a Christian origin of the thirteenth century. It was in all probability, they asserted, the work of Arnolfo di Cambio. Arnolfo may have been inspired by the statue of St Peter, once outside the old basilica and now in the crypt, which was undoubtedly transformed from that of an ancient philosopher by a change of head and the addition of the sacred keys. Schüller-Piroli[1] on the other hand claims that the bronze of the seated figure is composed of the same alloy of lead and silver as that found in coinage of the second half of the seventh century; that the warm brown-gold patina is only shared by bronze of the late medieval centuries. He does not exclude the remote possibility that Arnolfo di Cambio may have recast an ancient statue, substituted a new head, and provided keys.

At all events this deeply venerated image survived the destruction of Constantine's basilica and was given a place of honour in the new one. The present marble throne dates from renaissance times, and the plinth of Sicilian jasper inlaid with green porphyry panels was carved by Carlo Marchionni in 1756–7. It does not greatly matter precisely when the figure was made. There is about it a primitive dignity and sublimity which has awed generations of the faithful, who day by day congregate to salute the worn toe and rub their foreheads against the foot. Its symbolical beauty is not enhanced by the pontifical mitre and bejewelled raiments with which it is incongruously decked on high festivals.

Vain are the most exhaustive efforts of men, even of popes, to raise perennial monuments, however splendid as art, however rich in substance. Callixtus II (1119–24) reconstructed the Gregorian altar, using the same white marble so carefully selected by Pope Sylvester and the Emperor Constantine and wilfully discarded by the first Gregory. On the Feast of Our Lady, he laid the new altar stone, granting an indulgence of three years to those who might worship at it. His was probably the Gothic octagonal ciborium with finials clustering round a dunce-cap cupola, depicted on several late drawings and sketches of the interior. It too was to disappear in the Renaissance.

[1] 2000 *Jahre Sankt Peter*, 1950.

The venerated bronze statue of St Peter originally stood in the old basilica (see also p. 4)

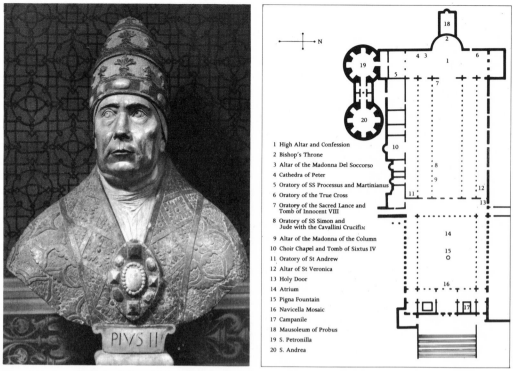

1. High Altar and Confession
2. Bishop's Throne
3. Altar of the Madonna Del Soccorso
4. Cathedra of Peter
5. Oratory of SS Processus and Martinianus
6. Oratory of the True Cross
7. Oratory of the Sacred Lance and Tomb of Innocent VIII
8. Oratory of SS Simon and Jude with the Cavallini Crucifix
9. Altar of the Madonna of the Column
10. Choir Chapel and Tomb of Sixtus IV
11. Oratory of St Andrew
12. Altar of St Veronica
13. Holy Door
14. Atrium
15. Pigna Fountain
16. Navicella Mosaic
17. Campanile
18. Mausoleum of Probus
19. S. Petronilla
20. S. Andrea

Pius II *left* embellished the old basilica. A plan of its final form by Tiberio Alfarano *right*

Even during the latter half of the fifteenth century, after pontifical schemes for the total demolition of Constantine's basilica had been ventilated, additions as well as restorations were still being made to the building. Lack of any concerted policy was due to a series of financial crises in the papal treasury, international distractions and the too quick succession of popes. Instead, muddle and makeshift in regard to the fabric's future ensued. In 1463 Pius II began reconstructing the tribune, or loggia of the papal benediction on the east front of the atrium and to the north of the entrance, which Innocent VIII (1484–92) completed in the renaissance style. Both popes must have known that when a comprehensive scheme of rebuilding was finally put in hand it would be swept away. It was demolished by Paul V after a hundred and fifty years' existence. Pius II likewise began the conversion, which Innocent completed, of Pope Symmachus's circular church of St Andrew to a sacristy. This fifth-century circular appendage, on the south side of the old basilica, joined to its fellow, the similar round church of St Petronilla (for a long time treated as an imperial mausoleum and sheltering the remains of the Apostle's daughter brought from the catacombs) made in old drawings and woodcuts a strange and picturesque group with Caligula's obelisk. When the transept was added the group formed a very uncomfortable tangent to the basilica, like a fractured limb. St Petronilla's church became a chapel under the patronage of the kings of France and in 1500 sheltered Michelangelo's Pietà. Minute detached churches, or sepulchral chapels, dedicated to St Martin, St John and St Paul, the deacons Sergius and Bacchus, and the senatorial family of Probus, were grouped about the west end of the basilica like satellite moons revolving round the planet Jupiter.

The Sacks of Rome

The picture of St Peter's throughout the Dark Ages must be seen against the sacks to which Rome was repeatedly subject. The process of disintegration of the Western Empire began under the absentee Emperor Honorius, who had fled to Ravenna on the first rumour that Italy might be invaded by the Goths. Here, entrenched between almost impenetrable marshes and the Adriatic Sea, he set up his capital. Honorius's terror of the Goths was only equalled by his ingratitude and folly. He put to death on the specious accusation of treachery his ward and protector, Stilicho, who had twice defeated Alaric, the King of the Goths, and thus deprived himself of the one general capable of defending him. He then refused to treat with Alaric, who begged him to do so in order that the city of Rome might be spared the fury of his troops. To the plea of this magnanimous enemy and the exhortations of the pope, Honorius turned a deaf ear. As a result, Rome fell to Alaric in 410 and suffered the first terrible sack at the hands of a barbarian invader. Within three days the Goths plundered everything they could remove from the city. Every church but two was entered and looted. The exceptions were St Peter's and St Paul's which Alaric commanded his men to respect and leave alone. The shrines of the two apostles were spared by the invaders who, regarded by the effete Romans as wild savages, were yet Christians, although Arians, in holy dread of disturbing places so sanctified by tradition. During the three day loot, a Gothic soldier came upon a girl in charge of a pile of treasure. He was about to fall upon it when the defenceless guardian remarked that he would do so at his peril. The things belonged, she said, to St Peter who would undoubtedly wreak his vengeance on the looter. The terror-stricken soldier not

Barbarian invaders. A Frankish foot soldier *left* and horseman *right*

only refrained from plundering, but escorted the girl and the treasure to the basilica where it belonged. On the journey, other soldiers turned from their booty and reverently joined the strange procession headed by the Roman girl and her Gothic accomplice, helping them to carry to safe custody chalices, crucifixes and lamps of gold and silver, encrusted with emeralds and amethysts.

The news of the sack of Rome by Alaric spread swiftly overseas, causing consternation and horror that the greatest and richest city of the civilized world, anciently the capital of the impregnable empire, and now the seat of the Christian religion, had succumbed so absolutely to a horde of barbarians. The lamentations of contemporary writers are still pitiable to read. St Jerome in his distant solitude at Bethlehem felt himself smitten to the earth. Never, he thought, would civilization raise its head again. He could not eat, nor think, nor act like a person of sound mind, so appalled was he by the first accounts of the Roman fugitives who had lived through the sack and now were reaching Palestine in dire distress. Other wretched victims, deprived of all their possessions, fled to Africa where St Augustine learned the dreadful story in Hippo. The catastrophe inspired his great treatise, *The City of God*, which was begun in answer to those pagans who claimed that the fall of Rome was owing to the abolition of heathen worship. On the contrary, Augustine postulated that out of the ruins of the Roman Empire would arise a far greater and more widespread hegemony of Christian rule.

Terrible as was the sack of 410, far worse sacks were to follow. Only moveable treasure had been carted in quantities out of the city by Alaric's Goths. The monuments and statues were unscathed. The citizens indeed were ruined temporarily, but the property and wealth of the papacy were little affected. In fact, a very short time was to elapse before St Jerome was reviling the sybaritism of the Roman clergy who were over-dressed and over-scented, who strutted about on tiptoe lest they dirtied their jewelled sandals, who wore rings on their fingers and had their hair curled and set. It was not because of these mincing popinjays nor of any display of lay leadership that Rome escaped the imminent destruction by Attila, King of the Huns. The extraordinary authority and courage of Pope Leo I, aided by an opportune vision to Attila of the threatening saints Peter and Paul, persuaded the terrible 'Scourge of God' to withdraw from the very gates of Rome. This miraculous delivery took place in 452.

Respite was not to endure for long. Only three years later, in 455, there occurred the sack of Rome by the Vandals under Genseric. These people, a migratory tribe originally from Scandinavia, and now come from Africa, likewise refrained from shedding blood – only the Emperor Maximus, while trying to escape, was slain by one of his own body-guard. But they too plundered, this time for fourteen days, palaces, houses, public buildings, churches and temples, taking away all they could lay their hands upon. The roof of the Temple of Peace being made of gilded bronze was stripped, and the sacred Jewish spoils, including the seven-branched candlestick captured by Titus in Jerusalem, were shipped on board Vandal vessels in the Tiber. But again, the shrines of the apostles were spared.

The decline of the Western Empire in the fifth century is tragic and unedifying. In 472 the third sack of Rome, this time under Ricimer, a Suebian prince, brought the city finally to its knees. In 476 the last sovereign, Romulus Augustulus, abdicated and the Roman Empire came to its inglorious end. Henceforward, Italy was ruled by barbarian kings. Then in the sixth century came the turn of the Gothic Kingdom to be destroyed.

The view up the Via della Conciliazione (see text p. 321). *Overleaf* The south fountain and façade of St Peter's (see text pp. 239, 288)

Between 535 and 553 Rome was occupied and sacked, first by Totila, King of the Ostrogoths, and, secondly, by the Eastern Emperor's general, Belisarius. Both these invaders offered gifts and prayers at the Apostle's tomb, which their troops were commanded to respect. The barbarian king, nevertheless, carried out his threat to turn the city into a pasture for cows by entirely depopulating it, and driving the miserable inhabitants into the Campagna. For forty days, not a soul was to be seen in the empty streets, where abandoned dogs, cats and cattle aimlessly wandered and foraged amongst the ordure, all that was left by the departed invaders and refugees.

Compared with the Lombards, Muslims, Magyars and Normans, who were the next invaders of Italian soil, the Goths, Vandals, Huns and Suebians had been civilized and romanized. Alaric, Attila, Genseric, Ricimer and Totila, names that sent a shudder down the spine of every Roman citizen of their times, were gentlemen in relation to the savage leaders of the hordes which were now to pour into the peninsula and inundate whatever region they passed through. Whereas the earlier invaders had admired and wished to preserve the Latin civilization, the later invaders were bent merely on its destruction. When the Lombards descended upon the valley of the Po, swarms of heathen savages attended them. Together they swept down Italy consuming and sacking, and leaving behind them a trail of pestilence, famine and want. Although Arians, the Lombards were the most rapacious of the invaders up to date, and throughout their long domination were more consistently feared and loathed by the Romans and the Church than any of their barbarian predecessors. Only the anarchy that prevailed in their ranks, and the persuasiveness and ransom money of Pope Pelagius II in 578 once again warded off an impending sack of Rome. The city was saved, but not by any intervention of the inhabitants, who by now lived in conditions of absolute demoralization and were quite incapable of making even a show of armed resistance.

The Lombards ruled Italy for over two hundred years until finally conquered by Charlemagne at the papacy's urgent instigation. Not until 756 did they besiege, without entering Rome. Nonetheless, they carried off from the catacombs in cartloads the sacred bodies of martyrs in order to enshrine them in the churches of their own capital, Pavia. This desecration so roused Pope Stephen III that he adopted a desperate method of eliciting support from the Franks. He sent a letter, signed in the name of the Apostle Peter himself, to their King Pepin, demanding in the most peremptory tones substantial aid, and threatening the loss of eternal life in the next world, if it were not instantly forthcoming. To Stephen's intense relief, the letter acted like a charm upon the devout Franks. Military relief was supplied without delay, and again the city escaped destruction.

Pepin's son, who was to bear a name even greater than his, was like the father to become supreme papal champion, first of Pope Adrian I against the Lombards and finally of Leo III against his mutinous subjects. Three times in the course of his long reign, he rushed to Adrian's rescue in Rome. He confirmed in the pope's favour the donation of vast territories in central Italy granted by Pepin, to which he continually added others. No wonder Charles looked upon himself as the patron as well as the saviour of God's Vicar on earth. No wonder too that he finally looked to the papacy for the supreme reward for more than twenty-five years' unremitting services. On Christmas Day of the year 800 one of the most solemn occasions in the history of St Peter's took place. Charles went to the basilica with a large retinue to attend Mass. He was on his knees meekly praying before the shrine of the Apostle. Certainly to the surprise of the congregation, if not of the Frankish

The view into the piazza and down the Via della Conciliazione from the roof of St Peter's (see text p. 322)

nno ættajo rēnunæ domno nſo gloriosissi

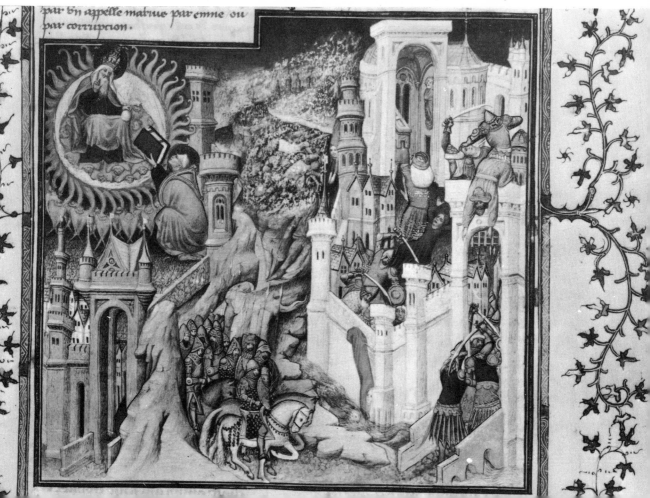

Invaders of Rome sacked the city on several occasions between the fifth and eleventh centuries. A Visigoth king and his court *top left*. The sack of Rome by the Goths, illustrated in a manuscript of St Augustine's *The City of God bottom left*. A Vandal horseman *above*. Attila the Hun *left*. Sword and helmet of a Vandal soldier *below*

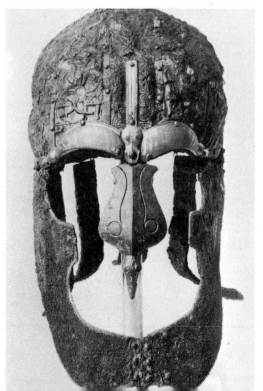

Charlemagne was crowned in St Peter's by Leo III; from a fourteenth-century French manuscript

king, Leo suddenly approached, and placing on his head a splendid crown, proclaimed him Caesar Augustus. 'God grant life and victory to the great and pacific Emperor!' he cried. Whereupon the priests, soldiers, nobles and common people present took up the words so that the whole basilica echoed to them. Then the pope actually bent the knee to the new emperor by way of homage. By this means, a barbarian monarch was made successor of the Roman caesars, and granted the rights and authority which were still nominally claimed, if no longer exercised by the Byzantine emperors in the East.

The great circular porphyry disc on which Charlemagne is said to have been kneeling at the moment of his coronation escaped the destruction of old St Peter's. It was relaid in the nave in front of the central door of the present basilica.

But in this terrible age the luck of St Peter's church could not be expected to continue indefinitely. Hitherto, her ancient prestige as the resting place of the first Christian bishop had worked wonders on the admiration and superstition of barbarian invaders. Soon, alas, depredators were to be at her gates who held her in no awe whatsoever. On

Charlemagne, first Holy Roman Emperor; a bronze statuette, believed to be a contemporary likeness

The worst sack of Rome took place in the reign of Pope Sergius II *left*, when the Saracens *right* despoiled the shrine of St Peter

the contrary, the followers of Mohammed both detested and despised all she stood for.

In short, the sack of Rome by the Saracens in 846 transcended in intensity and horror of human carnage any that had occurred previously. It was however different to all previous sacks in that this time the walled city was spared, whereas the basilicas of the two apostles and all the buildings that stood around them suffered cruelly. The attack did not happen unexpectedly. The Governor of Tuscany warned Pope Sergius II by letter of the approaching Saracen fleet. He cautioned him to remove for safety inside the fortifications of the city the bodies of the holy saints Peter and Paul, and the rich treasures that adorned their shrines, 'ne de tanta salute tra [? salutare re] gens nefandissime paganorum exultare potuisset', – to avoid the exultation by these most accursed pagans over their possible capture. His words were not totally unheeded. Father Engelbert Kirschbaum[1] believes that at this time the heads of the apostles were taken to the Lateran, where they

[1] *The Tombs of St Peter and St Paul,* trs. 1959.

have remained ever since. There is no doubt that, inflamed with righteous detestation, the Saracens raided the shrine of St Peter. They smashed to pieces the lower part of the *tropaion*, or tabernacle, which had been erected in the second century and was seen by the clerk Gaius; they destroyed the right side of the heavy stone ledge which rested upon the marble columns, and forced a way through the slab covering the grave below. The evidence of the recent excavations is that the jubilant Muslims penetrated the grave, robbing whatever treasure they found outside and in, and almost certainly desecrating, if not dispersing the Saint's remains. At last, the most sacred cynosure of all Christendom was violated by an enemy bent on striking a devastating blow at the very seat and centre of the Faith.

Finally, in 1084, the Normans, who were in Rome by papal invitation to fight the partisans of an antipope, pillaged, plundered and burnt the city. No previous raiders had wreaked quite such widespread havoc to buildings, nor caused such lasting confusion in papal government. Some English crusaders, happening to be in Rome a year or so later, left an account of the civil strife still raging. 'When we went into the Basilica of St Peter,' they related, 'we found before the altar the men of Guidbert the antipope [Clement II] who with swords in their hands wickedly seized the offerings laid on the altar. Others ran back and forth on the [ceiling] beams of the church and threw stones down upon us as we lay prostrate at our prayers. For when they saw any adherent of Urban [the lawful pope] they tried to kill him on the spot. We grieved not a little therefor in seeing such atrocity there.'

It is not a little surprising, when we consider the vicissitudes of Rome throughout the Dark Ages, that the shrine of St Peter survived so long the covetousness and savagery of successive invaders, heathen and Christian alike, only to be rifled in 846; nor surely that Constantine's basilica, battered, renovated and altered though it was, outlasted thirteen hundred years of violence, before finally being pulled down in order to make way for a more magnificent substitute.

One inevitable consequence of the repeated sacks of Rome which caused almost more distress to the Christian population than any other was the disturbance, and at times dispersal, of the relics of the saints and martyrs. Simple, devout persons derive no harm, and often much comfort, from objects that once belonged to those they loved and revered, or to those distant beings, now long dead but years ago specially blessed. It is when they attach supernatural powers to relics and when their veneration turns to worship that the sin of idolatry rears its ugly head. The temptation is apt to arise when they are desperate and life is dangerous and uncertain.

With the decline of Latin literature and scholarship in the West and the recrudescence of barbarian invasions there arose in an ill-educated and ignorant world a miasma of superstition. The wildest apocryphal stories were current, strange martyrologies were accepted, devils and sacerdotal powers were rife and relics were in fervent demand, often credited with miraculous cures. In the first and second centuries no interest had been shown in relics. The priest Gaius, writing in the late second or early third century about the shrines of Peter and Paul, merely referred to their triumphal memorials. But when St Cyprian was beheaded in 258 his flock mopped up the young man's blood with their own clothing which they preserved in his memory.[1] Already a mystic virtue was sensed

[1] The custom of preserving blood-soaked clothing of gladiators dates from pre-Christian times. See Masson, *op. cit.* p. 476.

in the physical remains of a specially holy man. By the fourth century relics were acquiring a sacred meaning, and were being venerated. Soon they were believed to be wonder-working. They began to accumulate in astonishing numbers. Not only bones and sinews of saints were collected, but objects associated with Our Lord were, after three hundred years of obscurity, conveniently assembled – the reed on which the sponge was offered to the crucified One, the sponge itself, the nails of the cross, the thorns of the crown and the seamless robe (the last of which is claimed by twenty different cathedrals). The holy blood and hair, the manger, the napkin which bound the sacred head in the tomb, and of course the cross, were discovered and apportioned among the treasure of Christian churches. Even the holy prepuce was formerly venerated in an obscure church in Latium, until a decree of 1900 forbade further mention of this detail. Relics of Our Lady were somewhat less numerous, but hair, milk, girdle, veil and shreds of her garments were claimed; and her home was miraculously transported from Syria to Italy by air. By the sixth century, godly people overstepped the limits of honour in acquiring relics by methods only matched by some stamp collectors of our own time. The richer and greater a person, the more over-reaching his or her unscrupulousness. Owners of private chapels in need of relics rifled tombs at night, purloined an arm or finger from coffins and bargained with venal custodians of cemeteries for pieces of cerecloth, which they took home and mounted in jewelled caskets. This pious mania persisted even into counter-reformation times. A lady devotee, in kissing the corpse of St Francis Xavier, is said to have bitten off a great toe which she carried away in her mouth.

The Influence of the Old Basilica

After the foundation of S. Sabina, no basilica in Rome derived from St Peter's until the ninth century. The first to do so was S. Prassede in 817–24. In addition to its plan of nave, two aisles and an apse, this little church has a confession for the repose and veneration of the saintly relics of the sisters Prassede and Pudenziana.

Even in remote England several Saxon shrines in churches were modelled on that contrived by St Gregory in Constantine's basilica. Peterborough Abbey Church, for example, may even have been founded with the express object 'that men who could not go to Rome might there be able to seek their patron', and that, 'just as blessed Peter was present in body in Rome, so he might also be present in this spot in spirit'.[1] The pope ordained that indulgences granted at Peterborough should be just as efficacious as those emanating from the Vatican Hill. Among other English cathedrals, Canterbury and Ripon offered the same vicarious privileges, and furthermore provided crypt chambers under raised presbyteries. In Brixworth church, Northamptonshire, and Wing church, Buckinghamshire, a raised presbytery survives in the apse with a semi-circular passage running beneath it. The purpose served by these confessions[2] was not practical but symbolic, and imitative of the mother basilica in Rome. Even the Saxon towers of English churches were influenced by the great campanile at St Peter's in that they were square and had windows of twin-arched lights divided by a baluster-like shaft. In the eighth,

[1] Quoted by A. S. Barnes in *St Peter in Rome*, 1900, from Dugdale's *Monasticon*.
[2] Barnes, writing in 1900, says that at Ripon and Hexham the crypts, according to local tradition, were used until the Reformation as confessionals, because when built they were termed 'confessions', and for no other reason.

The dome and one of the cupolas from the roof by day (see text p. 211)

ninth and tenth centuries, so many pilgrims from these islands reached Rome that the region in the forefront of St Peter's was named after them Burgus Saxonum (or the Saxons' quarter), which has given the suffix *in-Sassia* to the two churches of Santo Spirito and S. Michele.

The Vatican Palace

With commendable zeal Oddo Colonna, Martin V, on his return to Rome at the end of the Great Schism, set about restoring St Peter's Basilica and spending large sums on the patronage of artists like Gentile Fabriano and Masaccio. What was the Vatican Palace like which this determined man reached at the end of his long triumphal ride on an autumn afternoon in 1421 ? The crowds were huzzaing with relief and jubilation as their rightful sovereign advanced to reclaim his undisputed heritage. Flattered he may have been by this reception, yet surely filled with misgivings how to re-establish papal government after more than a century of papal exile. His capital was a desert, his vast church was tottering to decay. His palace by a merciful providence was about the only building in Rome that was remotely habitable.

The history of the papal palace of the Vatican is shorter than that of St Peter's Basilica by nearly eight hundred years. After the Emperor Constantine had given his wife's Lateran property to Pope Sylvester I, this place became the seat of papal government and the popes' only dwelling place. The Lateran we have to remember was just within the ancient walls of the city; the Vatican Hill was without, which accounts for the fact that for centuries after it was built St Peter's Basilica stood entirely exposed and isolated on its eminence. There were no residential nor office buildings of any sort attached to it. When Pope Symmachus, driven from the Lateran Palace by the antipope Laurentius, took refuge in St Peter's, there was not a single apartment outside the church where he could even spend the night. For five years, from 501–6, he dwelt in hastily constructed annexes, not amounting to more than a cluster of cells on the north and south sides of the aisles. As soon as the antipope was got rid of and because the Vatican was still defenceless against barbarian incursions, he returned to the Lateran Palace. Pope Symmachus's temporary refuge was only enlarged and improved by Leo III, who in honour of Charlemagne's coronation in 800 added a large banqueting hall. Then the Vatican became a guest's palace of some consequence. Emperors habitually stayed in it during their brief visits to Rome. With their large armed retinues, they were well able to defend themselves against a chance attack from outside the city walls.

There had indeed been nothing beyond a godly respect by Christian invaders for the shrine of St Peter – and also that of St Paul, likewise outside the city walls – to prevent a terrible disaster such as the one which befell in 846 at the hands of the Saracens. After the raid and the unprecedented violation by the unbelievers of both apostles' remains Christendom was jolted to its senses. The saintly Leo IV, who was elected pope in the following year, appealed for funds in order to build defensive walls round the Vatican. Christendom and the emperor responded. A stout chain of travertine and tufa forty feet high and linked by no less than forty-four towers enclosed what became known as the Leonine City. It was also joined to the ancient city across the river, long since protected by the Aurelian walls of the third century. Henceforth the Vatican became as safe a part of Rome to inhabit as the Lateran had been. But even after the creation of the

The dome from the roof by night

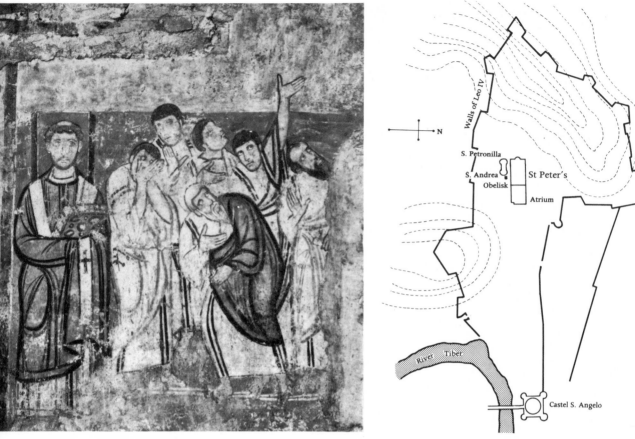

The Leonine city was created by Leo IV, shown with a square nimbus in a fresco painted during his lifetime *left*. Walls were erected around the Vatican area, linking it to the Tiber and the fortified Castel S. Angelo, as a protection against further attack *right*

Leonine City popes only passed an occasional night there during special, long drawn out ceremonies in St Peter's, ceremonies which did not allow time for them to return to sleep in the Lateran Palace.

Eugenius III (1145–53) was the first pope to begin building a papal palace attached to the basilica. It is remarkable that a pontiff so harried by St Bernard in his zeal for a new crusade and so persecuted by rebellious factions in Rome should have had the time and money to devote to the purpose. His successor, Anastasius IV (1153–4) went on with the work. Celestine III (1191–8) spent as much as half the year in the Vatican. Innocent III (1198–1216) was the first pope to concentrate on making it a permanent residence. He fortified the lower part lying on the south side of the basilica. But the pope who seriously got down to rebuilding the palace in anything like its recognizable form today was Nicholas III (1277–80). He transferred the residential part from the lower to the upper level of the hill, where it has always remained. The lower wing he gave over to the Curia and the papal chamberlain. He also joined the palace to the Castle of S. Angelo by a covered way, thus

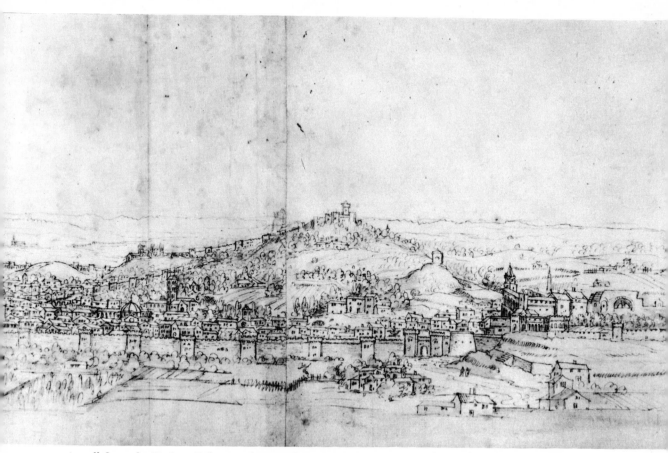

A wall from the Vatican Palace to the Castel S. Angelo contained a protected passage which provided a means of escape in times of danger; a sixteenth-century drawing showing the Vatican on the right and the Janiculum hill beyond the wall

providing in times of stress a desirable and frequently needed escape route to military security. Nicholas III greatly loved the Vatican, and had it not been for the impending exile of the papacy to Avignon, his successors would doubtless have felt obliged to complete what he only just had time to begin with so much zest and expense.[1] As it happened, Nicholas reached the northern limit of the terrain which determined the amount of building that could ever be possible, thus fixing as it were for all time the framework of the future Vatican City. He fortified the Leonine Walls, planted apple trees and laid out gardens on the site of the present Cortile di S. Damaso. For a century and a half afterwards the palace remained practically unaltered.

During the long absence in Avignon the Vatican Palace was not altogether uncared for. A disastrous fire at the Lateran in 1308 meant that Nicholas III's palace was to become the

[1] Of Nicholas III's work the Sala dei Chiaroscuri partly remains, with a contemporary painted frieze. Also the Sala dei Paramenti is mostly his.

The buildings of the Vatican Palace rising to the right of the basilica; a drawing by Marten van Heemskerk, 1533

popes' principal residence whenever they should return to Rome. Meanwhile, the new gardens were well cultivated and yielded welcome sales of fruit and watercress. When the last French pope, Gregory XI, reluctantly came back in 1377 he found a dwelling in tolerably good order. The Great Schism which followed the French exile brought more harm to the palace than absentee ownership had done, because fewer funds were available for the legitimate Italian popes to spend on proper maintenance. Nevertheless, when Martin V dismounted after his triumphal entry into the capital he was able to live perfectly well in the palace while repairs were put in hand. Eugenius IV (1431–47) planned to do all sorts of necessary works which his troubled reign and exile prevented. He got as far as building the Mint in the lower palace and enticing Florentine artists to decorate it. He commissioned Fra Angelico to embellish the palace with frescoes (they were destroyed a hundred years later by Paul III) and Filarete to cast the huge central bronze door to the basilica (it is still in place) in emulation of Ghiberti's doors in the Baptistry in Florence. It is strange to see on these beautiful panels the martyrdoms of Peter and Paul happily interspersed with the amours of Leda and the rape of Ganymede.

Not until the reign of Nicholas V (1447–55) were conditions settled enough to allow a reappraisal of the whole extraordinary jumble of medieval masonry, half fortress, half dwelling, with which this pope was confronted. Nicholas was determined to live as close as he could to the Apostle Peter's remains. Under his direction, the popes' private apartments were set like an eagle's eyrie in the upper citadel, of which the precipitous, cliff-like aspect is so familiar to all visitors to St Peter's. He built the wing in which the Borgia apartments and Raphael's Stanze were later to be fitted. He also began the original Vatican Library. In the reign of this enlightened pontiff, the dawn of humanism was slowly breaking. Soon the mists of terror and ignorance that had so long darkened Rome's horizon would be dissipated. With the brighter Renaissance a new chapter must open.

The great Filarete bronze doors to the old basilica were re-erected in the new

DESCRITTIONE FATTA
DELLA CHIESA ANTICA
E MODERNA
DI S. PIETRO,
con misure più
principali, e relatione
di pittura, scultura,
et architettura,
da Carlo Padre Dia.

4 The Renaissance Basilica

It is arguable how far the history of individual popes is relevant to that of St Peter's Basilica. I maintain that in so far as a person has played a part, however slight, in contributing to the fabric of a great monument, then his spiritual, or if you prefer it, his psychical qualities and indeed his general character must have considerable bearing upon its look. Certainly any artifact, whether building, painting, piece of sculpture or music, whether poem or work of literature, is made more comprehensible and interesting when we know something of the person, or persons who brought it about. From their particular natures we learn the motives which impelled them to create it. The joys, the sorrows, the exultations and the disillusions of the artist's, and to a lesser extent of the patron's life, colour very appreciably the essence of the thing created.

Because great art is more often the outcome of misery and unrest than of triumph and complacency, it goes without saying that artists and patrons are usually not the wisest or most stable of men. Thwarted ambition and accumulated disappointment, seldom to be dissociated from their labours, make them unfortunately over-sensitive, introspective and at times exceedingly malign. On the other hand, only success and content will make a man fitted to be a beneficent and wise ruler of his fellows. A list of those crowned heads who have been the greatest patrons of the arts will comprise some of the worst kings that ever reigned. So it is with the popes of Rome. Of their number John XXII (1316–34), one of the most bellicose of the two hundred and sixty-one popes to date – he engaged in endless warfare by means of interdicts, anathemas and excommunications, issuing it is said 60,000 decretals within eighteen years – whose name no successor cared to revive before the saintly old Pope Roncalli in 1958, sent from Avignon 500 gold gulden, which he could ill afford, towards the replacement of the perished beams of St Peter's. Had circumstances seen him settled in Rome instead of Avignon he would doubtless have initiated great improvements to the basilica, so genuine was his love of the arts.

Few popes, mercifully, have been as bad as John XXII, who was a sort of effluvium left behind by the Dark Ages. The Renaissance also produced popes whose private conduct was execrable and whose patronage of the arts commensurably praiseworthy. They will be discussed in due course.

Before proceeding with the subject of this book, which is St Peter's church, it seems only right and fair to interpolate here two points. They are that by far the greater number of renaissance popes were fundamentally good men by every standard; and even the bad minority put the glory of the Church as represented by their divine office well before all personal interests. A study of the times must lead to this conclusion, a conclusion which has not been reached by most Protestant historians. They have been far too ready to pick upon the evidence, irrefutable enough, that some renaissance popes unashamedly enjoyed the material privileges which attended their sacred office – without looking for

The renaissance popes were determined to replace the old basilica by one in the modern style of architecture; a seventeenth-century allegorical engraving of Julius II and Constantine

123

extenuating motives. The fact surely is that some supranatural dictation moved each one of these popes, whether ascetic or hedonist, to defend the Faith in which he implicitly believed by praiseworthy or reprehensible means. The most irresponsible cynic would be hard pressed to make a favourable case for, say, Alexander VI's character. Yet this Borgia pope, grossly amoral, certainly guilty of fornication and probably of murder too, was the consistent upholder of purity of faith and the rights of the Church. Where these principles were at stake, he would give way to no pressure from any source.

Among essentially good renaissance popes we must reckon Thomas of Sarzana, the son of a poor physician who became Nicholas V (1447–55). As well as being a most agile political figure in the European circus, he played – and this is our chief concern – a major rôle on the stage of St Peter's. This rôle would have been more momentous still were it not for the disasters of Nicholas's reign in the fall of Constantinople and the final, irreparable break with the Greek Church. They seriously hindered what was the chief ambition of this man of humble origin, namely to make Rome once again the capital of the cultural world. Nicholas attracted to his court distinguished scholars from overseas regardless of their religious opinions or their moral character. His overriding hobby was book collecting, and he was never happier than when cataloguing and arranging his shelves. He was the founder of the Vatican Library into which he garnered Greek manuscripts from distant lands. He restored many churches in Rome and brought the Acqua Vergine water supply back to the city. Yet he was not guiltless of despoiling ancient monuments in the process, and in one year took more than 2,500 cartloads of stone from the Colosseum.

Nicholas's election coincided with the end of the papal schism. The last of the antipopes was dead and there was now no one to call in question his sole right to wear the tiara. I have already referred to the serious disrepair to which the Vatican Palace and St Peter's succumbed during the Schism of the West. That no structural work had been carried out for so long accounts for the palace having entirely escaped alterations in the high Gothic style. It remained a tumble-down assortment of romanesque appendages. The condition of the basilica too was by now deplorable. During the past century and a half, it had often been used as a fortress and sometimes subjected to siege. It had suffered from damage by earthquake as well as from assualt and lack of maintenance. The southern wall leaned six feet out of the perpendicular and the mosaics on them were so covered with dust as hardly to be visible. Leon Battista Alberti in a report submitted to the pope warned him: 'I am convinced that very soon some slight shock or movement will cause it [the south wall] to fall. The rafters of the roof have dragged the north wall inwards to a corresponding degree.' Was it therefore surprising that a man of Nicholas's ambition to beautify Rome and of his newly restored powers should decide to pull down the whole antiquated structure, and raise a building worthy of the regenerated Church in the style of the new humanist age in which he lived? The famous words of his deathbed speech best express what was in his mind. 'To create solid and stable convictions in the minds of the uncultured masses,' he proclaimed, 'there must be something that appeals to the eye; a proper faith, sustained only on doctrines, will never be anything but feeble and vacillating. But if the authority of the Holy See were visibly displayed in majestic buildings, imperishable memorials and witnesses seemingly planted by the hand of God himself, belief would grow and strengthen . . . Noble edifices combining taste and beauty with imposing proportions would immensely conduce to the exaltation of the Chair of St Peter.' These magnificent sentiments were to be reiterated by the Jesuits in the age of the Baroque. There were also aesthetic and practical reasons in this pope's mind equally cogent. The medieval basilica was cluttered with haphazard monuments and accretions sadly detracting from that symmetry which the renaissance eye found decent. There was not room enough to accommodate the vast numbers of pilgrims then visiting Rome. In the Jubilee year of 1450, the crowds had been such that to the pope's great distress two hundred people were crushed to death on the Bridge of S. Angelo. Nicholas was determined to prevent a recurrence of this disaster, at any rate within the consecrated walls of the basilica.

Historians have always been uncertain how drastic Nicholas V's projects really were, considering what little they amounted to. They have found it hard to understand why, if he meant entirely to rebuild the basilica, he spent so much time and money on patching the old fabric. For he restored the nave, embellished the ceiling rafters and installed stained windows in the clerestory. Surely the answer is that at the beginning of his reign he had every intention of preserving the old basilica, but experience ultimately convinced him that restoration of so decayed a fabric was impracticable. When, after reaching this conclusion, he decided upon total rebuilding, it was too late.

Nicholas's projects were indeed far more impressive than his achievements. We know all about them from the detailed life of the pope by his secretary, Giannozzo Manetti. The man he chose to carry them out on paper was the Florentine sculptor, Bernardo Rossellino. How far Rossellino was advised by Alberti, his senior in age, is still uncertain. At all events Rossellino came upon the scene first. He worked for the newly elected pope outside Rome; then he restored the walls of the city and several churches within them. Vasari claims that 'at the time when Nicholas V had thrown the city of Rome into utter confusion with his peculiar manner of building, Leon Battista Alberti arrived in that city, where . . . he became known to the pontiff'. That thenceforward Rossellino proceeded under the counsel of Alberti, such being the will of the pope. Thus together they 'brought many useful and praiseworthy labours to conclusion' in Rome.[1] At least there is evidence that Nicholas, who directed his own building operations, sought the advice of Alberti. He accepted a copy of the great architect's famous treatise, *De re aedificatoria* and, presumably, heeded the report which Alberti presented to him on the parlous condition of the church's structure. Ludwig Pastor even goes so far as to suggest that perusal of the book was the immediate cause of Nicholas's change from preservation tactics to a policy of total rebuilding.[2]

In any event a plan by Rossellino for a new basilica survives. There is reason to presume that it was dictated by the pope, whether or not the sculptor was advised by Alberti. The strange thing about it is the similarity to the plan of Constantine's basilica. For a renaissance plan it was old-fashioned, which makes us wonder in what respect Nicholas's 'peculiar manner of building' threw 'the city of Rome into utter confusion'. The plan consists of a nave and four aisles, with the addition of a deep apsed choir, to become known as the Tribuna di San Piero[3] (which was ultimately built), flanked by chapels, and

---

[1] Georgio Vasari, *Lives of the Most Eminent Painters, etc.* 1550 et seq. See chapter on L. B. Alberti, vol. 2 in translation by Mrs J. Foster, 1888.

[2] Ludwig Pastor, *History of the Popes from the Middle Ages*, trs. 1906–53, vol. 2.

[3] Not San Pietro, as might be supposed.

a transept of the same width as the nave. The nave was to be carried on freestanding columns. Some ancient columns were actually brought ready for this purpose. The same old Constantinian roof construction was to be repeated in open timber. Over the crossing however there were to be a dome and cupola, and the apse was to contain the papal throne. Five doors were to lead from the nave and aisles to a columned atrium, in the centre of which the famous pine-cone was to be re-erected. Nicholas and Rossellino's aim was to give strict symmetry, previously lacking, to the façade. At the western end of the atrium were to rise a pair of bell towers. The vestibule, separating atrium from piazza, was to take the form of an arch of triumph, faced with marble, but fortified. Defence was still a serious consideration, for the prolonged troubles of medieval times and the recent fall of Constantinople to the Saracens were by no means forgotten. The project would in fact have repeated the ancient layout to a notable extent, only on a scale even larger than that of the present St Peter's. It was markedly in contrast with the total disregard by the later renaissance architects of Constantine's plan of basilica and atrium. Although not executed, Rossellino's project became the model for important fifteenth-century churches elsewhere. The pope and his architect designed that from the piazza three spacious streets should radiate. They were to be provided with continuous colonnades on ground level, with closed galleries overhead.

What precisely did Nicholas V accomplish? It was very little. First of all, he swept away the unsightly stalls and shops which for centuries had congested the atrium steps. Then

The first steps to rebuild St Peter's were put in hand under Nicholas V; a portrait attributed to Simon Marmion *left*. A plan was prepared by Rossellino *right*

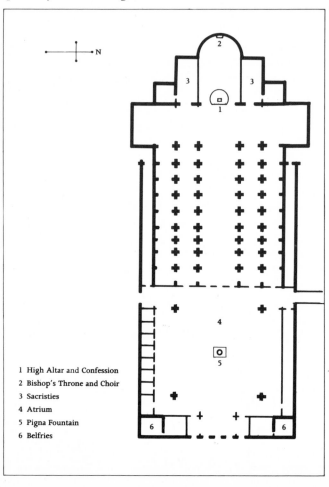

1 High Altar and Confession
2 Bishop's Throne and Choir
3 Sacristies
4 Atrium
5 Pigna Fountain
6 Belfries

The Loggia of the Benediction was reconstructed to the right of the entrance to the atrium by Pius II; a sketch by Marten van Heemskerk

he made a start on the new choir considered essential for the clergy. This was to be an extension behind the apse of the Constantinian church and involved the demolition of the Templum Probi, or so-called house of St Peter, which, when its foundations were laid bare, disclosed a mortuary chamber of the Roman Anicii family built against the west end. Work on the choir – or Tribuna di San Piero – took ages to get going. It was stopped on Nicholas's death and resumed in the reign of Paul II. Apart from these two positive steps towards a new church, Nicholas's work can only be described as negative.

It turned out that the walls of the new choir had reached a height of six feet, and the first demolitions of the old basilica were just put in hand, when Nicholas V died. Superstitious persons were not wanting to warn the new pope, Callixtus III (1455–8), what fate had in store for him, if he were to continue tampering with a building of such age and sanctity. True, work was suspended for a time, but the real reason was probably Callixtus's disinterest in renaissance humanism and art, his pressing endeavour being to save Western civilization from further Turkish encroachment. The next pope, Pius II (1458–64), can certainly not be accused of indifference to the humanities and the arts. Aeneas Sylvius Piccolomini was one of the most cultivated popes to grace the throne of St Peter. He was a poet and descriptive writer of a high order, a most discriminating patron and remorseless critic of the second-rate in writing and painting. Unfortunately, his brief reign was handicapped by ill-health – he was crippled with gout in the feet contracted in Scotland – by poverty, and agonized concern how to rally the squabbling Christian powers to expel the Turks from Europe. In spite of these harrassing worries, he began to build an arcade for the new piazza before the church. It got no further than the three-storeyed Loggia of the Benediction, a fragment which survived until Paul V substituted the present façade. The loggia features prominently in numberless views of St Peter's during the sixteenth century. This paragon of popes died before he was sixty at Ancona, desperately awaiting the promised Venetian crusading fleet which never came.

Paul II (1464–71), a genial, handsome and somewhat vain Venetian, loved splendour and carnivals, but associated humanism and art with atheism and political subversion. Yet he was the ardent promoter of printing and restorer of Roman arches and equestrian statues. He built the Palazzo Venezia, Rome's finest *quattrocento* palace. Not until 1470, when he had only one more year to live, did Paul resume the suspended work upon Nicholas V's Tribuna di San Piero. In this short time progress did not get very far. More interesting is Paul II's association with the transept of old St Peter's. In drawings made before 1470, there are no signs whatever of any arms to Constantine's church. Until this reign then did the basilica's plan of naves, aisles and sanctuary preserve an absolute classical rectangle, broken only by the western apse? In other words, did Paul II add the dwarf through-transept (amounting to terminal chapels projecting a short distance through a pair of columns), which is shown in the well-known plan published by Tiberio Alfarano in 1589–90, long after the transept had been demolished? Pope Pius XII's excavators were satisfied that the transept shown by Alfarano was Constantinian. More recent scholars have thrown doubts on their archaeological discoveries and incline to the 1470 attribution.[1] In this case it is extraordinary that at so late a stage of the old basilica's existence and after Nicholas V's abortive efforts at patching, a large-scale alteration should be undertaken to a fabric universally recognized to be worn out and perishing.

Paul II's work on St Peter's proceeded along the lines begun by Nicholas V before his decision had been taken to rebuild from the ground upwards. He entrusted it to Giuliano da Sangallo, then a young man, who had begun life as a wood carver under Lorenzo the Magnificent in Florence, and was to crown it by designing the lovely little Villa Medici at Poggio a Caiano. Giuliano, during the short time available to him before the pope's death, was busily engaged on the tribune. In 1471 his association with St Peter's came to an abrupt halt. As far as we know, he did not resume it for well over thirty years.

Sixtus IV (1471–84), although a Franciscan monk, was hardly as pious a man as his pleasure-loving predecessor. He was actuated by a strange mixture of celestial and sublunary motives. Passionately devoted to the cult of Our Lady, he fervently desired to promote the glory of the city of Rome. An ecclesiastical scholar of renown, he was a patron of learning and art second only to Nicholas V. Like other priests promoted from a sheltered life of extreme poverty and obedience to one of limitless authority, he became inordinately profligate of money. He was totally unaware of the word's meaning and gaily dispensed as if they were water whatever funds he could lay his hands upon. He was, admittedly, generous to a fault and cared deeply about the welfare of his subjects. Unfortunately this astute yet simple man allowed himself to be influenced by three acquisitive nephews who took advantage of his open-handed ways. At a time when the Turkish

[1] Admittedly it is rash to dispute archaeological evidence when one has not participated in its investigation. Nevertheless my inclination is not to accept the transept of old St Peter's as Constantinian. There is as yet no proof that Constantine gave transepts to any of his other basilicas in Rome or elsewhere. The earliest Christian churches of the fourth century followed the juridical basilican plan. Later centuries found it inconvenient especially where great numbers of pilgrims congregated at a shrine. To make more room transepts were often added.

Paul II *left* appointed Giuliano da Sangallo *right* as Architect to St Peter's, but his plans were never proceeded with

menace was at its most dangerous – in 1480 the fall of Otranto to the infidel caused the utmost terror and dismay throughout Italy – Sixtus's favourite nephew, Cardinal Pietro Riario, chose to give a banquet in honour of the Princess Leonora of Naples, which excelled in extravagant luxury the fabled feasts of the gods on Mount Olympus. The Lucullan meal lasted six whole hours. Forty-four dishes were served, including 'stags roasted whole, and in their skins, goats, hares, calves, herons, peacocks with their feathers, and finally, a bear with a staff in his jaws'.[1] Sugar fortresses from which banners waved, a mountain with a living serpent coiled upon it, ten great ships made to sail into the room laden with sugared almonds, were among the delicacies. Allegorical figures were presented, the triumph of Venus was enacted and a ballet danced on the stage by ancient heroes and their mistresses.

In spite of the tense international situation and the acute financial embarrassment caused by the cardinal nephew's excesses, Sixtus issued a bull for renovating Rome, built the Ponte Sisto across the Tiber, prolonged the Acqua Vergine water supply, rebuilt the hospital of Santo Spirito for orphaned children, restored countless churches and built those of S. Maria del Popolo and S. Maria della Pace. He also founded St Luke's Association of painters and re-established the Vatican Library.

[1] Ludwig Pastor, *op. cit.* vol. 4 pp. 243–5.

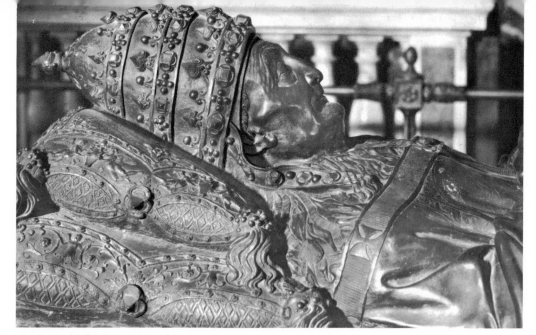

Sixtus IV built the Sistine Chapel in the Vatican but halted the plans for rebuilding St Peter's; detail of the head from the monument on his tomb, now in the crypt of St Peter's

Sixtus's building activities at the Vatican were feverish. His greatest contribution, which bears his name, was the chapel for the Sistine choir. To embellish this uncomfortably deep rectangular block some of the world's leading painters were summoned by Sixtus, whose impatience was only matched by Julius II's with Michelangelo a generation later. In addition to completing the chapel, he refitted the palace. He strengthened the tottering fabric of St Peter's, restored the roof, inserted more windows and provided a new pavement. He likewise repaired the old sacristy and chapel of St Petronilla. Sixtus scrapped the tabernacle of the confession, which dated from the twelfth century, and erected a new ciborium over Peter's tomb while incorporating the four surviving porphyry columns of the altar raised by Callixtus II. Sixtus's ciborium remained in place until Bernini erected the present baldacchino in the 1630s.[1] The ciborium was enriched with bas-reliefs representing Christ delivering the keys of heaven to St Peter. Clearly then this pope had no intention of carrying on Nicholas V's project of pulling down the old basilica and building a new one.

Sixtus IV's finest memorial is his tomb by Antonio Pollaiuolo, now preserved in the crypt (Grotte Vecchie). It is a renaissance bronze of incomparable workmanship. The old pope lies with his head on a tasselled pillow, wearing the tiara. The head is a masterpiece. The cheeks are hollow, the eyes sunk from age. Yet the puckered forehead gives a lively, quizzical expression. Refinement of taste is suggested by the long curved nose, and strength of character by the jutting chin. If ever there was a portrait of cultivated intelligence Pollaiuolo achieved it here. The reliefs of the catafalque symbolize the theological virtues, and are in themselves flawless gems of the sculptor's art.

[1] Bernini re-used two of the porphyry columns for the altar of Saints Simon and Jude in the south transeptal apse (now known as the altar of the Crucifixion of St Peter), and two for that of the martyrs Processus and Martinian in the north transeptal apse.

Innocent VIII *left*, from his monument in St Peter's (see also p. 134). Alexander VI, by Pinturicchio, *right* left no mark on St Peter's but commissioned the Borgia Apartments in the Vatican

The reign of Innocent VIII (1484–92), a benevolent, easy-going but irresolute individual, was made so hideous by the squabbles among the Italian sovereigns and their attacks upon the Church's authority that the pope even threatened to live in France. Almost the only redeeming event of his reign was the propitiatory gift by the Sultan Bajazet II to Innocent of the head of Longinus's spear which had pierced the side of the Saviour upon the cross. Its reception in St Peter's was marked by hysterical rejoicing as much on account of the nature of the sacred relic as the indication – which proved illusory – of the Turks' favourable disposition towards the papacy. Bajazet's real motive was to bribe the pope to retain in Rome his captive brother and hated rival for as long as possible. Innocent's seated effigy on Antonio Pollaiuolo's bronze wall monument has a likeness of the spearhead triumphantly displayed in the pope's left hand. It is the only monument from the old basilica to be re-erected in the new.[1] The delicate beauty of this renaissance tomb becomes almost insignificant in its present opulent surroundings. In the course of re-erection, the supine figure of the pope was set below instead of above the seated figure, which was the original position. The face shows tenderness and simplicity, but the receding chin affirms that Innocent was not a man of action. He conscientiously carried on Sixtus's work of church restoration and the completion of S. Maria della Pace. But the arts and scholarship did not prosper under him as they did during the previous pontificate.

The Vatican Palace was at the end of the fifteenth century still a congeries of piecemeal structures making no concession to their surroundings, and scarcely deserving the name of architecture. Innocent rebuilt the lower palace, or Curia Innocenziana, in which to lodge foreign embassies (it was swept away by Paul V). Depressed by the sorry muddle

[1] Against the second pier of the south aisle.

of buildings in which he was fated to live, he set about erecting an entirely separate dwelling, yet within the Vatican walls. He chose a site at the furthermost northern point of the Leonine City which was also the highest, and so most salubrious. The Belvedere, designed by Pollaiuolo and carried out by Iacopo da Pietrasanta was, like the Villa Medici at Poggio, one of the first villas to be built since Roman times. It had an immense influence upon subsequent renaissance villa architecture. The pope called on Pinturicchio and Mantegna to decorate it. There Innocent could retire, away from the bustling offices and embassies, in detached splendour, confronting an intermediate garden landscape. The core of the Belvedere has survived to this day, but no longer in isolation. It forms the extremity of the present Cortile della Pigna, hidden partly behind the great hemicycle of the pine-cone, which was later attached to it at an oblique angle. For centuries now it has enshrined the Laocoon, Apollo Belvedere and other classic works of Vatican sculpture round a central octagonal court.

At the southern extremity of the Cortile del Belvedere, and separated from the Cortile della Pigna by the library block, the battlemented tower and the Appartamenti Borgia recall the contribution of Alexander VI (1492–1503). The three pokey, tenebrous rooms decorated for the Spanish pope and his children by Pinturicchio still exhale, in spite of centuries of shuffling tourists, the sinister atmosphere of that cloak and dagger family. Elected to the papacy through the rankest simony, Rodrigo Borgia was infinitely amoral. Nevertheless, he was extremely clever and practical; and he was not wholly unpopular with his lenient subjects, who derived entertainment from the sight of his children involved in political intrigues, annulments, assassinations and poisonings with the apparent connivance of their indulgent parent. Alexander left at the Vatican little material evidence of his nine-year reign, apart from the Borgia apartments. But the uneasy atmosphere of these apartments and the ghost of his murdered son, the Duke of Gandia, which accompanied by torches carried by unseen hands used to haunt the old basilica, were held in terror by his successors. On his agonized deathbed the pope was heard to cry out, 'I am coming. It is right so. Only wait a little.' After these desperately ambiguous words, he closed his eyes. Before the breath was out of his body, his servants plundered his wardrobe and every stick of furniture in his rooms, leaving nothing but some torn fragments of tapestry nailed to the plastered walls. Succeeding popes reviled his memory and would never set foot inside the apartments which had been the scene of so much scandal and blasphemy.

The election, not without bribery, of Cardinal Giuliano della Rovere as Pope Julius II (1503–13) brought about a crisis in the history of St Peter's. I have told how Nicholas V's conclusion to demolish the Constantinian basilica and build anew came too late in his lifetime. His successors during intervals between coping with urgent affairs of state and parrying threats of Saracen invasion did no more than toy with the problem. Each continued the process of patching and renewing in the hope that the onus of demolition might be deferred to the next reign. For fifty years they procrastinated. Pope Julius, on the other hand, was not the man to shrink from any undertaking that was in his eyes necessary. No task, however unpopular, was too disagreeable for this pope of iron will and undeviating determination. Here was a challenge that appealed to his imagination, his love of the arts and his desire to raise a splendid edifice which would be a fitting symbol of papal prestige and power. Julius was made in a gigantic mould. He saw himself

The portico (see text p. 242)

a mighty prince as well as the spiritual representative of a meek creed. Fully aware of the short duration of papal reigns and made wise by Pope Nicholas's experiences, he lost little time in setting about the task which even he, dauntless and indefatigable though he was, learnt towards the end of his life could never be accomplished by one incumbent of St Peter's throne.

First of all this martial pontiff set about establishing a permanent papal army. It appeared to him intolerable that the meanest baron was stronger than the Pope of Rome, who was obliged to depend in emergencies upon unreliable mercenaries. In 1506 he founded the Swiss Guards, who to this day defend with pikes, halberds and other archaic accoutrement all entrances to the Vatican City. An agreement with the Swiss Confederacy raised a force of 6,000 fighting men. The army existed until 1825 when Pope Leo XII converted it to a domestic bodyguard. Today it consists of a mere hundred men, including four officers, a chaplain, twenty-three non-commissioned officers, two drummers and seventy halberdiers.

These fine, upstanding northerners, with their fair hair and clear complexions, are carefully selected for their looks as well as dependability. And a splendid sight they make in their sixteenth-century uniforms. They stand guard day by day in slashed doublets and baggy hose of violet and orange stripes, with berets drawn down over one eye. This is their undress uniform. On state occasions they wear a steel cuirass and helmet and carry a halberd. In recent times they have been supplemented by the Noble Guard, recruited from patrician Roman families, who wear glistening helmets with blood orange osprey plumes; the Palatine Guard, enrolled from the Roman middle-class, who wear gold-braided scuttle caps with a pom-pom in front; and the Papal Gendarmerie, who are the police of the Vatican, and wear the uniform of Napoleon's grenadiers, with busbies and a red pouffe, jackets with heavy epaulettes, and tight white inexpressibles.

The High Renaissance coincided with an enormous increase of wealth to princes and potentates. The discovery of the New World and the opening of mines of gold, silver and diamonds led to an influx of riches and jewels from the Americas to Europe. The popes' coffers benefited as much as those of the sovereigns of Christendom from the cataract of treasure. Julius had plenty of revenue to draw upon. The papacy too had never seemed more stable. The days of Lutheranism and Reformation lay ahead unperceived. So discerning a patron was well able to attract to Rome the greatest artists of the age. Painters, architects and sculptors basked in the sun of the new papal Maecenas until such time as they crossed his path. Whereupon they had a rude awakening from any misconceived dreams of giving easy satisfaction. Composers too found opportunities of commissions. Julius loved music and one of his first acts was to endow the papal choir chapel, known as the Cappella Giulia, in order to train native Roman voices. He wished to ensure the singing of the religious offices in a manner befitting the majesty of a renaissance church.

Julius was blessed with that merit common to most great men, a supreme confidence in initiating schemes of such magnitude and expense that posterity has no alternative to complying with them. Such too was the grandeur of his conceptions that he attracted men of a like calibre to carry out his schemes. As one would expect, the coincidence of two minds of this metal sometimes resulted in sparks which, when fanned, turned rapidly to conflagrations. We shall touch upon the storms between Julius II and Michelangelo in another chapter.

Julius had not been pope for longer than a year and a half before he decided to build

The south aisle; water colour by Louis Haghe (see text p. 237)

close to the old basilica a mausoleum to contain the colossal monument of himself which Michelangelo had already been commissioned to execute. He was encouraged in this undertaking by Giuliano da Sangallo, who was then the architect in whom he placed most confidence. His bond with Sangallo had been a mutual loathing of Alexander VI. While the Borgia pope was on the throne Sangallo had been the companion of Cardinal della Rovere during his exile in France. Julius however soon abandoned the project of a detached mausoleum and in the spring of 1505 was intent upon fulfilling the work begun by Nicholas V on the basilica, work which Sangallo, then a young man, had resumed under Paul II. By the summer he changed his mind once again. He concluded that nothing was acceptable less than complete rebuilding on absolutely contemporary lines and in the grandest conceivable manner. This decision was the pope's last; and was irrevocable. It had been brought about by his conviction that the old basilica was now to all intents and purposes ruinous and in a highly dangerous condition.

Needless to say, he encountered much opposition. The Curia and the Romans were now more than ever attached to the Constantinian building. They looked upon it with veneration and a good deal of superstition. Had it not existed practically since the Christian religion was founded, certainly ever since Christianity was accepted as the religion of imperial Rome? It was insufferable that a new pope should lightly take upon himself the responsibility of sweeping away a building twelve hundred years old, a building which was the tangible link with Rome's glorious past. Nearly all the cardinals opposed the decision; and the city was enraged. Satires – always a sign of Roman indignation – were posted at street corners. Pasquino[1] was particularly vociferous. Undeterred, Julius issued an appeal for funds to the Christian monarchs, including Henry VII of England, the bishops and the nobles throughout Europe. Progress was so rapid that on 18th April 1506 the pope laid the first stone of his new basilica twenty-five Roman feet below the pavement of the old. It was to be the foundation of the St Veronica pier at the south-west corner of the crossing. On a block of white marble Julius inscribed his intentions. Under it he placed a pottery vase containing freshly minted ducats, some gold and bronze medals displaying his effigy and a model of the future church. The occasion was one of much formality and splendour. The pope, wearing his mitre and grasping a trowel, descended into the deep abyss with a few attendants. But the crowd so pressed against the edge of the cavity that the pope below feared lest a collapse of the earth might bury him alive. Anxious and alarmed, he hurried through the ceremony to the extent of laying the first stone crooked before scrambling up to the surface. For four months he followed the course of building with the most lively interest. Then on 27th August, accompanied by his architects, he marched to war against Bologna, expelled the usurping Bentivoglio tyrant, and retrieved the province to the Papal States, thus vastly enhancing his prestige among the nations.

When Julius finally made up his mind to rebuild he had before him the choice of three different schemes. The first was Rossellino's dormant plan, which had been prepared for Nicholas V at much trouble and expense. Julius disliked it, and at once dismissed it as thoroughly out of date. The second scheme was presented by his old companion and ally, Giuliano da Sangallo. Giuliano's scheme we may suppose also not to have been contempor-

---

[1] Pasquino, a mutilated Hellenistic torso, on a pavement close to the Palazzo Braschi, was famous for the satires attached to the pedestal at times of controversy.

It was Julius II who put in hand the definitive plan for the new basilica; a portrait by Raphael *left*. The architect of his choice was Donato Bramante *right*

ary enough to satisfy the go-ahead pope, and to hark back to the architect's youth when he was first commissioned by Paul II more than thirty years before. At any rate, the old man's proposals were not accepted. Giuliano retired in high dudgeon – but with liberal rewards – to Florence, declaring that he had been unjustly deprived of work promised him. After six months' lapse however he was persuaded to return and finish the fortifications of Nicholas V's round tower of the Vatican Palace on which he had been previously engaged. The third scheme to be presented, which by its splendour, beauty and novelty captured the imagination of Julius II so as to be accepted without demur, was Donato Bramante's.

The story of the rebuilding of St Peter's is immensely long and complicated. It is nowhere more difficult to follow than during the earliest years of Pope Julius's pontificate, because documents other than drawings are lacking. The number of preparatory sketches on the other hand is vast. Among the Uffizi Gallery archives are preserved about nine hundred folios of studies and models from the hands of Bramante and his pupils, Peruzzi and Antonio da Sangallo; but their history and chronology have not yet been sorted out.

There is no doubt whatever that Julius II and Bramante made a very united partnership. Both were filled with zeal, possessed of a demonic energy and quite without scruple in a determination to see their work fulfilled, no matter what the obstacles or cost. It has been stated that the architect played upon the pope's desire for self-gratification, and persuaded him to rebuild totally. This is unlikely. No one could have persuaded Julius to do anything that did not originate, or that he did not believe to originate in his own mind. Nor were the pope's motives solely personal aggrandizement. The glorification of the

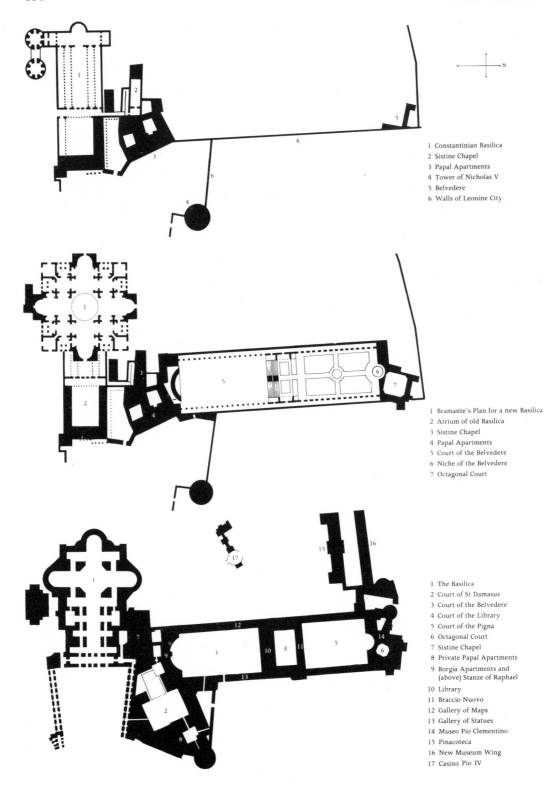

1 Constantinian Basilica
2 Sistine Chapel
3 Papal Apartments
4 Tower of Nicholas V
5 Belvedere
6 Walls of Leonine City

1 Bramante's Plan for a new Basilica
2 Atrium of old Basilica
3 Sistine Chapel
4 Papal Apartments
5 Court of the Belvedere
6 Niche of the Belvedere
7 Octagonal Court

1 The Basilica
2 Court of St Damasus
3 Court of the Belvedere
4 Court of the Library
5 Court of the Pigna
6 Octagonal Court
7 Sistine Chapel
8 Private Papal Apartments
9 Borgia Apartments and
  (above) Stanze of Raphael
10 Library
11 Braccio Nuovo
12 Gallery of Maps
13 Gallery of Statues
14 Museo Pio Clementino
15 Pinacoteca
16 New Museum Wing
17 Casino Pio IV

The development of the Vatican Palace and St Peter's. At the end of the fifteenth century *top*.
A project by Bramante, 1503, which was only partially realized *middle*. Today *bottom*

Church and the papacy was behind his every endeavour, whether in warfare against the Bolognese, in argument with an obstinate Curia, or in raising a church of stupendous proportions. It is true that Bramante handled the pope with delicacy and skill. His tactics were very different from those of the imperious and highly irascible Michelangelo who respected no man, and dared to flout princes and popes. Bramante never opposed Julius, but identified his ideas with his master's, and was always ready to embark upon a new project with the least delay. Vasari stresses his singular promptness to act so long as he felt confident of his client's willingness to pay. Of Pope Julius's compliance in this respect he seemed never to have any doubts.

To the end Bramante remained high in favour with Julius, who was genuinely attached to him. His rise to papal favour was spectacular. He first left his native Lombardy for Rome in 1499 when he was already fifty-five years old. With astonishing enthusiasm he studied and measured all the ancient buildings in the city, the Campagna, Tivoli and Hadrian's Villa. Although of ripe middle age, Bramante allowed his art to be revolution-ized by his Roman discoveries. They were to stand him in excellent stead in the great work of the few years ahead of him. According to Vasari, Bramante had been appointed sub-architect at Alexander VI's court on the strength of the chaste little cloisters he built for the monks of S. Maria della Pace at the expense of Cardinal O. Caraffa. In the first year of Pope Julius's reign, he received 100 florins for some unspecified work at the new court. Bramante was cultivated, well read in Dante, and devoted to music and poetry. Vasari says that he improvised on the lyre, and composed several sonnets; but none of his verse has survived. He was of a cheerful and amiable disposition, and generous to other artists. Indeed he was extravagant, lived in too splendid a style, and was constantly in financial difficulties. He frequently sued his friends for money. He had an immoderate appetite for pears. We have few other particulars of his tastes.

Bramante had a professional's mastery of the building science and technique. Un-fortunately he was far too precipitate to be thorough, or rather too casual to supervise his subordinates properly. Shortly after his death, faults appeared in his workmanship which had to be rectified at much cost and inconvenience. His intensive study of the methods of the ancients enabled him to revive for the first time a cement mixture for friezes and cornices. Vasari gives unstinted praise to Bramante's cornices and to the beauty of the capitals of olive leaves he used on his Corinthian order. In vaulting he invented a method of construction by means of a framework of stout beams, on which the friezes and foliage decoration were carved and then covered with castings in gypsum. He used a novel form of movable scaffolding for centering his arches, of which he was justifiably proud.

Before helping to oust Giuliano da Sangallo from the office of Architect to St Peter's, Bramante had prepared designs for alterations to the Belvedere and the making of the great Belvedere Court of the Vatican Palace, the care of which was traditionally entrusted to a different architect to that of the basilica. The designs are dated 1503 and 1504. Briefly, Bramante's project was to transform Pollaiuolo's isolated Belvedere Villa into a sculpture gallery and to join it to the Vatican offices by a long imposing court, where hitherto vineyards and gardens had been. Corridors were to form the connecting arms. Bramante was the first architect to relate the Belvedere to the rest of the palace. To do so he was obliged to tilt, so to speak, the face of the villa several degrees from east to south in order to set it at right angles with the long arms of his court.

The court of the Belvedere, looking south, with a tournament in progress; an engraving of 1565

The architect's principal objective was to treat this northern end of the great court to be built against the sixteenth-century Belvedere, in imitation of the ruins of the Roman Praeneste, or Palestrina. At the head of the long, stadium-like court stretching southwards there was to be a modified adaptation of the Temple of Fortune. A great niche, or rather hemi-cycle, with flanking walls of blind arcades, separated by twin pilasters, was to be an echo of the semi-circular colonnade of the famous Latin backcloth at Praeneste. Bramante's next idea, never realized, was to fashion an open arcade within the niche. In front of a wide platform there was to be a double ramp descending in terraces. A contemporary perspective sketch by Del Dosio in the Uffizi Gallery shows the partial realization of Bramante's scheme before his niche was raised and given a half-dome, and before other tampering took place a generation later. The somewhat absurd curved colonnade made by Pirro Ligorio to crown the great raised niche is a less effective reminder of the Praeneste prototype than Bramante's sober design would have proved if only it had been carried out.

Before his death, Bramante completed the eastern side of the great court up to the second of its three storeys[1] – of which the lower Doric order was copied from the Theatre of Marcellus – the foundations of the western corridors, and the transformation of the

[1] The third storey was completed by Antonio da Sangallo.

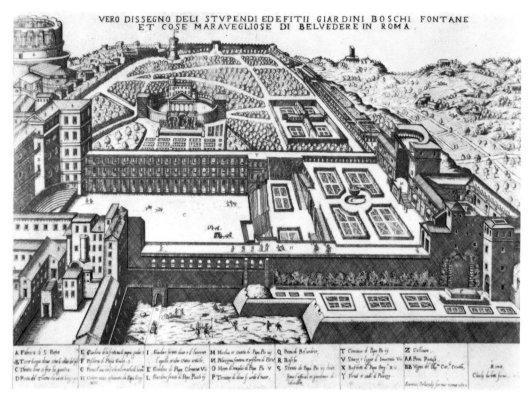

The court of the Belvedere, looking west, with the Vatican Gardens beyond; an engraving of 1579

octagonal statue court within the old Belvedere Villa. The last achievement, which survives, was well in progress by 1506 when the Laocoon group was dug up in Nero's Golden House, and put into one of the corner tribunes. In 1511 the Apollo Belvedere was installed in another. The following year the beautiful spiral staircase, known as La Scala a Chiocciola, was under way. Bramante projected it from the north-eastern angle of the villa. Its purpose was to enable horsemen to ride up to the Belvedere from the lower ground by a short route. An unbroken ramp of soft worn brick, supported by four orders of elegant columns of white stone, one above another, curls gently upwards like a frozen breath. In 1531 a long stretch of Bramante's eastern corridor caved in owing to the architect's careless and hasty construction, or rather to his men being made to work day and night without proper supervision. It had to be rebuilt. Again, two hundred years later the pilasters had to be strengthened. They were so enlarged in the process that they now look disproportionately broad in relation to the space between them.

We must return once more to the activities of Julius II and Bramante at St Peter's in 1505. Those people who look upon renaissance architecture as cold, pompous and imitative – and in the nineteenth century these were common charges – have delighted in abusing this pope for wantonly destroying Constantine's basilica and dispersing the accumulated treasure of centuries which it contained. The accusation is unjust. As we have seen, the

A temporary structure was raised over the shrine of St Peter during the demolition of the old basilica; a drawing attributed to Marten van Heemskerk, 1533

old basilica had been unquestionably ruinous for a very long time. The patching of half a century had been of no avail, besides wasting an enormous amount of money. Wanton Pope Julius certainly was not. Bramante on the other hand was. He was in such a turmoil of hurry to get on with the job – we have to remember that he was far from young, and life was then short and uncertain – that he respected nothing inside the old basilica, neither tombs, statues, mosaics, nor moveable works of art like candelabra, icons and even altars. All these things he threw out as useless, antiquated lumber. He did not bother to have inventories made of the things he destroyed. For several weeks on end he employed 2,500 workmen on this wholesale destruction. Rightly he earned the title of *il ruinante*. Not content with iconoclasm, he urged the pope to have the setting of the new church altered from that of the old. He wanted to make his main front face southwards so as to have Caligula's obelisk, then standing close to the sacristy, in the foreground. The displacement was to involve shifting the Apostle's tomb to another site. Pope Julius to his credit was scandalized, and resolutely refused to countenance the proposal. He would not allow the tomb to be touched. On the contrary, he ordered the architect to raise a temporary structure of *peperino* over the presbytery and the confession, including the Constantinian apse, to protect them inviolate during the demolitions and rebuilding. The structure is shown in several sixteenth-century drawings, a pleasing Doric affair of three arches and a pediment, too good one would suppose for so ephemeral a purpose. It survived until 1592.

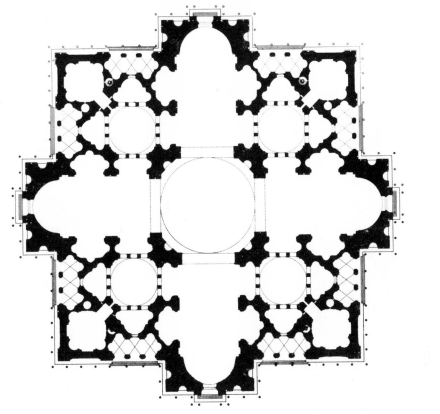

One of Bramante's early plans for the new basilica, based upon the shape of the Greek cross contained within a circle, with a central dome surrounded by lesser domes

Ruthless though Bramante was, he was by no means free to do just what he wanted. There was the restraining hand of his master, which he dared not defy. There were the unfinished walls of Pope Nicholas V's choir, or tribune, and the still more extensive west foundations of the apse and transepts, which he was bound from reasons of economy to take into account. To a large extent, they determined the dimensions of his overall plan for the new basilica (they were only scrapped in 1585 on advice given years previously by Michelangelo). Lastly, there was the prevailing fashion of his day that only a centralized plan was suitable for the mother church of Christendom. In other words, the old, strictly basilican plan, long, rectangular or transeptal, could no longer be entertained. The symbol of the universal Christ expressed in the Greek cross within a circle, geometrically relating a central dome to a series of lesser domes, was deemed essential to the new humanistic approach to religious architecture.[1] Bramante designed on this pattern a vast building to cover 24,000 square metres, which was 9,500 more than the area finally covered by Michelangelo's church before the nave was lengthened in the seventeenth century. The diameter of Bramante's Greek cross would have been nearly two fifths greater than the length of the old Constantinian nave and over three fifths greater than its width.

[1] The abstruse theological and architectural doctrines of the Greek cross are the subject of R. Wittkower's *Architectural Principles of the Age of Humanism*, 1949.

The Greek cross design as the ideal shape for a church had inspired Perugino in a mural for the Sistine Chapel in 1482

Bramante had already experimented with the Greek cross within a circle in Milan.[1] He had been inspired by Leonardo da Vinci's paper plans and drawings of churches in this idiom. Leonardo had not executed any of them. Bramante however was determined to make the attempt. Both Leonardo and Bramante had closely studied the fifth-century church of S. Lorenzo in Milan, which was of centralized plan with four large apses. Its influence is very apparent in Leonardo's sketches and Bramante's actual work, for which the first opportunity arose when he was called upon to enlarge the church of S. Satiro. This was in either the late 1470s or early 1480s. Bramante was at once impressed by the existing church which dated from the ninth century. No larger than a small chapel it too was of centralized plan. The architect not only incorporated it in his larger scheme but adapted the design to the baptistry which he added to S. Satiro. Thus Bramante's baptistry at Milan became the prototype of all renaissance centrally planned churches and chapels. His designs for St Peter's were, however, not his first attempt in Rome at this form of architecture, derived as it was from early Christian churches. In 1502 he built the circular Tempietto in the courtyard of S. Pietro in Montorio, on the site then erroneously claimed to be that of St Peter's martyrdom.

The Tempietto design, although on an infinitely smaller scale, can be detected in Bramante's ambitious scheme for St Peter's. The culminating feature of the centrally planned church is of course the dome; and the peristyle and dome of the Tempietto are

[1] For the information in this paragraph I am much indebted to Mr Peter Murray's *Architecture of the Italian Renaissance*, 1963, chapter V.

Bramante's design for the Tempietto of S. Pietro in Montorio in 1502 *left* and the front elevation of St Peter's as illustrated on a medal of Julius II, 1506 *right*

reflected in the colonnade of the drum and the dome of Bramante's St Peter's, as indeed we can judge from the relief of a medal struck by Julius II and in Serlio's woodcut in his treatise on architecture.[1] The colonnade of St Peter's drum was to be closely packed with Corinthian shafts, whereas the peristyle of the Tempietto is composed of Doric columns comparatively widely spaced. Nevertheless, the conception of both is the same. In each building the dome is a hemisphere, crowned by a finial motif in the smaller, and a proper lantern in the larger. In the St Peter's design, the dome is raised from the base by steps so as to bear out the architect's boast that he was going to put the dome of the Pantheon over the vault of the Temple of Peace, which was the renaissance name for the dominating Basilica of Maxentius in the Roman Forum.

In 1506 a foundation medal was struck showing Bramante's final intention. It depicted a hemispherical Pantheon-like dome, as in Serlio's woodcut. In addition, there were to be four lesser domes (of which two only appear on the relief) over the arms of the Greek cross church, and a fifth over the portico entrance. This entrance was likewise derived from that of the Pantheon, and Bramante actually made his masons begin copying the Hadrianic capitals of the original, only on a larger scale. As early as 1508 contracts were made for carving them as well as the balustrade of the balcony to be reserved for the papal blessing. A pair of very tall bell towers were to flank the portico. The necessarily rough medal relief was no doubt a general indication of what Julius and Bramante hoped would come into being.

[1] *Tutte L'Opere D'Architettura et Prospetiva*. The first two books were published in 1537 and 1540.

In the autumn of 1506 the victorious pope returned from his military campaign against Bologna accompanied by Bramante. At once the two men resumed work upon St Peter's with increased gusto. On 10th April 1507 the Archbishop of Taranto laid the foundation stones of the three other piers of the great crossing to support the dome. Since the crossing piers were the first part of the structure to be raised, they were largely to dictate the size and even shape of the future basilica, no matter how far subsequent architects deviated from the original scheme. Alas, work on the colossal undertaking took its time! There were other pressing demands upon Julius's energies, and funds were not disgorged quickly enough even from the fat papal coffers. In 1513 the pope issued a bull announcing to the world that the new basilica would eclipse in size and magnificence every church in Christendom. Graciously he promised an extension of indulgences to those pious benefactors who agreed to pay contributions on an annual basis.

The idea that a generous offering to some good cause, made with the right intentions, should be rewarded with an indulgence from 'the Church's treasure chest', is quite in accordance with Catholic doctrine. But, inevitably, it came to be interpreted that anyone could buy remission from his time in purgatory. Indulgences in fact were offered by some preachers as if they were for sale. The abuse was subsequently forbidden by the Council of Trent; but it was too late. It provided the spark that ignited the fires of the Protestant Reformation which consumed the chaff and the grain alike. One of the ironies of history is that the means devised to finance the building of a great shrine over the tomb of the first pope should have done much to destroy the authority of his successors.

Soon after his magnanimous gesture Pope Julius II, worn out by excruciating pain from stone in the bladder, died. Bramante, crippled with gout in the hands, lost heart and in 1514 followed his master to the grave. At his death the four great piers were complete up to the cornice, and the connecting arches, now adorned with sunk panels in the Roman fashion, were in place. The form of the piers was never to be substantially altered. It remained the governing factor of every subsequent plan of St Peter's, including the final and actual one.[1] Furthermore, the walls of the projecting choir (the Tribuna di San Piero) were completed on Nicholas V and Rossellino's foundations; and vaulting was begun on the south transept, where until very lately St Petronilla's chapel had stood.

Bramante had always been generous in helping and promoting fellow artists. Very wisely he had rallied round him a band of the brightest of the younger generation to collaborate at St Peter's. They greatly respected and loved his memory. In consequence, the Bramante tradition was upheld without question for many years after his death. Not until the death of Paul III in 1549 were definite changes brought about. Bramante's plan for St Peter's was then jettisoned. Even so there is evidence that his disciples made modified use of his designs for lesser Greek cross churches, such as S. Maria di Loreto in Rome, the lovely S. Maria della Consolazione at Todi, and possibly S. Biagio at Montepulciano.

As early as 6th April 1506 a money order had been issued, doubtless at Bramante's request, enabling him to pay for the services of five sub-architects. Of these Antonio da Sangallo the younger, who had followed his uncle Giuliano to Rome, became indispensable to Bramante, and towards the end of his life completed the drawings which the old man's trembling fingers could barely sketch in outline.

---

[1] H. von Geymüller (*Les Projets Primitifs pour la Basilique de St Pierre de Rome*, 1875) is insistent on this point.

Bramante's stature in the history of St Peter's is immense. The trust reposed in him by the pope, once he had approved each project, was implicit. The architect was regarded as the divinely inspired instrument of Christ's Vicar in the creation of the greatest temple of the Christian world. His design for St Peter's was commensurate with the authority of the papacy as regenerated by a civilization newly based on principles of humanism and the rules of art according to the classical masters. The Renaissance was very conscious of its break with medieval philosophy and art; and Bramante's projected basilica was the symbol of a new manner of thinking and more glorious mode of living. Moreover he raised the profession of architect to one of the most honourable and coveted posts in renaissance Rome. Hitherto, architects were recognized under the names of *muratore*, *tagliapietra* or *faber lignarius*,[1] and were treated merely as master craftsmen. Bramante earned the title of *Messer*, which was accorded to his successors at St Peter's in tribute to a highly responsible office. Not only was he sole creator of the basilican design but the controller of a huge army of workmen attached to innumerable crafts. On the pope's behalf, he drew up contracts with the master craftsmen, who were paid by a conventional tariff for each square foot of wall, pavement and roof, and an agreed sum for each specially applied feature, whether column, capital, vaulting panel or niche shell-head. The master craftsmen in their turn paid the artisans whom they employed by the day.

Julius II's successor, Leo X (1513–21), was an oldish-young Medici of thirty-seven. The favourable circumstance of birth rather than brain had made him a prodigy. He was ordained priest at the age of seven, and created a cardinal at thirteen on the marriage of his sister to the son of Pope Innocent VIII. Privilege and precedence were his as though by right. Pleasure he demanded and got. 'Let us enjoy the papacy since God has given it to us' are words which may have been put into his mouth. They certainly express the behaviour by which we may judge him. At the same time this spoilt prince was of true piety and blameless morals. He was modest and gentle. Unfortunately his appearance, which may have determined his career, was unprepossessing, for he was puffy, flabby and unhealthy. This was not owing to good living for he eat and drank sparingly. All his life he suffered severely from chronic fistula, on the pretext of curing which a young cardinal attempted to poison him in 1517, but was discovered and put to death. In spite of physical disabilities, Leo exercised undeniable charm. His tastes were spontaneous. As well as hunting and coarse buffoonery, he dearly loved music and literature. The greatest achievement of his reign was the promotion of painting. He got Raphael to finish decorating the Stanze of the Vatican Palace and to design cartoons of tapestries for the Sistine Chapel. His affection for Raphael was demonstrable. He made him a papal chamberlain and, according to Vasari, actually contemplated making him a cardinal. When the painter addressed to the pope his famous request of 1520 that the antiquities of Rome ought to be respected, Leo at once complied and commanded that the greatest care should be taken of them in the future. When Raphael lay dying Leo sent daily to ask after him, and in anxiety for his friend's soul despatched the Fornarina[2] from his house while at the same time providing her handsomely with money. On Raphael's death the pope was plunged into such distress that for weeks he was incapable of attending to business.

[1] Literally builder of walls, stone carver and carpenter.
[2] Raphael's mistress.

Leo X, *left* in a portrait by Raphael, appointed Fra Giovanni Giocondo *right* as assistant to Bramante

Leo received at his court painters, musicians and writers on the level of patricians and would allow no class distinctions where the aristocracy of the mind was concerned. His thirst for the company of creative artists was unquenchable. 'He spent his life', the historian Ranke declared, 'in a sort of intellectual intoxication.' In this respect he was indeed a renaissance prince and a true chip of the Medici block.

Leo X was however by no means as discerning, or eclectic a patron of the arts as Julius II. Sculpture and architecture did not move him as much as painting, stucco work and the ancillary decorative arts. Consequently, he carried on the building of St Peter's from a sense of duty to his great office rather than enthusiasm for participating in an architectural masterpiece. All the same, no sooner was he elected than he was obliged to take instant action. The death of Pope Julius and the fatal decline of the architect, Bramante, had removed the two great impulses behind the whole project. Leo was confronted with the ancient basilica partly demolished and the new one only just begun. Confusion was appalling. The crossing still lacked a roof; the Constantinian nave was exposed to wind and rain. Debris and dust were everywhere and nowhere could Mass be celebrated. Something had to be done. The pope ordered the demolition work to continue. By November 1519 the Constantinian portico had fallen beneath the pickaxes. An urgent need now was to ensure adequate funds. So the pope confirmed Julius's special indulgences to subscribers towards the building expenses. For a time this source of supply continued to function. But after the abuse of indulgences was turned into one of Luther's chief weapons against the papacy, contributions from the faithful through this channel were soon reduced to a trickle. Lastly, a successor to Bramante had to be appointed.

On his accession, Leo at once recalled from Florence old Giuliano da Sangallo[1] to become partner to the man who had superseded him in 1505. Bramante was by this time extremely feeble and, as I have pointed out, almost wholly dependent upon young Antonio,[2] the son of Giuliano's sister, to whom the uncle was also devoted. So the appointment may not have been as tactless as it otherwise seems. Giuliano was now nearly seventy and himself required assistants to share the heavy responsibilities of his duty. Four and a half months before Bramante died, the pope thereupon appointed two other partners, Fra Giovanni Giocondo and Raphael. Within less than six years, all the members of this triumvirate were dead.

In 1514 Fra Giocondo was seventy-nine years old. He was a jolly old Dominican monk of many accomplishments who originally hailed from Verona. He was a Greek scholar of some renown and an engineer, whose skill in hydraulics and bridge building was widely extolled. He was much travelled, had harnessed a water supply at Blois and built a bridge over the Seine for the French kings. He was besides the intimate friend and adviser, perhaps even the spiritual confessor, of Raphael. Unfortunately, Fra Giocondo died very soon after his appointment,[3] but not before fulfilling a most useful function. His experience detected weaknesses in Bramante's structure, and he lived just long enough to school his colleagues in the way to overcome them by reinforcing the foundations. But now Raphael was likewise deprived of his 'administrator and coadjutor', as he described Giuliano da Sangallo. On the very day of Fra Giocondo's death Giuliano, worn out and ailing, retired to Florence, where in 1517 he died. The youngest and surviving member of the triumvirate was thereupon left sole Architect in Chief of St Peter's.

As we have seen, Leo's devotion to Raphael even exceeded that of Fra Giocondo and Giuliano da Sangallo. Indeed everyone loved Raphael, whose singular sweetness captivated the hearts of his contemporaries, and cast a spell over posterity. It accordingly invested his art with a veil of romance which, until lifted this century, prevented an objective view of its proper merits.

Raphael's charm was in a sense his undoing. Not insensible to the adulation which his genius and beauty of person induced, he allowed himself to be smothered by the attentions of his devoted admirers. Never had an artist been more lionized. At the height of his fame, he moved like a prince rather than a painter. When he went to court he was often accompanied by as many as fifty artists gathered to do him honour. Patrons overwhelmed his slender shoulders with commissions which he was not always able to fulfil.

Raphael had first come to Rome on the recommendation of Bramante in 1508, when he began painting the Stanze for Pope Julius II. He threw himself with the fervour of faith into celebrating the divine pre-eminence of the papacy, a doctrine soon to be passionately controverted. Pope Julius was so delighted with his frescoes that he dismissed Perugino, Pinturicchio and the other painters working at the Vatican Palace in favour of his new protégé who was then barely twenty-five years old. Whatever architectural qualifications the young painter acquired, he owed to Bramante, who even sketched for him

---

[1] Giuliano da Sangallo's actual appointment was dated 1st January 1514 (N.S.).

[2] In 1510 Antonio da Sangallo received 200 ducats for centring the four arches supporting the dome. He was also that year called in as Master of Work upon alterations to the Torre Borgia to Bramante's designs.

[3] 1st July 1515.

the perspective of buildings on the School of Athens fresco. His single experience of church design was the little chapel of S. Eligio degli Orefici, lying between the Via Giulia and the Tiber, which he planned as a Greek cross and to which he gave a shallow drum and hemispherical dome in the Bramantesque style. But in Bramante's admiring eyes this limitation was no reason why Raphael should not ultimately be entrusted with carrying on his tremendous scheme of rebuilding the first Christian church of the world. After all he too had been primarily a painter who only took to architecture in his advanced middle age. In renaissance times artists were not expected to specialize in only one field of activity. Therefore there is nothing surprising in Pope Leo's brief of 1st August 1514 to Raphael in which he wrote, 'At his [Bramante's] death he justly opined that to you might be confided the building commenced by him . . .'

As time went on, Raphael became more and more troubled by the responsibilities of his post of Architect in Chief to the basilica. His heart and soul were concentrated upon painting the Stanze and decorating the Loggie which bear his name. Their completion was, he felt, the principal motive of his life. At first he embarked upon his new rôle fairly happily because he knew that he had Leo's wholehearted backing. As early as July 1514 he had written to a friend that the pope 'has associated me with an aged monk who has passed his eightieth year. The pope sees that he cannot live much longer, and His Holiness has therefore determined that I should benefit by the instructions of this distinguished craftsman and attain to greater proficiency in the art of architecture, of the beauties of which he has recondite knowledge; his name is Fra Giocondo. The pope gives us an audience every day, and keeps us long in conversation on the subject of the building.' After the aged monk and the ailing Giuliano had withdrawn from the scene, Raphael was left to hold the heavy baby on his own. He was obliged to continue remedying Bramante's faulty work on the lines indicated by Fra Giocondo, and propping up what was left of the old basilica, tasks which frankly bored him. He was distracted how to raise funds. There was little time, and less money, with which to make headway with the new building.

It was some relief to have Antonio da Sangallo with whom to share responsibilities. On 22nd November 1516 the nephew of his old friend, Giuliano, had been appointed coadjutor. This had entailed getting the consent of Antonio's patron, Cardinal Alessandro Farnese. It was willingly given. The two artists worked in happy collaboration and the past experience of Sangallo as assistant to Bramante on work at St Peter's gave much support to the harassed painter. Antonio had apparently criticized in a friendly and helpful spirit and even amended Raphael's first model for a basilica, which was on a plan different to Bramante's, namely that of a Latin cross. This happened soon after Raphael's appointment as Architect in Chief in 1514. Whether the Latin cross plan was entirely Raphael's idea is not known. Certainly Leo X was delighted and thought it more practical than the Greek cross plan. Bramante may have come round to its possibilities just before his death. Raphael's manuscript drawings have not been preserved, nor have the two models he is known to have made. His second plan can only be judged from a moderately accurate woodcut which Serlio gives of it in his treatise.[1] Raphael's basilica, according to Serlio, was to consist of a nave and two aisles, instead of four, separated by pilasters against narrow piers. The whole exercise cost the artist much tribulation and anxiety how it was to be carried out. 'Vitruvius gives me of course considerable guidance,' he wrote

[1] Geymüller, op. cit., is emphatic that Serlio's woodcut had nothing to do with Raphael's design.

The interior of the dome (see text p. 225)

ruefully, 'but not enough.' He looked to antiquity for beautiful forms, all of which were supplied by his own keen observation of Roman remains and what Bramante's more scholarly studies had imparted to him. Alas, his fears how he would acquit himself in directing the actual construction were unnecessary! One afternoon in the spring of 1520 he hurried from the Villa Farnesina on foot and arrived at St Peter's in a great sweat and fever. Within a period of days he was dead. He was thirty-seven years old.

During his six years as Architect in Chief, Raphael had executed two models of St Peter's, of which the first was praised and the second accepted by Pope Leo. His actual achievement however amounted to little more than the raising of one or two columns and the continuation of Bramante's vaulting. On his death the Latin cross project was abandoned. Leo came to the reluctant conclusion that it was too expensive. The Greek cross was once more in favour as entailing less stone and mortar. The varying plans in this form by Antonio da Sangallo may date from this period of uncertainty. As we shall see, they too came to nothing because of lack of funds. Yet Leo was somehow induced to advance 60,000 scudi to pay for consolidating Bramante's foundations and existing walls, the labour and expense of which had so greatly harassed his beloved Raphael.

The name of another great architect associated with St Peter's now comes into prominence. Baldassare Peruzzi belongs to the same generation as Raphael and Antonio da Sangallo the younger, being only two years their senior.[1] He had been architect of the Villa Farnesina which Raphael was busily decorating at the time of his death. Pope Leo came to the conclusion that the plans for St Peter's by all the preceding architects were on too large a scale, and 'that the various parts of that vast fabric were not in harmony with each other', according to Vasari. He resolved therefore to have a new model constructed by yet another architect. Peruzzi was appointed coadjutor to Antonio in 1520. Like many of his distinguished brethren he spent much of his working life at St Peter's, left behind him a mass of projects on paper and very little to show for them. Scores of drawings by Peruzzi survive which pose numerous problems. He had even prepared a plan for a new basilica as early as 1505 when he was twenty-three years old. In a general history of St Peter's there is little point in analysing projects which in any case came to nothing. It is enough to state that the plan which met with the final approval of Peruzzi himself, Pope Leo and his successors was of a Greek cross with apsed arms, each apse opening upon a semi-circular colonnade. The central dome was to be flanked by four lesser cupolas. At the angles were four, square projecting towers. The high altar was to be in the centre under the dome. Whether Peruzzi's plan would have provided a church practical or large enough is doubtful. But it might have been a building of the greatest beauty, to judge from his perspective drawing for it.

Pope Leo's old enemy the fistula finally got the better of him, and carried him off in 1521. For a year the papacy underwent a marked change of incumbency. No greater contrast to the pleasure-loving, art-dedicated Medici of princely lineage and splendid upbringing could be imagined than the ascetic, academic Fleming of low birth and impoverished background who now succeeded. Adrian VI was serious, good and pious. But he genuinely disliked all forms of display, and mistrusted artists and intellectuals, who during his

---

[1] He was born in 1481. Raphael and Antonio da Sangallo were both born in 1483.

The interior of a cupola (see text p. 237)

A self portrait by Raphael, *c.* 1504 *above left*, and his plan for St Peter's *above right*. The perspective drawing by Peruzzi for a Greek cross church with a portico, *c.* 1529 *below*

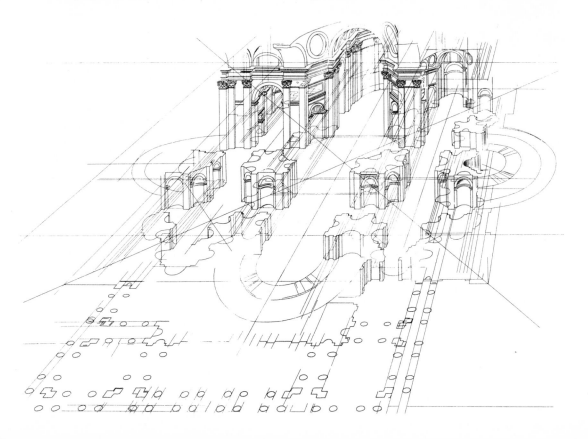

Pope Clement VII and the Emperor Charles V, by Vasari

brief reign lay low. Moreover, he was quite without humour, and bent upon reforms. In consequence, the Italians were utterly bewildered by this unsophisticated northerner. They had no use for him whatever. Adrian's unpopularity, the progress of the Lutherans, the fall of Rhodes to the Turks, the political dissensions raging among the French, English and Germans, and the plagues in Rome hastened his death. He was succeeded by the most tragic and pitiable of all the popes of the Renaissance, if not of all the ages, Clement VII (1523–34).

Clement was, like Leo X, a Medici, albeit an illegitimate Medici. Not prodigal like Leo, but parsimonious, not frivolous but frugal, and naturally procrastinating and indecisive. He was the victim of his predecessors' mistakes and of ineluctable circumstances. The landslide which had begun to rumble during the reign of Leo – who, warned by the Catholic sovereigns to heed the anti-papal propaganda and avoid further abuses, merely turned a deaf ear – and to rattle down the slopes during the reign of Adrian, fell in a cascade of destruction upon the whole fabric of Christendom during that of the unfortunate Clement. England, Scandinavia and half of Germany were

At the time of the Sack of Rome the troops of the Emperor parodied a papal procession and made mockery of the papal blessing; a sixteenth-century engraving

lost to Catholicism in the Protestant apostasy. The Turks gained further victories in Eastern Europe. The fatal rôle of temporal sovereignty long since adopted by the papacy now exposed Clement's weakness to the voracity of the Christian princes. The Emperor Charles V, parading as the secular champion of the Faith, profited from the disturbances of the time by quarrelling with the pope and turning northern Italy into a battlefield. The factious Colonna family, encouraged by the emperor, marched into Rome in 1526 and looted the Vatican Palace. One member strutted upon the piazza in the pope's vestments while making mockery of the papal blessing. These calamities and insults were pin-pricks compared with the bloody wounds which were to follow. In May 1527 occurred the Sack of Rome, which was one of the most terrible of the many incidents of the sort to befall the ancient city. No pope before or since suffered worse indignities and humili-ations; and few of his attendants escaped physical violence of the utmost cruelty. In his defence the whole body of the gallant Swiss Guards was wiped out to a man.[1] The

[1] It is pleasant to record that after the sack Clement VII in gratitude reaffirmed the duties and re-established the privileges of the Swiss Guards, when he recruited them anew.

barbarity of the invaders far exceeded that of the Goths and Vandals. The destruction of buildings and works of art within so short a time was never before so widespread. And by whose hands were these indescribable things perpetrated? And for what reason? By the imperialist troops of the avowed enemy of Lutheranism, the healer of schism, the pious devotee, the eldest son of Mother Church, the Holy Roman Emperor, Charles V, in requital for the pope's endeavour to free Italy from foreign domination.

The emperor's henchman in this nauseating business was a hired Frenchman, the Constable of Bourbon, who commanded a mixed bag of Protestant German and Catholic Spanish troops. Under his leadership, they desecrated the churches and tore the Blessed Sacrament from the tabernacles, submitting it to every blasphemy. The head of St Andrew was thrown to the ground, St Veronica's napkin was offered for sale, the Holy Lance was fastened by a German soldier to his pike and marched through the Borgo. Pictures and sculpture were smashed, treasures melted down and tapestries plundered in endeavours to extract the gold and silver thread. One of the least misfortunes of the sack was the destruction of the building accounts relating to the new basilica. The actual tomb of St Peter was however untouched, not we may imagine through special reverence of the invaders, but because of its immunity within Bramante's protective structure. Instead, the mercenaries murdered every ecclesiastic on whom they laid hands, and violated and sold nuns to the brothels. It was estimated that 6,000 to 10,000 inhabitants of the city were put to the sword and two-thirds of the buildings destroyed. For fifty miles around Rome, the country was made into a smoking wilderness.

For several months Pope Clement remained shut in the Castle of S. Angelo in conditions of appalling want and misery. In December the imperialists were bribed with what money the pope could rake together to quit. In the confusion Clement slipped away to Orvieto, where in time he recovered his health and senses.

Clement VII *left* was broken in mind and spirit by the experience of the Sack. He gained safety in the Castel S. Angelo by escaping along the secret passage from the Vatican *right*

The central crossing under construction, looking west; a drawing by Marten van Heemskerk

When Clement VII was elected pope he had made it clear that he wished to continue Leo's Medici patronage of art and letters. Accordingly, the artists and intellectuals, whom Adrian had discouraged, flocked back to Rome. Painting in the Stanze was resumed, and additions were made to the Vatican Library. But the events which I have described drastically curtailed papal patronage. The Sack of Rome caused the dispersal of Raphael's surviving band of artists, which was never reunited. Indeed the sack is often said to have ended abruptly the phase called the High Renaissance. The terrible bloodshed and destruction had an instantaneous effect upon artistic style. The tranquil course of classical art was broken. Gentle pastoral scenery and idyllic figures of swains and shepherdesses now seemed irrelevant to landscape painting, totally unrealistic and out of date. The horrors men had recently endured were henceforth reflected in different scenes and figures. Artists concentrated upon acts of brutality and moods of passion. Architecture too was shaken out of the classic repose which had suited the sleepy opulence and security of Leo's reign. Instead, the design of buildings became contrary, harsh, even cruel. An element of defiance of and hostility to the past was to be detected in the new style, which we today call mannerist, of buildings by contemporaries like Giulio Romano and Michelangelo. These men had lived through and participated in events which seered their very souls.

Clement's first act on his election had been to set up a commission to investigate how funds were being spent on work on the new basilica and to ensure that henceforth they should be properly spent. He instituted the Congregazione della Fabbrica di San Pietro, which has taken charge of the fabric ever since. His second act was to appoint Peruzzi Architect in Chief of St Peter's. He made him devote much work upon embellishing the Chapel of the Sacrament, which was later demolished with the rest of the old basilica.

The west end of the new basilica under construction; a drawing by Marten van Heemskerk

Needless to say, Peruzzi's achievements as principal architect amounted to little during this reign. In the sack he only just got away with his life. He was captured trying to escape from the city; and suspected of being a high-ranking prelate because of his grave appearance. To prove his claim to be an artist, he was forced to draw the corpse of the Constable of Bourbon who had met his deserts in the fighting. The sketch was considered by his captors so convincing that he was spared.

Such was the resilience of Clement VII and so great his love of the arts that by the time of his death the effects of the Sack of Rome were at least superficially repaired. Owing to his particular patronage of jewellers, much of the treasure of the papacy was replaced. The Court of St Damasus, contiguous to the south-east corner of the Court of the Belvedere was begun. Only St Peter's remained in a state of suspension; and grass and weeds were now growing upon the crevices of Bramante's great piers and arches. There are records of what St Peter's then looked like. The very year of Clement's death, Marten van Heemskerk, a Flemish painter and engraver, on a three-year visit to Rome, began making a number of sketches of the constructions. They show the arched but still roofless crossing of the new basilica towering above the remains of the old, and dwarfing the adjacent Vatican Palace on the north. From now on, innumerable topographical artists, many of them foreigners, illustrated the consecutive phases of the rebuilding. Likewise, we begin to get eye-witnesses' accounts in writing. For instance, in 1535, the last year in which Heemskerk was sketching, one Johann Fichard, a lawyer from Frankfurt, was jotting down his detailed impressions of St Peter's and the Vatican.

Very different was the character of Paul III (1534–49) from that of Clement VII. Cardinal Alessandro Farnese, builder of the Palazzo Farnese and patron of Antonio da Sangallo the

Paul III was determined to carry on with the rebuilding of St Peter's; a fresco by Vasari showing the basilica from the west, with Rosselino's choir of S. Piero in the foreground

younger, was sixty-seven at his election, which took place without lobbying and without opposition. He was able, diplomatic, crafty and very popular. He knew how to withstand the voracity and self-seeking of the European princes and the emperor. The figure and features of this old man are familiar from Titian's portrait – the head thrust forward from the shoulders, the eyes penetrating yet betraying nothing of what they see, the chin slightly jutting and the long beard spade-shaped; the nose straight and narrow and the mouth foxy. It is the face of a man ruthless and cruel enough when provoked to strike. No one has yet fully revealed how barbaric were the sentences of the Inquisition which he established in Rome. When Ludwig Pastor was writing his *History of the Popes from the Middle Ages* he was never allowed to investigate the proceedings of the Sacred Congregation of Propaganda. Even the Emperor Charles V had occasion to remonstrate with Pope Paul III over his severe dealings with heretics. Yet this stern pontiff was determined to grapple with the reform of the Church which he saw to be absolutely necessary; and it was during his reign that the Council of Trent was convoked. He was hardworking and allowed himself few relaxations. One was to watch the traditional carnival sport of pushing a herd of swine off the summit of Monte Testaccio to be hacked in pieces below by riders armed with lances.

Paul III was a generous contributor to the Vatican Library. Although he patronized men of learning, theologians were more welcome to his court than poets. He gave a sitting to Titian in 1543, it is true; otherwise he employed only second-class painters. Architecture however was another matter, and the Farnese Palace, one of the undoubted masterpieces of the Renaissance, will be his lasting monument. In the Vatican Palace he was responsible for the Cappella Paolina and the Sala Regia, the construction of which unfortunately involved the destruction of the chapel painted by Fra Angelico for Nicholas V. But Paul was not the man to be over-scrupulous when making room for something he wanted. And although he issued stringent commands that the ancient monuments of the city must be protected, he nevertheless removed from them large blocks of marble for the building of St Peter's and, in laying out new streets, razed several historic temples to the ground.

In December 1534 Pope Paul summoned Peruzzi, who since the Sack of Rome had established himself in Siena, to resume his duties at St Peter's. The architect was immediately directed to carry on work at the Belvedere. Before he could turn his attentions to the basilica, he died in January of 1536. Paul was not to be deterred by this misfortune. He was absolutely determined to continue the rebuilding of the church of Peter begun with such impetus by Pope Julius II and Bramante, but practically static since their deaths. The obvious architect of great experience, long association with St Peter's and faithful service to himself was Antonio da Sangallo. To him the task was now solely entrusted; and he was exhorted to proceed with promptness. Pope Paul's fanaticism in prosecuting a decision was no less formidable than that of Pope Julius, but there was one thing he lacked in which the other abounded, and that was money. He had the greatest difficulty in raising funds, and he set about the attempt by questionable means. He pilfered part of the contributions from Spain towards the crusade against the Turks, and re-embarked upon the dangerous course of selling indulgences.

As long ago as 1520 Antonio da Sangallo, in reversal of Raphael's Latin cross plans, was experimenting upon Greek cross designs for Pope Leo. He did not depart from them now. In fact the Greek cross plan he prepared for Pope Paul III approximates to Bramante's far more closely than Peruzzi's had done. We are able to judge it minutely, because the detailed model which he submitted to the pope has survived.[1] Very large and made of wood, it took seven years to finish and cost as much as the building of a fair sized church. It shows how closely Sangallo repeated the Lombardic features which Bramante had introduced to the Roman Renaissance. They constitute the design's chief weakness which critics were not slow to pounce upon. Antonio's spaces were far too cluttered with

[1] The model was made for Sangallo by Antonio Labacco and is a marvel of joinery.

Antonio da Sangallo's projected scheme for the completion of St Peter's. Plan *above*; model *below*

closely packed orders, tabernacle windows and arcades. Vasari referred deprecatingly to 'all those minute pyramids of which he proposed to form the finish, seeing that in all these things the model does rather seem to imitate the Teutonic or Gothic manner than the good and ancient one now usually followed by the best architects'. Vasari was right in considering Sangallo's design overwrought and fussy. His dome was a mixture of Bramante's St Peter's dome and S. Maria delle Grazie cupola in Milan, and made to rest upon a drum of two orders of arcades. The crowning lantern was packed with columns, and fairly bristled with pyramids. The distinguishing feature was two immensely high towers flanking a porticoed vestibule which projected towards the east. Sangallo's vestibule is unlike anything we have considered hitherto, and if carried out would seemingly have extended his centralized plan into a Latin cross.

Sangallo's model has distinct likenesses to Bramante's project, but is without the older architect's ultimate grasp of the ancient Roman economy. It is full of motives taken from the Colosseum and the Theatre of Marcellus, but unassimilated and unrefined, of such sort as Bramante adopted from text books in his Milanese days before seeing and studying these things for himself at source. Certainly Michelangelo thought he filched his master's schemes without improving upon them in the process. It is true Michelangelo's well-known dislike of Sangallo was not directed exclusively against his architecture. He gravely resented Sangallo's explosion of ill nature in his presence when Paul III approved of Michelangelo's design of a cornice for the Palazzo Farnese. The occasion was almost a reflection of the uncle Giuliano's resentment years previously at being superseded by his superior in talent, namely Bramante. Michelangelo was also involved in a row with Antonio over the Borgo fortifications, when he caused work on the other's Santo Spirito gateway to be discontinued. Antonio was undeniably touchy and jealous. He was also snobbish and unfeeling. He allowed his wife, a beautiful but spoilt and haughty girl, to insult his poor relations; and he is said to have been so disagreeable to his old father that he died of a broken heart. These failings doubtless exacerbated Michelangelo's antipathy. But above all the great sculptor genuinely disapproved of the other's methods of composition, his insensitivity in assembling his masses and his overall heaviness. He found Antonio's architecture derivative, stodgy and dull.

Once Sangallo's model was approved by Pope Paul, work was put in hand, and there was a spurt of activity. The architect hastened to enlist as many of his relations as he could muster on whose complacency he could rely. Vasari refers to them as *la setta Sangallesca*, the clique or mutual admiration society, whose greed in making money out of St Peter's filled Michelangelo with intense disgust. In 1538 Sangallo raised a divisional wall across the nave of the old basilica in the thirteenth bay towards the east at a point which was to terminate his new building. In 1540 he was diverted to tackle work on the Sala Regia in the Vatican Palace. Between 1544 and 1546 he was back at the church engaged upon the inner ring of piers on the apsed transepts. All was proceeding smoothly when the pope sent Sangallo to canalize the waters of the river Velino near Marmora. The heat was intense; Antonio was old and delicate. He caught a fever and died.

Once again, another long and carefully prepared scheme for the new St Peter's went by the board. There is no reason to regret that Sangallo's design was not carried out. It is enough to have it in the beautifully made model. It is too eclectic, too pernickety and too tasteless to have been a success. With Sangallo's death, the Bramante school may be said to have come to a close. His programme was then finally jettisoned as we shall

An engraving of 1548 showing the front elevation of Sangallo's design

shortly see. Even so, Sangallo's work went far enough to settle once and for all the interior volumes of the future basilica. This architect also determined the level of the pavement by raising it above that of Constantine's, and so forming the height of the crypt, or Grotte as they are called, below. Finally, a debt of gratitude will always be due to him for having strengthened the fabric which he inherited. Vasari gave him unstinted praise for the precautions he took to prevent further cracks appearing in Bramante's piers. 'If this masterpiece of care and prudence were upon the earth,' he observed justly, 'instead of being hidden as it is beneath it, the work would cause the boldest genius to stand amazed . . .' How much more amazed and grateful should not we be who are able to enjoy the great building which rests solidly upon these very piers four centuries after Vasari's words were written.

The immediate action of Paul III and the Congregazione della Fabbrica was to invite Giulio Romano, then at work in Mantua, to fill Antonio da Sangallo's place. Before Giulio could persuade his employers to release him, he too died. The Congregazione thereupon invited Jacopo Sansovino; but he resolutely refused to leave Venice. After these reverses, the pope in great anxiety not to waste further time – he was already seventy-nine – decided upon a course of action which secretly he had always wanted to take, and for some reason not in accord with his imperious character had failed to take. Now he would delay no longer; he would brook no refusal. He would issue a command which had to be obeyed. By this decision he altered the whole history of St Peter's.

5 Michelangelo and his Followers

In 1546 Michelangelo Buonarroti was seventy-two years old. Ever since Pope Paul III's election twelve years before, he had been in papal employment intermittently, but not in any capacity concerned with St Peter's Basilica. One of the first acts of Paul's reign had been a visit, accompanied by a retinue of cardinals and prelates, to Michelangelo's modest dwelling in the vicinity of Trajan's column. 'For thirty years', the formidable new pontiff addressed the artist, 'I have longed to employ you, and now that I am pope shall I deny myself the fulfilment of my wish?' Any other artist than Michelangelo would have succumbed with awe and gratification to such blandishments. But politely and with dignity he declined. He was unwilling, he replied, to be committed at his age to regular duties and was only anxious to complete at his own leisure the monument to Pope Julius II, undertaken so many years ago. The imposing deputation withdrew and the cavalcade trotted back to the Vatican without having accomplished its purpose. Nevertheless, in the following year Michelangelo was persuaded to become a member of the papal household. He was appointed by brief the principal architect, sculptor and painter of the Vatican Palace. This was the sequel to the consent he had already given to Clement VII to paint the Last Judgment in the Sistine Chapel. He had then demanded and was granted the condition that he should be protected from all importunities of papal servants and fellow artists. Apart from the Last Judgment commission, over which he was allowed to take his own time, the high-sounding appointments were rather honorary and advisory than obligatory duties. Michelangelo had not yet capitulated.

Now Pope Paul, deprived of Antonio da Sangallo's twenty-six years' services as Capomaestro, and disappointed by Giulio Romano's death and Jacopo Sansovino's refusal to come to Rome, issued a command which Michelangelo, then in the Holy City, could hardly disobey. He was to direct affairs at St Peter's. Even so, the septuagenarian sculptor laid down and obtained his own terms. He prefaced them by reiterating his genuine reluctance to take over so onerous a work. How was he, an old man, to succeed where many of his predecessors had failed? There are frequent references in his letters written at this time and at later dates to dislike and fear of the new responsibilities thrust upon him. He regarded them as a visitation from the Almighty, a penitential discipline to be endured with the best grace possible. Therefore in his deep humility, and for the good of his soul, he tells the Holy Father, he will receive no salary over and above the fifty scudi a month which he is already receiving by virtue of his advisory post at the Vatican Palace. His new office shall be undertaken 'only for the love of God and in honour of the Apostle', Peter. Secondly, he stipulates that if he is to succeed, he must have complete freedom of action. The pope is so anxious to endorse Michelangelo's appointment that he agrees unreservedly to the last condition to the extent of absolving him from the tedium of keeping accounts. Moreover, he gives him full authority over the

Michelangelo, the greatest of the architects who played a part in the design of St Peter's

administration of the Fabbrica, and confers on him the right to adopt, amplify or reject all previous plans for the church and to formulate entirely new ones, if he thinks fit. His trust in the artist could hardly go further.

Michelangelo to his credit fully acknowledged the generous manner in which Paul III conferred upon him the duties of Chief Architect of St Peter's. 'He never showed me anything but kindness', were his words written after this pope's death. They were about the only unqualified appreciation of the many popes he served. Indeed, the Farnese pope remained his consistent supporter even after the alluring and elusive bird had finally been netted. Michelangelo was soon in dire need of support, for his appointment and the terms of its acceptance raised him bitter enemies. The *setta Sangallesca*, who were well and truly organized to carry out their master, Antonio da Sangallo's, long-laid plans, were infuriated by the imputation in Michelangelo's refusal of a salary that they had been feathering their nests out of St Peter's over the past decades. They were also intensely jealous of the pope's absolute confidence in their rival. Michelangelo, fortified by the papal authority, thereupon dismissed the whole clique. His high-handed action was confirmed in 1549 by a written *motu proprio* from the pope. The effect of the new broom was to sweep away many abuses and to instil the basilican workmen with a fresh enthusiasm and zest for the great and holy task ahead of them.

There is no doubt that the responsibilities of Chief Architect of St Peter's brought Michelangelo's old age intense tribulation and suffering, which were greatly exacerbated by his own intransigence and unevenness of temper. Yet he looked upon the work at St Peter's as the crowning achievement of his life. His letters, although full of complaints and anxieties, bear this out. Writing to his friend, Vasari, in 1554 he says that it is his duty to see the work on St Peter's through, come what may; and that, were he to throw it up, he would be committing a very grievous sin. Again in 1557, when eighty-three years old, he writes: 'I believe . . . that God entrusted me with this labour.'

I have now reached a stage where it is necessary to interrupt the chronology of my story. I must retrace the years as far back as to the fifteenth century, when Michelangelo made his first historic contribution to the priceless treasure which St Peter's Basilica enshrines. The famous marble Pietà was commissioned from the young sculptor, then in his twenty-fifth year, by a nobleman from Gascony, Jean de Bilhères. He was a Benedictine monk who became Abbot of St Denis, a member of the French Royal Council and President of the States-General. He was sent by the King of France in 1491 as Ambassador to Rome, where he was soon made a cardinal. He was a great promoter of the arts. He enclosed St Petronilla's altar in the chapel attached to the south-west angle of the old basilica. It was for this chapel, or rather French mausoleum, which it soon became, that he intended the Pietà. In May 1499 the group was finished just in time to be set over the saint's altar. In the following August Cardinal de Bilhères died and was buried a little to the right of the masterpiece which he had commissioned and paid for. The Pietà remained in place until the demolition of the mausoleum in 1544.

Michelangelo's Pietà is the only one of his works to be signed. It is said that the sculptor, having overheard another claim the work for his own, went one night by stealth into St Peter's and carved his name on the Madonna's girdle. The group shows no sign of that terrible spiritual anguish conspicuous in the sculpture of Michelangelo's later years. The tenderness of the stylized composition, the grace verging on insipidity of the figures, and

A liturgical ceremony; the congregation around the high altar at a Papal Mass (see text p. 290)

of course the sanctity of the subject (which, incidentally, Michelangelo's contemporaries were shocked to see treated at all) have made it one of the most popular works of sculpture in the world. The symbolism of eternal motherhood and the incarnate crucified accounts for the incongruity of a young matron supporting in her lap a son of apparently riper years than her own. The situation in which the Pietà was placed in 1749, skied above an altar that had been erected for it, was most unsatisfactory, because the group was created to be seen at eye level. In the old basilica it was correctly sited. Francis I's request in 1507 that the precious work of art might be sent on loan to Paris was rightly ignored. Until 1964 it had never left St Peter's. In that year it was shipped to the United States for exhibition. A subsequent Vatican decree forbidding the future exportation of major works of art for exhibition is clearly a wise and welcome measure.

The Pietà aroused unstinted admiration in those people to whom great art meant more than faithful representation and religious instruction in iconographical form. There are reasons for assuming that one of its first competent admirers was Pope Julius II. He decided in 1505 that the young sculptor's services must be enlisted. So he instructed his old friend and favourite architect, Giuliano da Sangallo, to bring about an introduction. Michelangelo, who was then in Florence, put aside his work on the Battle of the Cascina cartoon for the Sala del Consiglio, thus forfeiting 3,000 ducats which was to have been his payment, and obeyed the summons to Rome. In this manner was brought about the ill-fated conjunction of two impetuous, uncompromising minds. Irritation, frustration and anger were to be engendered by the white-hot love-hate which developed between them. At first, however, all went merry as a marriage bell. The two men took to each other in ecstacies of mutual harmony. The sculptor was raised high in the pope's graces to the extent of causing much resentment among the numerous competitive artists who had flocked to the court of the new papal Maecenas in search of patronage.

Pope Julius's first command was that the young artist should create his tomb on a stupendous scale. The original contract stipulated that it must contain forty statues, to be delivered within five years. The finished thing was to be erected in the fifteenth-century choir designed by Rossellino. Accordingly, Michelangelo was despatched with every flattering demonstration of favour and promises of liberal reward to the Carrara quarries to mine the finest marble. There he spent at least eight arduous months selecting 110 tons of flawless blocks. On his return to Rome, he set up at much cost and trouble a workshop and lodging for himself in front of St Peter's. Meanwhile, Julius's enthusiasm for the tomb had waned. The volatile old tyrant was now conceiving grandiose plans for Michelangelo to paint the vast expanse of the Sistine Chapel ceiling. By the spring of 1506, the sculptor had received no money with which to pay for the freight of marble coming by sea from Tuscany and the workmen he had hired there. Several times in April he begged to see the pope, and each time was put off with an excuse. At last Julius grudgingly granted an interview. Michelangelo complained that being owed money he was seriously in debt. The pope flew into a rage and had him driven from the room. This behaviour was too much for Michelangelo's spirit. He felt insulted, and immediately fled to Florence.

Michelangelo recounted the story of Julius's stingy and insolent treatment of him, the flight and subsequent pursuit, in letters to friends years later.[1] What was the real cause

[1] Letters to G. F. Fattucci, emissary of Clement VII, in January 1524: and to Luigi del Riccio, in October 1542.

High Mass in the tribune on the Feast of Saints Peter and Paul, 1966 (see text p. 292)

It was Paul III, *left* by Titian, who appointed Michelangelo *right* Chief Architect to St Peter's

of the artist's sudden fall from favour? Julius was exacting, mercurial and autocratic. On a whim he would change his mind, no matter what the consequences. Michelangelo supposed that Raphael and Bramante's envy poisoned the pope against him; that the latter mischievously whispered to Julius that it was tempting providence to proceed with plans for a tomb while yet living. The two rivals 'wanted to ruin me', Michelangelo wrote in 1542, 'and Raphael had a good reason indeed, for all he had of art, he had from me'. This accusation made thirty-six years after the row over Pope Julius's tomb need not be taken too seriously. A desire to ruin a successful rival was not in accord with Raphael's gentle nature; and Michelangelo's memory having brooded so many years over past grievances became notoriously unreliable. Bramante, on the other hand, had more reason to feel hostile. He saw Michelangelo as a dangerous competitor for the post of Architect in Chief of St Peter's; and he had not forgotten how readily Pope Julius over-threw his old friend, Giuliano da Sangallo, in his, Bramante's, favour. Moreover, he was aware that Michelangelo had complained to the pope of his shocking destruction of the classical columns of the old basilica and also of Mino da Fiesole's tomb of Nicholas V.

Vasari has put forward another cause of the pope's displeasure. Michelangelo would allow no one to look at his work in progress, and suspected that sometimes during his absence his workmen admitted strangers. One day the pope, having bribed an assistant, entered the Sistine Chapel while the artist, unbeknown to him, was engaged on the ceiling. Michelangelo, hearing an unbidden visitor whom he did not at first recognize, seized a

Michelangelo's Pietà; detail of the head of the Virgin (see also pp. 191, 192)

God creates the sun and the moon; detail from the ceiling of the Sistine Chapel

plank and in a fury chased His Holiness out of the chapel. The incident may possibly have happened at a later date, but certainly not in 1506 when work on the Sistine Chapel had not begun.

Before leaving Rome, Michelangelo just had time to scribble a note to Pope Julius as follows: 'Most Blessed Father, this morning I was turned out of the palace by your orders; therefore, I give you notice that from now on, if you want me, you will have to look for me elsewhere than in Rome.' The pope sent in pursuit five horsemen who caught up with the sculptor at Poggibonsi that evening. But they could not persuade him to return. The fugitive proceeded to Florence. The Signory of that city were then submitted to three imperious briefs demanding Michelangelo's extradition. The members were worried and alarmed. The Gonfalier Soderini sent for Michelangelo and told him he had treated the pope in a cavalier manner which even the King of France would not dare assume. He urged him to go back to Rome at once, since Florence had no wish to be at war with the pope. The sculptor was impenitent. He was still enraged. He replied that he would sooner go to Turkey and work for the Sultan. The message was transmitted to His Holiness through a cardinal sent specially to mediate. Meanwhile, Michelangelo resumed work on the cartoon for the Sala del Consiglio. Graciously he conceded that if the pope would give him a five-year contract with advance payment he might consent to carve the papal tomb in Florence, but not in Rome. He feared that if he returned to Rome his life would be in danger from jealous rivals. Had he done so, he remarked years later, 'my tomb would have come before the pope's'.

The long and the short of the story is that before the year 1506 was out Michelangelo's proud spirit was broken. The incident had sorely shaken him. His poems of this date reflect irritability and bitterness. They complain of the corruption and depravity of Roman society, and of the pope's perverseness. 'You have believed all empty words, and done favours to foes of truth', he addresses him. 'The more I sweat and show my skill, The less you seem to care for what I've done.' Gradually his passion and resentment cooled. The reluctance of the Signory to be involved in trouble with Rome undoubtedly induced Michelangelo to leave Florence. In November he agreed to meet the pope at Bologna. The interview began inauspiciously. Michelangelo felt he was there under compulsion as he was ushered in. Sulkily he fell on his knees. Julius sat victorious and frowning. Then the situation was saved by the tactlessness of a bishop in attendance. He had the folly to observe that Michelangelo was merely an artist with bad manners. The remark provoked the pope to round upon the surprised prelate with his stick, and to fall upon Michelangelo's neck with a bear-like embrace.

The tomb seemed to be forgotten. The pope, having won Bologna back to the Papal States without resistance, was very much alive and jubilant. He preferred to concentrate upon scenes of victory. So until June of 1507 Michelangelo was obliged to make and cast a huge bronze effigy of Julius in an attitude of triumph. The work was acclaimed by contemporaries; but it did not survive for long. It was destroyed by the partisans of the Bentivoglio tyrant in their revolt a year later against the papal subjugation.

In May 1508 the contract with Michelangelo for painting the Sistine Chapel ceiling was concluded, and work began. The feverish haste in which the tremendous task was carried through is well known. The picture of the artist labouring in solitary confinement for months on end, cramped and on his back under the ceiling so that at the finish he could barely straighten his stiffened limbs, is apocryphal. It is true he spent consecutive days and nights at the top of his scaffold tower, directing the operations to which his whole soul was dedicated and occasionally snatching an hour or two's sleep. He had also to master the unfamiliar technique of fresco painting and the avoidance of mould formation from damp. But he was assisted by an army of labourers, who were well trained and drilled. They prepared the wet plaster in advance by lime washing, nailed the sections of cartoon to the vaults for outline tracing by stylus point, and dusted them over with black powder. The extent of this daily task has been accurately determined by a minute examination of the edges of each application of lime wash.

Characteristically, Michelangelo began by a row with Bramante who had somewhat officiously provided a scaffolding suspended from the chapel ceiling. He saw at once that the arrangement did not suit him and, no doubt tactlessly, however justifiably, scrapped it. Instead, he devised an alternative moveable scaffolding built from the ground upwards. Bramante took great umbrage and urged the pope to entrust the remainder of the chapel decoration to Raphael. It may have been awareness of this mischievous suggestion that led Michelangelo to number Raphael among the enemies anxious for his ruin. Work on the ceiling however, once started, proceeded fast and furiously. Michelangelo's chief complaint was not so much physical discomfort as irregular supply of funds with which to pay his workmen. The pope, having returned to Bologna to settle fresh troubles there, was now in great straits for money. He could only send payments to Rome at intervals. Within twenty-two months, the central ceiling vault was more or less finished. On 27th June 1511 Julius, disappointed with the results of his expedition, was back in Rome anxious to see the frescoes unveiled. His presence was an embarrassment and irritation to the artist. The old pope, gouty and tormented by gall stones, would nevertheless insist upon climbing the scaffolding before the final touches had been put. Then in his impatience he ordered the scaffolding to be taken down before Michelangelo was ready. Not content with doing this, he asked for gilding to be added to the garments of the prophets in the lunettes. This last interference provoked an inevitable snub from the artist. Irritated beyond all endurance, he reminded His Holiness that the poor men depicted never wore gold in their lifetime, and he would not be a party to their doing so now.

When in 1512 the whole Sistine Chapel ceiling was completed, Michelangelo turned again to the tomb. But no agreement could be reached either as to the monument's form or the artist's payment. In October Michelangelo wrote to his father, 'I am still doing no work and am waiting for the pope to tell me what to do.' One of the difficulties, now that Julius's original intention to preserve Rossellino's tribune had been abandoned, was where to put the tomb. Nothing was settled before Julius's death; and the 10,000 ducats left in his will for the monument to be completed and erected in the Sistine Chapel only led to infinite posthumous troubles, whereas total abandonment at this stage would at least have avoided a prolongation of them. In May 1513 a second contract was agreed with the pope's executors, whereby a revised design was to be executed within seven years. Henceforth the story of the ill-fated project no longer has any concern with St Peter's. A third, fourth and fifth contract were drawn up, while the sculptor's original splendid conception was curtailed and successive inferior designs were churned out. Money disputes, frustrations, disappointments and rages made it the wasting tragedy of Michelangelo's life. 'I see', he wrote in 1542, when its completion was finally entrusted to inferior artists, 'that I lost all my youth chained to this tomb.' The final monument, reduced in size, disproportionate in scale, and mean in design, is to be seen in the church of S. Pietro in Vincoli, a failure only redeemed by the stupendous figure of the sculptor's Moses, serving as a memorial to the two men whose conflicting wills made a conciliatory whole impossible.

In the end, Pope Julius II's remains were to have no resting place of their own. His coffin was eventually shovelled into the grave of his uncle Sixtus IV, and left there with no epitaph to record his extraordinary character and the remarkable incidents of his reign. *Sic transit gloria mundi!* Such are Fate's rewards for the ambitious!

Leo X, as was to be expected, cared little about the memory of his predecessor. He was not going to encourage its immortalization by an enormous tomb by Michelangelo. On the contrary, his ambitions were fixed upon the embellishment of that church of which his family were the principle patrons, namely S. Lorenzo in Florence. Because of Michelangelo's equivocal attitude towards the Medici family, Leo was not particularly well disposed towards him. The sculptor for his part was torn between personal loyalty to the

The figure of Moses for the monument to Julius II

Medici, who had been his earliest patrons and benefactors, and political allegiance to the free institutions in Florence which the ruling dynasty had overthrown. In fact a mutual embarrassed antipathy prevailed between the new pope and the great artist. 'He is an alarming man,' Leo remarked of Michelangelo, 'and there is no getting on with him.' Although the pope did not welcome him in Rome, he was ready enough to entrust to him the design of a façade for S. Lorenzo in his distant native city. After years of frustration, this project came to nothing. The sculptor was then directed by the pope to the Medici tombs. In this way Leo X successfully kept the man at arm's length from Rome while retaining the services of the greatest artist of the age. The next Medici pope was far more friendly and forgiving. The election of Cardinal Giulio de' Medici was hailed by Michelangelo as offering rare opportunities to artists. The gentle Pope Clement VII made much of his compatriot and bore his rudenesses with docility. On one occasion, he gently admonished him with a reminder that even he, Michelangelo, was mortal and could not in a lifetime do everything he wished. When the second Florentine revolt, brought about by the Sack of Rome and the belief that the Medici pope was utterly routed, had been put down, Clement shielded Michelangelo from the reprisals which befell many leaders of the insurgents, and resumed their old acquaintance. In 1534 the pope commissioned him to paint the Last Judgment in the Sistine Chapel. Michelangelo's work in Florence being finished, he moved in September to Rome, never to leave it for the remaining thirty years of his life. Two days after his arrival Clement VII died.

Pope Paul III confirmed his predecessor's commission and until 1541 Michelangelo was engaged upon the largest fresco painting in Rome, 48 feet broad and 44 feet high. It covers the whole of one end wall of the Sistine Chapel from ceiling to dado. Such overall treatment of an altar end of a chapel was an unorthodox lapse from tradition on the part of the patrons. It involved the removal of a pre-existing fresco by Perugino and two lunette paintings by Michelangelo himself. Windows in the altar wall had to be blocked up and plastered over, and the whole surface made to slope so that the top overhung the bottom by a foot in order to prevent any accumulation of dust and dirt. All preparation of the ground in lime and mortar, and the actual painting were done by the artist with the help of a single colour-grinder. When Paul III saw the finished fresco, he was so overcome with emotion that he broke into loud paeans of thanksgiving and praise.

The Last Judgment evoked an unprecedented applause from the theologians. The size, the nature and the treatment of the subject were exceptional and novel. It was as though Michelangelo were revealing a vision of the cosmic fate and interpreting, as no layman had done before him, the awful sanction of God's covenant with mankind. It was the most fervent spiritual expression of this astonishing genius who had wrestled with the mystic experiences of the soul. In every one of the scenes depicted, there was evidence of the artist's terrible awareness of the *Dies Irae* and the retributive justice of the Old Testament. The influence of the Last Judgment upon contemporary artists was equally profound, for it created a new style of centrifugal painting of a single grand theme which was to endure until the close of the baroque era.

The last echoes of applause had scarcely died away before the theologians, and men of letters too, whipped up a hostile criticism of the fresco on the plea of indecency. Irreverence and impudicity were now the charges levelled against it. 'Such things might be painted in a voluptuous bathroom,' wrote Pietro Aretino (author incidentally of a set of obscene sonnets, accompanied by pornographic illustrations), 'but not in the choir of the highest chapel.' Michelangelo's retort was to introduce in the fresco the angry critic in the likeness of St Bartholomew and his own tortured features in the folds of the flayed skin. But the ridiculous objections nearly brought about the fresco's complete destruction. The Council of Trent loudly denounced the use of unsuitable subjects in religious art, and as soon as Michelangelo was dead Daniele da Volterra was made to paint over all the nudities. Successive mutilations in the interest of purity have so altered the Last Judgment that it is practically impossible to imagine it in the original condition. Had the counter-

The crossing, looking north. The Pope is being carried on the *sedia gestatoria*. Water colour by Louis Haghe, 1864 (see text p. 291). *Overleaf* The nave. Oil by Pannini (see text p. 264)

reformation objectors attacked the Last Judgment on artistic rather than ethical grounds, their criticism might have been valid. For the fresco does convey, in a different sense to that meant by Pietro Aretino, the impression of a public bathroom – as it happens a quite respectable and in no sense voluptuous one. The area covered is an enormous ocean of swirling trunks, arms and legs. These do not form a composition which the eye can assimilate. Nor is it easy, owing to the paucity of natural light and the awkward height of the chapel to concentrate in any comfort or satisfaction upon individual scenes and figures.

On completion of the Last Judgment, Michelangelo promptly undertook the frescoes of St Paul's Conversion and the Crucifixion of St Peter in the Cappella Paolina of the Vatican Palace. He was then well over seventy years of age but, he complained ruefully, could refuse nothing to Pope Paul III. Both frescoes have suffered grievously from fire and over-restoration, with the result that the outlines are now harsh and the colours somewhat brash.

We are now back at the crucial phase in the history of St Peter's when Pope Paul III entrusted to Michelangelo the immense responsibility of Chief Architect to the basilica. What were the architectural qualifications of the renowned sculptor and painter now in the twilight of his age? Vasari, who was Michelangelo's friend and earliest biographer, was not unduly exaggerating when he prefaced an account of his life with this high-flown paragraph: 'While the best and most industrious artists were . . . struggling to attain that high comprehension which many call intelligence, and were universally toiling, but for the most part in vain, the Ruler of Heaven was pleased to turn the eyes of his clemency towards earth . . . to send to the world a spirit endowed with universality of power in each art . . . one capable of showing by himself alone what is the perfection of art in the sketch, the outline, the shadows, or the lights, . . . nay, who was so highly accomplished in architecture also, that he was able to render our habitations secure and commodious, healthy and cheerful, well proportioned, and enriched with the varied ornaments of art.' In discounting Vasari's implication that his hero left behind him some domestic architecture, let us for the moment bear in mind the phrase relating to Michelangelo's 'perfection of art in the sketch, the outline, the shadows [and] the lights,' which applies as much to his architecture as to his painting and sculpture.

In actual fact the buildings of which this old man could boast were few indeed. The façade of S. Lorenzo church in Florence, which he designed, had come to nothing. The group on the Capitoline Hill in Rome was not to be finished until many years after his death. The Farnese Palace was chiefly Antonio da Sangallo's work, and only the upper storey his. His buildings wholly completed from beginning to end amounted to the New Sacristy and the Library of S. Lorenzo in Florence. They were all.[1] An exiguous list perhaps, and the buildings not of monumental size. But in style they were revolutionary and extremely important as foreshadowing a new epoch in European architecture.

Michelangelo frequently denied that he was an architect. The denial was strictly true in the professional sense, and was not made in false modesty. On the other hand, as J. S. Ackerman[2] has pointed out, in it lies the strength of our claim that he was one of the greatest architects of all time. The claim is not as paradoxical as it sounds. Michelangelo

[1] The Porta Pia gateway in Rome was to follow in 1561–5.
[2] *The Architecture of Michelangelo*, 2 vols., 1961.

The cattedra. The Pope presiding at High Mass on the Feast of Saints Peter and Paul, 1864. Water colour by Louis Haghe (see text p. 278)

The central group from the Last Judgment in the Sistine Chapel

was first and foremost a sculptor, as he himself declared. Did he not say, 'with the milk of my nurse [who was the wife of a stonecutter] I sucked in the chisels and hammers wherewith I make my figures'? 'Endowed with universality of power in each art' though he was, he tried to resist Pope Julius's command that he should paint the Sistine Chapel ceiling and Pope Paul's that he should build the new St Peter's, because he considered himself neither painter nor architect, but sculptor. Sculpture was the art he believed to be most expressive of his genius. It was the lamp of painting and 'between them there is the same difference that there is between the sun and the moon'. Again, 'I say that painting is to be considered the better, the more it approaches relief', an opinion notably borne out in the essentially sculptural quality of his Sistine Chapel figures. He adopted exactly the same approach to architecture; therein lies the novel quality of his buildings.

Michelangelo's buildings were treated like sculpture, and this is how they are to be understood. He first conceived them in his mind as – I cannot explain better than by quoting Mr Ackerman – 'organic forms capable of being moulded and carved, of expressing movement, of forming symphonies of light, shadow and texture, like a statue'. This in a nutshell explains the originality of Michelangelo's architectural conceptions. They inaugurated a totally novel manner of building which persisted so long as the baroque style endured. They marked a basic departure from the renaissance manner, which was to

The Crucifixion of St Peter in the Pauline Chapel

resolve abstract geometrical problems. With Michelangelo architecture ceased to be a coldly mathematical and static science to be wrestled with on the drawing-board. It became a dynamic and dramatic force to be released from within the teeming imagination. The artist identified the physical functions of the human form with the structure he was assembling. This structure became a pullulating, sensuous thing from his hands. The material of Michelangelo's building surfaces was as responsive to his fingers as the marble representing the flesh of the model he might be sculpturing.

No wonder that the great sculptor's revolutionary methods met with the disapproval and resentment of specialist architects. These people were often genuinely shocked by his unorthodox and to them seemingly amateur methods. They were certainly jealous of his original genius. Even Vasari tacitly admitted that, whereas 'he composed a decoration of a richer and more varied character than had ever before been adopted', very different from what was in common use, yet he wilfully deviated from 'what was considered measure, rule and order, by Vitruvius and the ancients, to whose rules he would not restrict himself'. Such snapping of the fingers at established authority was all very well for Michelangelo, Vasari opined, but when 'this boldness on his part' encouraged lesser artists 'to an injudicious imitation' it became deplorable. His imitators among the younger architects did more damage than his detractors. How comparable was his example to that

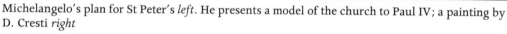

Michelangelo's plan for St Peter's *left*. He presents a model of the church to Paul IV; a painting by D. Cresti *right*

of Picasso in our time! Both have led to ignorant travesties of the truth and a quantity of second-rate and vulgar counterfeits.

In spite of having suffered injustices from Bramante, Michelangelo repeatedly gave tribute and praise to the older man's scheme for St Peter's. In a letter to Bartolomeo Ammannati in 1555 he wrote that Bramante had been as gifted an architect as any since the times of the ancients. His plan for St Peter's was concise, straightforward, luminous and beautiful. To Vasari he professed to carry on where Bramante had left off, while reiterating that he who first devised a great project ought in fairness to be respected as its true author. In consequence, he upbraided Bramante's successors who out of ignorance and arrogance sought to depart from it. Notwithstanding his pious profession to be returning to Bramante's design, he departed from it in several respects, notably in the shape of the dome and the abandonment of corner towers. Indeed, his rather ostentatious praise of Bramante largely disguised his contempt and dislike of Antonio da Sangallo and his lot. He never missed an opportunity of railing against the *setta Sangallesca*. The letter to Ammannati eulogizing Bramante contained a direct criticism of Sangallo. In departing from Bramante's project, Sangallo was departing from truth. 'The first thing that Sangallo's plan does,' he says, 'with that ring of chapels on the exterior, is to deprive Bramante's plan of all light; and that's not all, it has no light of its own. And its numerous hiding places, above and below, all dark, lend themselves to innumerable knaveries: such as provide shelter for bandits, for coining money, ravishing nuns, and other rascalities, so that in the evening, when the church is to be closed, it would take twenty-five men to seek out those who are hiding inside, and because of its peculiar construction, they would be hard to find.' This passage is certainly an illuminating commentary upon the day to day dangers of renaissance life, even inside St Peter's holy basilica. But, he goes on to complain, Sangallo's proposed far-reaching ambulatory, with its concatenation of little chapels and vestibule projecting from the northern side of the church would involve the destruction of the Pauline Chapel and possibly of the Sistine Chapel as well. Michelangelo's famous letter to Paul III of 1544 laying down the principles of correct architecture – a disingenuous letter, to say the least, considering how far his own work deviated from them – had likewise been a denunciation of their infringement by Sangallo in practically every particular.

Vasari in his life of Antonio takes up the theme where Michelangelo's published letters on the subject leave off. I have already referred in the last chapter to the biographer's objections, doubtless echoes he had repeatedly overheard from Michelangelo's lips, to Sangallo's model. In short, Michelangelo was genuinely offended by his predecessor's intention to limit the grand spatial effects which Bramante had conceived.

Paul III, who had approved Sangallo's model readily enough when it was presented to him, now heartily endorsed Michelangelo's rejection of it. The new Capomaestro, after attempting several models in clay, produced his first in wood towards the end of 1547. It was made within fifteen days. It is now lost. It was doubtless nothing like as detailed as Sangallo's which has survived. Michelangelo's basilica was to be of lesser dimensions. The space round the central dome was to be narrower; more light was to be allowed; and the destruction of salient parts of the Vatican Palace was to be avoided. The scheme would, he claimed, be cheaper than that envisaged by Sangallo.

The new zest which Michelangelo's appointment and his immense prestige had instilled into St Peter's workmen slackened on the death of Paul III in 1550. This gifted and determined pope had been not merely the architect's friend but active champion. His protection and help enabled him within three years to complete the south transeptal arm. His successor, Julius III, likewise treated Michelangelo with signal honour. He made the architect sit beside him in the presence of several standing cardinals. He heaped upon him liberal rewards. But the new pope did not readily make up his mind, and stick to a policy. He was inclined to listen to too many advisers and detractors of Michelangelo's schemes. The pope's confirmation of his predecessor's brief in Michelangelo's favour raised a storm of complaint among the Sangallo faction against what they described as the Capomaestro's despotism. Members of the Fabbrica di S. Pietro addressed a letter to Julius accusing the architect of secrecy and withholding from them his intentions. In particular, they objected that he was not going to admit enough light into the basilica – a silly objection considering that it was precisely what Michelangelo had levelled against Sangallo. It is true that Michelangelo seldom settled the design of an important feature until the very last moment, and would habitually alter his plans as he went along; yet he had always intended to put extra windows above those which already existed in the

The front elevation as it might have been completed by Michelangelo. An engraving after Domenico Fontana *left*; a medal of the reign of Gregory XIII *right*

arms of the church. The pope, ever anxious to behave fairly, summoned members of the Fabbrica to hear Michelangelo justify himself. Cardinal Cervini damaged the Fabbrica's cause by reviling the architect in the most intemperate language. Michelangelo in a spirited reply completely demolished the cardinal. It was none of the Fabbrica's business, he told them, to question his intentions, but to procure money to enable him to carry them out. The designs for the building, which they were not competent to judge, were solely his affair. Then, turning to the pope, he said, 'Holy Father, if the labours I endure, do not benefit my soul, I am losing my time vainly over this work.' To which the pope, gently putting his hand on his shoulder, replied, 'You are gaining merit for both body and soul. Have no fear.' Whereupon he sanctioned everything Michelangelo had so far done, and strengthened his authority. On the other hand, the much needed funds were not forthcoming. Michelangelo feeling thoroughly frustrated threatened to leave Rome for Florence and was only prevented by Pope Paul IV, who again confirmed the privileges granted him by Paul III. Still money was withheld and building was accordingly halted. In May 1557 Michelangelo wrote to Vasari that if only the pace of things begun under Paul III had been maintained he would by now have been able to return to Florence. As it was, work 'is slowing down just as we are facing the most exhausting and difficult part'.

There is no doubt that Michelangelo's great age and infirmities were a cause of embarrassment to the Fabbrica. The Chief Architect went less and less often to St Peter's. In his last years he was obliged to direct affairs from his home through a not very efficient deputy. Numerous misunderstandings and some mistakes resulted. For example, the master builder miscalculated the measurements of the ceiling over one chapel, and a large

Pius IV *left* protected Michelangelo. His chief rival, Pirro Ligorio, was diverted from interfering with St Peter's by a commission to design the Casino Pio in the Vatican Gardens *right*

section had to be taken down in consequence. 'If one could die of shame and suffering I should not be alive', Michelangelo remarked, when informed of the humiliating incident.

It is greatly to the credit of Pius IV, the last of many popes Michelangelo served, and incidentally a Medici, although unconnected with the Florentine dynasty, that he treated the old man with affection and tact. He was tenderly solicitous for his health, and sent him presents for his comfort and 200 gold scudi. Michelangelo the year before his death wanted Daniele da Volterra to act as his deputy. But the Sangallo faction recommended instead Nanni di Baccio Bigio whom the Fabbrica appointed Superintendent of the basilica. Bigio, an undistinguished sculptor, was a professed enemy of Michelangelo who was naturally greatly affronted and upset by this flagrant act of hostility. Pope Pius with much diplomacy dismissed Bigio and resolved the differences with the Fabbrica. Others envious of the Chief Architect's authority were not backward in trying to poison the pope's ear against him. Amongst them was Pirro Ligorio who with remarkable assiduity and expressions of concern pointed out that Michelangelo was in his dotage and positively endangering the church fabric. The pope, however, would not turn against his Capo-maestro. To keep Ligorio quiet, he made him Palace Architect and commissioned him to build in the Vatican Gardens the enchanting little Casino Pio with its loggias, grottoes, fountains and incrustations of pagan relief.

This typical renaissance pleasance set among trees and enlivened with flowing water was designed for dalliance and tranquility. It was admirably expressive of its creator's talent for stage scenery and decoration. Ligorio was aristocratic in his tastes as well as birth, whimsical and fickle in temperament, steeped in pagan mythology and even a falsifier of ancient reliefs and inscriptions. In the words of Ackerman, 'For Ligorio antiquity was a storehouse of motives rather than a source of architectural principles.' In his capacity as Architect to the Vatican Palace Ligorio added the half-dome to the great exedra in the Court of the Pine-Cone and, as an afterthought, crowned it with the incongruous semi-circular loggia. He also covered the brick façade with stucco drafted to imitate masonry, which altered its entire character. Michelangelo's sole contribution to these changes was the double-ramped stairway, a replica of the one he put in front of the Senator's Palace in the Campidoglio. Ligorio then built the theatre recess at the southern end of the court, in front of which on festal occasions the pope and cardinals would sit on the open-air seats watching dramas, pageants and tournaments.

Michelangelo died on 18th February 1564 in his eighty-ninth year. His body was escorted from his studio near the Forum of Trajan to the church of the SS. Apostoli by a long procession of friends, admirers and all the artists in Rome, assembled to do him honour.

What stage had St Peter's church reached by the time of Michelangelo's death? The south transeptal arm with its apsed chapels and vaulting was complete inside, except for the decoration; on the exterior the entablature of the main order was reached, but the attic storey had not yet been put on. The north transeptal arm, begun later than the other was nearly complete, the vaulting of its apse only half done. The drum of the dome was almost finished. The foundations of the corner chapels on the north side of the basilica had been dug. The Pantheon-like portico, meant to be set directly against the eastern arm still remained merely a scheme on paper.

In assessing the achievement of Michelangelo, it is necessary to consider how much his hands had been tied at the outset of his task as Architect in Chief of St Peter's. Bramante's four great central piers, the determining factor of the dome and so in a sense of what the whole basilica would ultimately look like, could not of course be altered. The outer rings of Sangallo's transeptal arms were already in place, the southern one, it is true, reaching only just above ground level. Michelangelo was obliged to keep the inner rings. He largely rebuilt them, strengthened the piers of the two hemicycles and formed within them spiral staircases to enable panniered donkeys to carry material to the roof. The outer rings he lopped off entirely. In other words, while reducing the total volume, he was obliged to maintain the form of the interior which had been bequeathed to him. What he was able to do was to get rid of Sangallo's ambulatories and excrescences. In the hemicycles he substituted three chapels for five. He simplified the interior by reducing it from multiple components to an entity and in the process introduced a system of direct lighting by the addition of attic windows.[1] Thus his service to the interior of St Peter's was to render it into a cohesive whole. Otherwise there are but few and superficial traces of his style inside because nearly all the decoration belongs to a subsequent period.

The exterior of the basilica as seen from the sides and especially from the rear is Michelangelo's main contribution to St Peter's, even more so than the dome, which is only his by implication. It is a pity that this great man's work can only properly be seen and understood from the Vatican Gardens to which the public now has no access. Here Michelangelo's genius was not restricted. The composition that he fashioned is really most

[1] These of course were built to his design after his death.

The Pietà (see text p. 168)

peculiar. Since its size prevents the symmetry of the west end being taken in at one view, a jagged rhythm of geometrical forms is presented – great semi-circle, diagonal, jutting angle, diagonal, and again semi-circle. The rhythm is of course calculated, but to the casual viewer does not at first appear so. It is made more difficult to appreciate by the extreme complication of pilasters and recessed strips, which are followed into the entablature in a seeming infinity of backward and forward breaks. The effect is uneven, staccato, and restless. Upon the intervening spaces Michelangelo crammed windows and niches. On the wider surfaces he put two great projecting tabernacles with pediments alternately pointed and curved, quite out of scale with the space provided. On the narrower surfaces between the coupled pilasters he packed three round-headed, slit-like openings. The lack of any relation between the levels of the tabernacles and slit openings is most irrational and disturbing.

Michelangelo deliberately departed from Bramante's horizontal design in his extraordinary emphasis upon a vertical effect. It is at once apparent that he meant to lead the eye up from the ground to the culminating dome. Bramante's emphasis was to have been the other way round. His great fat dome on a spreading podium would sit like a broody hen on a comfortable nesting-box. From the body of the church excrescent chapels would protrude here and there like baby chickens peeping under the mother's wing. Yet Michelangelo controlled his upward surge of writhing, thrusting walls by his horizontal attic, which binds these revolutionary forces tightly together with a gigantic belt, the entablature. Wölfflin, writing in the last century, saw in the tribune apse of St Peter's the beginnings of baroque flow, what he called 'the final calming of a violent upward surge'.[1] But we, accustomed to a clearer differentiation between the renaissance and baroque styles find the deliberate disharmony of the surfaces an essentially mannerist expression of unease. To our way of thinking there is nothing rhythmical or flowing about St Peter's apse. No wonder that Milizia, writing at the height of eighteenth-century reposeful classicism, candidly disliked what he considered the ill-formed windows with unsightly pediments, the over-elaborate ornament and the top-heavy attic storey.[2]

Almost stranger than the actual disharmony of Michelangelo's design of the exterior, which is so strongly apparent when one looks closely into it, is the apparent calm and majesty when one does not. Until one starts analysing the ingredients, when the 'dichotomy within the surface filling', to quote Wölfflin again, shouts stridently and defiantly, the great perpendicular bulk merely serves its admirable purpose as foothills to the lofty dome. There is no instance in Western architecture of a building so flagrantly, so hideously discordant, achieving such a rousing success. It combines the astringency of Stravinsky's themes with the distortion of Picasso's figures, at once repellent and magnificent. Like them it is the offspring of an old man's disillusioned and expended genius.

In other words, what survives of Michelangelo's exterior of St Peter's (remember that the main façade has nothing to do with him) cannot be considered without the dome which it serves and upon which it is so dependent that, taken on its own, it is an unpalatable fragment. Michelangelo died before his final dome design was settled. This accounts

---

[1] *Renaissance and Baroque*, 1888, trs. 1964.

[2] Francesco Milizia, *Lives of the Celebrated Architects*, 1768, trs. 1826.

Detail of Christ's head for the Pietà (see text p. 171)

Michelangelo's work on St Peter's. The exterior and interior at the time of his death *top left and above*. A view from the southwest *bottom right*. Details of the west end *bottom left and top right*

The North East prospect of St. PETER'S CHURCH in Rome

Sold by Henry Overton at ye white horse wout Newgate London

H. Hulsbergh Sculp:

for the attic of the basilica, constructed in 1557, having been left at the time of his death without a facing, in case of last minute changes in the dome design.[1]

The idea of a grand cupola to surmount the Apostle's tomb was as old as the dawn of the Renaissance. It was first conceived by Rossellino to cover the crossing of his otherwise medievally planned church. Rossellino's choir, a constant embarrassment to his successors, even influenced the shapes of all the domes that were ultimately designed. Bramante's dome was intended to dominate the entire structure beneath and around it. It was to be a hemisphere stepped, on the model of the Pantheon dome, from a drum encircled with columns. Bramante expressed an ideal – it is illustrated in volume III of Serlio's *Architettura* – rather than a project. Because he had carried out a hemisphere so successfully on the tiny Tempietto of S. Pietro in Montorio, he would not necessarily have found it simple to execute on the vast scale of St Peter's. In any case he never got far enough to make the attempt. Antonio da Sangallo, faced with the immediate translation of ideal into project, was obliged to sacrifice aesthetics to technical design. He therefore presented in his model an ovoid profile over a drum composed of two storeys of arcade, the whole thing crowned by a huge Christmas-cake lantern.

Michelangelo at once rejected both Bramante's and Sangallo's conceptions. Boldly he determined to combine the aesthetic with the technical in his design. To bring about a satisfactory visual and stable effect, he increased the dimensions of the drum and brought it into far closer relationship with the rest of the building. In fact, he knitted the two together in such a way that they became interdependent and an inseparable entity.

In turning away from his predecessors' projects, Michelangelo did not immediately resolve one of his own. On the contrary, there are good reasons for supposing that at his death he was still undecided what precise form his dome should take, even though he had long ago settled the general pattern. As early as 1547 he was writing to Florence for measurements of Brunelleschi's octagonal dome over the cathedral there. He always greatly admired and was much influenced by it. He took from it the double-shell construction. For his first project he adopted Brunelleschi's raised profile, the ribs, the little eye-windows of the drum and the octagonal lantern. His sketches[2] of the late fifteen-fifties show that he was still undecided whether to have a dome of raised profile with low lantern, or a hemispherical dome with high lantern. His choice of the second coincided with the model he was designing in 1559–60 for S. Giovanni de' Fiorentini.[3] His final dome design for St Peter's – or rather, to be accurate, his last known design – was slightly more elevated than a hemisphere, whereas the inside shell was exactly hemispherical. Between 1558 and 1561 he made a wooden model, or half section of dome and drum, which survives.[4] Although giving a good indication of what was in Michelangelo's mind during these latter years, it is a less reliable guide to the evolution of his creative processes than the series of undated sketches by his hand. The model too has been altered since his death by subsequent architects, Della Porta, Carlo Fontana and also Vanvitelli. Even so,

---

[1] Michelangelo's dome studies were revised over and over again while work on the body of the basilica proceeded.

[2] Precisely five sketches by Michelangelo for the dome survive. They were done at different stages.

[3] It came to nothing.

[4] Michelangelo's first model in terra cotta was made at some unknown date. A second in wood was made for the complete church in 1546–7.

A view of the west end

198

THE EFFIGIES OF M
GIACOMO BAROZZIO
DA VIGNOLA

W Sherwin sculpsit et excudit

The dome of Michelangelo's model, as subsequently altered *top left*. Pius V, portrait by
Zuccarelli *bottom left*, was insistent that
Michelangelo's plans should be carried on
and he appointed Vignola *top right* to succeed him

its principal features (which have been carried out) were Michelangelo's conception. For he designed the buttresses to the drum in free-standing, coupled columns, linked to the dome by great, stout scrolls. The scrolls in turn were linked to the lantern by ribs lashing the swelling volume, like ropes across the envelope of a rising balloon. By this means action and reaction, form and weight were forcibly and tellingly suggested.

For five months after Michelangelo's death, Pope Pius IV (1559–65) could not bring himself to replace him. During that time he called for discussions among the Fabbrica how best to finish off the dome. He attended every meeting of the Fabbrica which eventually decided to enlist the opinion of the leading architects in Italy and abroad. Still the pope was too stricken by Michelangelo's loss to take any positive action. Finally, with a great effort, he pulled himself together. He nominated Pirro Ligorio Chief and Vignola Second Architect to St Peter's. The two men were given strict injunctions not to deviate in any respect from those of their predecessor's plans which had been accepted. Needless to say, on the election of Pius V in 1566 Ligorio, thinking to take advantage of the former shepherd from Piedmont, a Dominican monk of extreme sanctity and lack of worldly interests, dared to make the attempt. Much to his surprise, the saintly pope, who although no aesthete yet cherished great veneration of Michelangelo, dismissed Ligorio without a moment's hesitation.

Pius V (1566–72) was a typical pope of the Counter-Reformation, that is to say a pope in complete contrast with his pleasure-loving renaissance predecessors. He established a new standard of papal morals that was long overdue. He was devout in his religion, and correspondingly strict in his discipline. Yet his outlook was depressingly narrow. In fact he did not seem to care for people enjoying themselves. He put a stop to the spectacles in the Court of the Pine-Cone. He instituted rigorous punishments for immoral conduct among his subjects, and frequently burnt alive those found guilty of sodomy. On the other hand, he tried but failed to stop bull-fighting, which he declared to be 'more suited to devils than men', a sentiment over which one cannot quarrel with him. He wanted to dispose of the collection of pagan sculpture in the Belvedere Court, but on being dissuaded merely stripped the walls of the reliefs and closed the court to the public. He did however present to the Roman Senate, whose gravity and years rendered them, he supposed, immune to irregular susceptibilities, the sculpture on the stairs leading to the Belvedere. He cleared the Villa Giulia of statuary and threatened to destroy the monuments of the ancients in the city because they had been raised by pagans. Popes, he said platitudinously, should rejoice not in their buildings, but in their virtues. In spite of these views, he carried out several building activities of a useful and religious nature. He erected the library across the great courtyard, thus cutting it in half – in order to destroy the open-air theatre as much as to encourage learning. He built the Torre Pia to contain three additional chapels; and he restored the Sistine Chapel ceiling which was in danger of collapse.

On the whole, this stickler for moral rectitude – the 'terrible' pope he was called in Rome – blissfully unaware of Michelangelo's emotional propensities, revered his memory. Having appointed Vignola Architect in Chief to St Peter's in Ligorio's place, he called upon Vasari to control him and prevent a further risk of deviation from the master's plans. Vasari, anxious at all costs to preserve his beloved friend's drawings for posterity, and wise to the traditional disfavour that overtakes the reputation of the greatest men

The condition of St Peter's in 1575. A bird's eye view *left* showing the atrium and east end of the old basilica still standing, with the new building rising behind. A view within the atrium *right*

soon after they are dead, carefully hid them. Little in fact was done to St Peter's in the way of building throughout the reign of Pope Pius V, whose pressing concerns were an unrelieved struggle against the caesaro-papalism of Philip II of Spain, the issue of a bull excommunicating Queen Elizabeth of England, the prosecution of a brutal campaign under Alba against the heretics of the Low Countries and, last but by no means least, the resistance of Muslim advances.

The new Architect in Chief had, before working under Ligorio, been assistant to Michelangelo at St Peter's from 1551 to 1555. He therefore knew the building intimately and, although disapproving of his superior's lack of orthodoxy where the rules of the orders were concerned, was nevertheless able, and obliged, to carry on the Michelangelo tradition.

Jacopo Barozzi, a native of Vignola in Emilia, was, after Michelangelo, the most important architect of the later Roman Renaissance. His *Regole delli Cinque Ordini*, in which he summarized a lifetime's evaluation of the Vitruvian doctrines, was the most influential textbook upon classical architecture to be written since ancient times. It fulfilled a need for recording the classical tradition of building during a period of dangerous architectural heresies. Clearly the author had Michelangelo in mind, for he went back to Bramante and Antonio da Sangallo for examples of pure classical forms in the contemporary idiom. Even so, he was highly selective, rejected whatever he deemed irrelevant motifs, and would not countenance the repetition of outworn formulas. Vignola was a sifter and amplifier of long established truths rather than a discoverer of new ideas. There was something a little colourless about his personality, which is often the case with professional men who entirely subordinate all private concerns to their livelihood. His own architecture could be dynamic – the Palace at Caprarola is indeed dramatic and forceful – without being strictly original. But Vignola's architectural achievements are scanty. Most of his buildings were either left unfinished, to be altered by successors, or were done with the cooperation of others. Even the Gesù church, which has made his memory famous, was given the façade by Della Porta. In the middle of the sixteenth century patrons were seldom able to employ a single architect for long. Instead they had to employ several at a time, or one after another. Ever since the Sack of Rome artists were constantly on the move, seeking commissions in provinces remote from their homes, turning their talents to whatever job was offered and seldom concentrating upon one from start to finish. The times were unsettled and remained for half a century out of joint. They were the sequel to fundamental religious disturbances and a series of wars in Italy.

Vignola too was a poor man of business. Unlike many of his less gifted contemporaries, he did not make a great deal of money. He was a perfectionist who had to design every-thing himself down to the last detail. He could not delegate work. Nor could he cooperate with partners. He was embarrassed with his subordinates, supercilious with his equals, proud and reserved with his superiors. He seldom spoke well of other architects and often picked quarrels with his clients. Lacking all graces and charm, he was suspicious of these qualities in other people. He was totally devoid of humour.

The interesting thing about Vignola is that he was about the first professional architect. In every sense he was professional. Unlike contemporary renaissance artists who were mostly versatile and ready to turn their hand to painting, sculpture or goldsmiths' work, Vignola was exclusively an architect. He had none of the attributes of the universal man. His designs were thought out with the painstaking thoroughness of the master-builder, which he was; and he insisted upon their being carried out in the same disciplined and meticulous spirit.

After his appointment as Deputy to Ligorio in 1564, Vignola was at first virtually, and after 1566 when Ligorio was dismissed, absolutely in charge of all works at St Peter's. He held the office of Architect in Chief until his own death in 1573. The period was not one of great activity owing to Pius V's preoccupation with crusades against infidels and heretics. Vignola spent the whole year of 1565 at St Peter's. Throughout the other years he was largely absent, and during the two last of his life he left affairs in the incompetent hands of his son Hyacinth. Vignola initiated few projects at the basilica, and we cannot help wondering whether he felt his position to be a false one. Did he resent the strict papal injunctions faithfully to follow Michelangelo's plans? Did he secretly sympathize with Ligorio's revolt against the Michelangelesque Mannerism? At least he had the tact and good sense not to say so. His labours were certainly confined to carrying on where Michelangelo had left off. He completed the drum of the dome above the entablature where the great garlands are now carved. He finished the attic of the north transeptal arm.

The piazza outside the atrium at a papal blessing, 1567. The drum of the dome is now complete

Vignola then left little mark at St Peter's. Mr John Coolidge[1] has disposed of the long accepted claim that he was responsible for the two lesser domes which flank the great dome on its east side. These little cupolas, most beautiful in themselves but not prominent enough from a distance and practically invisible from the piazza, cover the Gregorian and Clementine chapels, which constitute the north-east and south-east angles of Michelangelo's plan. Mr Coolidge points out that the free-standing columns, in front of an unconventional form of bent pilaster against a pier, are contrary to Vignola's invariable treatment of continuous surfaces as single planes; but quite in accord with some of Della Porta's architecture.[2] What Vignola probably did was to finish off the Cappella Gregori-

[1] 'Vignola's Character and Achievement', *Journal of the Society of Architectural Historians,* October 1950.
[2] *Vide* his Cappella Sforza in S. Maria Maggiore.

The west end of the new basilica with the Vatican Gardens; a painting by Henry Van Cleve, 1589

ana to Michelangelo's design and merely re-erect the inner dome which is below the roof level. The outside, visible cupolas of both chapels were completed by his successor.

Vignola was buried in the Pantheon close to Raphael. His coffin was accompanied by a concourse of Romans who with their quick intelligence recognized that, although he was not one of the great creative architects, he deserved, as the upholder of the pure classical tradition, their respect and their mourning.

The septuagenarian Boncompagni who succeeded as Gregory XIII in 1572 was a complete contrast to his saintly predecessor. He was not particularly devout. Montaigne remarked that during the pope's Mass in St Peter's Gregory and his cardinals gossiped together unconcernedly. The pope had a son, Giacomo Boncompagni, born it is true before the father became a priest, to whom he was devoted but whom he kept under control.

Gregory made no pretence to understand art. Nevertheless, he was a man of learning and a great patron of the Vatican Library. He contributed generously towards the embellishment of the Gesù church, the Oratory church and the Collegio Romano. He built the Quirinal Palace. He installed fountains throughout the city, and made the Association of St Luke into an Academy of Art. He resolved to complete all the works begun by Pius V and for love of him to press forward with the building of St Peter's.

Gregory XIII reigned, rather surprisingly, for thirteen years, dying at the advanced age of eighty-three. He achieved a good deal of work at St Peter's, but like so many of his predecessors nothing like as much as he confidently set out to do. The first thing he turned his attention to was the dome. On the death of Vignola in 1573 this sensible pontiff appointed the Genoese, Giacomo Della Porta, Architect in Chief to the basilica. It was indeed granted to Della Porta to complete the dome but not to Pope Gregory to witness its completion. Instead, the pope saw the transept and the western arm of the basilica vaulted, the Cappella Gregoriana built and named after him, and its decoration put in hand. This chapel was the pope's pride and joy, on which he lavished funds and attention. Nearly every day he went to watch its progress. He transferred to the altar the remains of his namesake, S. Gregorio di Nanziano, from a tomb in S. Maria in Campo Marzo, much to the dismay of the Benedictines whose church it was. They were loath to part with the precious relics, but their remonstrances were in vain. Gregory XIII was obsessed by relics and attached great importance to the trappings of death. He ordered his own body to be buried in balsam and aromatic herbs, wearing full pontifical robes of ruby red

Gregory XIII *left* was responsible for the decoration of the Cappella Gregoriana *right*

Cupolas above the Clementine and Gregorian chapels were designed by Della Porta (see also p. 115)

and a golden mitre. He raised above the Gregorian altar four ancient columns of African marble and two of *verde antique*. The rich marbles and brilliant mosaics were considered by contemporaries the acme of expensive taste. Expensive the chapel certainly is, but taste is clearly wanting. With relief the eye dwells upon the touching little twelfth-century Madonna del Soccorso, painted upon a sawn-out segment of marble column from the old basilica and now incorporated among the lavish polychrome over the altar. Della Porta was wholly responsible for the decoration which was still being applied after Gregory's death. He then constructed the outside cupola, and that of the balancing Cappella Clementina on the south, to reflect the ovoid contours of the great dome, which he was about to alter from Michelangelo's hemispherical design.

6 The Dome and the Obelisk

The reign of Sixtus V (1585–90) witnessed a really spectacular advance in the building of the renaissance St Peter's. For nearly one hundred and fifty years a succession of popes, beginning with Nicholas V, had entertained magnificent schemes of leaving behind them a complete new church to the glory of the titular Apostle and, not a little, to their own. One by one these popes came, stayed a short while, and went. Many left no mark whatever on the new fabric; several advanced it a trifle. Of no pope up to date can we say that he was solely responsible for raising as much as an aisle, a transept, a façade or a dome. And of all the basilica's features the great central dome caused most expectation and anxiety. It was looked upon as the most ambitious architectural venture of modern times. We have seen how since Rossellino's day a number of dome projects were put forward and discarded. Bramante and Antonio da Sangallo each evolved a highly individual dome. Michelangelo started afresh and produced one of his own on entirely different lines. Della Porta, after certain modifications, finally carried out Michelangelo's conception. That he was able to do so was owing to the dynamic determination of Pope Sixtus V.

Felice Peretti was an individual of immense stature. No other renaissance pope, apart from Julius II, matched him in will-power and energy. His spirit was indomitable before every conceivable misfortune and opposition. A Franciscan monk of humble origin and poverty – of which circumstances he was very proud – he had suffered all his life from bad health, contracted in earliest youth when he was a swineherd in the savage passes of the Marche. During his election at the age of sixty-five, he was seriously ill, but by a supreme effort recovered. 'The papacy is the best medicine', a friend said to him at the time by way of encouragement. Sixtus was doubtless to agree that the prospect of his reign was a more potent prophylactic than the actuality. He suffered in the summers from the heat of Rome and in all seasons from acute insomnia, which his doctors vainly endeavoured to alleviate. A hopeless patient, he argued and expostulated, for he was one of those tiresome laymen who always know better than the experts.

Sixtus's reign lasted a mere five years. Yet his building activities within the short space allotted to him are almost incredible; and make one question whether he had planned them in anticipation of his election. His parents had always been convinced that in spite of his low station in life their son would one day wear the tiara; and it seems that he had never doubted it. On becoming pope, his first move was to restore the third-century water supply of the Emperor Severus, to be called after him the Acqua Felice. He repaired the aqueduct all the way from Palestrina to Rome, which covered twenty-two miles of artificial channel passing mostly overhead and sometimes by pipe underground. The source fed twenty-seven fountains in the city, thus bringing fresh solace to the inhabitants and fertility to the gardens. Sixtus's next move was to link the major basilicas together

The obelisk in position before the domed basilica; the façade is from a design by Domenico Fontana based upon Michelangelo's intentions. An imaginary view published in 1600

and the hills to the heart of the city with a network of straight streets, among them the Via Sistina and the Via Felice. He raised four obelisks at strategic junctions of these streets. He built the Sistine Loggia at St John's Lateran and the Cappella Sistina in S. Maria Maggiore; and made additions to the Quirinal, Lateran and Vatican palaces. At the last he finished the library begun by Pius V across the Court of the Pine-Cone, and formed the Court of St Damasus by extending the papal apartments in an easterly direction. He threw several bridges across the Tiber. It is true that he saved the columns of Trajan and Marcus Aurelius by turning them into pedestals for statues to Saints Peter and Paul. But he had absolutely no respect for ancient monuments, many of which, including the three-storeyed Septizonium, he destroyed without compunction. Indeed, he boasted how, given time, he would 'clear away the ugly antiquities'. His vandalism was by no means moderated by his Chief Architect, Della Porta, who took terrible toll of medieval monuments in the old Basilica of St Peter.

In 1585 Pope Sixtus confirmed Della Porta in his post of Capomaestro of St Peter's. At the same time he appointed Domenico Fontana as his assistant. In both these architects he reposed the utmost confidence. This pope made no deliberate changes in Michelangelo's plans for St Peter's, leaving their execution entirely in the hands of his Chief Architect. He was merely determined to see the work carried through with the utmost speed, and above all the dome erected. He provided ample funds, took keen interest in the proceedings and was kept informed of their minutest particulars. As far as the architect and his assistants were concerned, he was a model patron. He was generous, enthusiastic and, what is unusual, not interfering. But he was a taskmaster. Work never went fast enough for him, and the older he got the more he chafed at delays and exhorted urgency. By 1589 relays of eight hundred labourers were kept busy day and night without respite. Sixtus's haste brought inevitable trouble upon his successors. Careless workmanship led to serious cracks in the St Veronica pier of the crossing. But the pope was blissfully unconcerned with the consequences of his impetuosity. With admiration and stupefaction the citizens of Rome, accustomed to their basilica's slow progress, watched the dome's development day by day. Their eyes could hardly credit the magical thing soaring into the blue skies. For we must remember that the only large domes in existence at this date were those of Hagia Sofia in Constantinople, the cathedral in Florence, and the Pantheon. To the majority of Romans only the last, comparatively low and saucer-like, was familiar. It is not surprising therefore that they were overcome with pride and emotion like the historian Procopius, who, seeing the dome of Hagia Sofia for the first time, exclaimed that so beautiful an object could not possibly be supported on piers raised by human hands, but must be suspended from heaven on an invisible golden string.

How far did Della Porta depart from Michelangelo's final design for the dome? Scholars are still arguing the point. Some claim that Della Porta's profile actually follows projected alterations made by Michelangelo at the time of his death.[1] They suggest that, as Michelangelo constantly changed his mind at the eleventh hour, and at the end of his life was still pondering whether to have a hemispherical or elliptical dome, Della Porta, who was in most respects faithful to the great master's projects, would not have altered

[1] D. Gioseffi, *La Cupola Vaticana*, Istituto di Storia dell'Arte, no. 10, 1960.

One of the holy water stoups (see text p. 299)

the dome's outline if he knew he was thereby departing from a final decision. Did he not pull down Rossellino's provisional choir, and in its place build the western head of the basilica in order to conform with the two transeptal arms, because Michelangelo had so designed it? Furthermore, they point out, some of Michelangelo's sketches exist to prove his experiment with a pointed form of dome. He may well then have reverted to this profile on his deathbed, a fact of which Della Porta would have been fully aware.

Against this argument there is Della Porta's admission to Pope Sixtus that he had not the courage to complete the dome projected by Michelangelo, whose ideas were conceived by intuition rather than technical experience. He, Della Porta, on the other hand, had made exhaustive scientific investigations, which precluded the advisability of a hemispherical dome. The thrust would be too great for its safety. Therefore, he proposed instead to make his dome ovoid. This protestation may have been disingenuous and merely an excuse for his arbitrary change of outline. Della Porta in fact returned more or less to the dome outline of Antonio da Sangallo's wooden model upon which Michelangelo had poured much ridicule.[1] If he consciously adopted Sangallo's design, he kept the secret to himself. Most probably he decided – and I am sure he was right – that a raised outline would be more satisfactory aesthetically than a hemispherical one.

At all events Sixtus V invited Della Porta to prepare on paper a working drawing of his intended outline. It was spread out on the nave floor of St Paul's outside the Walls, which was the largest covered space available in Rome, and duly examined by the pope from the gallery above. Thus was Della Porta's raised profile for the dome approved. The architect made in addition a few changes of no insignificant sort. He altered Michelangelo's arrangement of openings in the second and third stages of the dome, substituting eye-windows surmounted by volutes, like those on the lowest stage, for angled and segmental heads. His change of dome profile necessitated the narrowing of the ribs and the projections at their base. He also added the lions' masks over the swags of the drum since they were the heraldic device of Pope Sixtus. Lastly, his most important change of all was the lowering of the lantern because of the heightening of the dome. Michelangelo had always been greatly concerned over the relationship of the two and, until the end of his life, found it difficult to decide 'which should play the chief rôle in accentuating the aspiring forces'.[2]

In 1569 Stefano du Pérac published engravings of the exterior and a section of the future St Peter's which he claimed to be Michelangelo's final solution. This was three years after the architect's death and long before Della Porta's alterations to the dome. The dome in du Pérac's engravings differs considerably from Michelangelo's wooden model, which is thought to have been altered by Della Porta and others after the actual dome was built. Du Pérac's section agrees, however, with the model in showing that the inner shell was always meant to be hemispherical. Della Porta did not change the inner dome which is today just as Michelangelo designed it. The outer shell in du Pérac's engraving is on the other hand only slightly ovoid, the degree being measurable by the space between the inner and outer shells widening as it reaches the summit. Michelangelo expressly intended the divergent space to make ascent to the lantern comfortable and maintenance of the dome easy; also to avoid dampness percolating through the decorated inner shell.

[1] The relation between radius, base and height of Sangallo's and Della Porta's domes is the same.
[2] J. S. Ackerman, *op. cit.*

The baptismal font (see text p. 289)

Sixtus V *above left* energetically pursued the building of St Peter's with Della Porta and Domenico Fontana *above right* as architects. The dome *right* was completed by Della Porta to a more ovoid shape than was originally envisaged by Michelangelo *below* (see also pp. 93, 115 and 116)

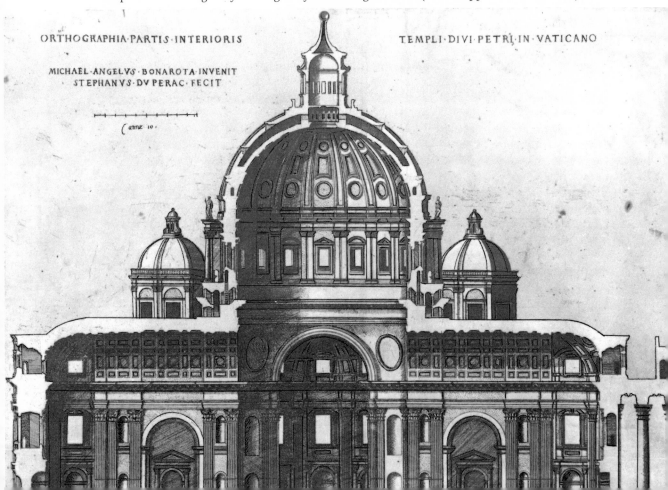

ORTHOGRAPHIA·PARTIS·INTERIORIS   TEMPLI·DIVI·PETRI·IN·VATICANO

MICHAEL·ANGELVS·BONAROTA·INVENIT
STEPHANVS·DV PERAC·FECIT

Della Porta made the actual outer shell far more ovoid than it appears in du Pérac's engraving. However he kept intact Michelangelo's drum, only making a few minor changes to it. Michelangelo provided paired columns to act as buttresses to counter the the mighty thrust of his hemispherical dome. When the thrust was largely removed by the dome of more vertical dimensions, these buttresses accordingly had little part to play. They are now practically inactive; and they seem merely to compress the drum. Moreover, the feeling of unease is intensified by the omission of the statues designed by Michelangelo (and illustrated by du Pérac) to stand upon the buttresses. Luigi Vanvitelli and Antonio Corradini in the eighteenth century both deplored this omission. The former advocated linking the dome ribs to the drum columns with great scroll supports in order to stabilize the ponderous mass. The latter, in 1743, suggested putting figures of prophets where Michelangelo meant statues to stand, in order to provide extra weight and emphasis for the buttresses. But neither of these proposals was adopted. Both however were carried out on the model.

Distant views of St Peter's. From the Pincio; 'The Fountain of the Academy of France' by Corot *above*. From the Tiber; an engraving by Piranesi *below*

Although Della Porta was constrained to lower the lantern because he raised the dome, he nevertheless made its pyramid higher than Michelangelo intended. This was doubtless because of his introduction of a row of vase-shaped finials, or candles set round the base of the pyramid, which if kept low would have been totally submerged by them. Michelangelo never meant to crown his lantern with candles, as du Pérac's engravings prove. He wished it to resemble the lantern he put over the Medici chapel in Florence in 1521 – namely, a lid with a fairly squat knob linked to an order of columns only by scrolls. Both the heightened pyramid and the candles were also added by Della Porta to Michelangelo's wooden model, presumably before building, so as to show the Fabbrica what the finished structure would look like.

The history of St Peter's dome is one matter, the appearance is another. The memory of Michelangelo has always been held so sacrosanct that the shape of the actual dome was for centuries ascribed to him exclusively. It was thought sacrilege to call something so beautiful anyone else's creation. Then, after it became established that the shape was not entirely his, learned scholars took to criticizing it. If only, they complained, Della Porta had never come upon the scene and had left well alone: then we should have had the master's hemisphere to admire. I, for one, rejoice that Della Porta made the dome's outline as it is, whatever his reasons, technical or aesthetic. I believe that there is only one dome in existence of more satisfying form than St Peter's, and that is St Paul's in London, which came after it. This opinion does not prevent me from regretting certain omissions and minor malformations, for which Della Porta must be held responsible. I think it a pity that he did not allow the statues to stand upon the entablature of the drum peristyle. I think he did not improve the slender lantern by introducing the circlet of candles. In spite of raising the pyramid, he detracted from its elegance by these fussy little spikes which, by veiling the base, make the whole lantern seem too wide and heavy.

It is a truism to point out that St Peter's dome can be appreciated only from a distance whence the angle of vision is not distorted by upward tilting. Excellent views are still obtainable from well-known vantage points on the seven hills, where the viewer is more or less on a level with the dome. From the Pincio in the morning, or the Janiculum in the evening when the rising or setting sun is behind you, not only can St Peter's be taken in but the whole constellation of lesser domes which like satellites have evolved from and now revolve round it. In contemplating this sun of domes, you may judge how successful are the moons which are dwarfed by its bulk and made pale by its radiant splendour. There is the Gesù dome, a squat lid like a skullcap; the S. Giovanni dei Fiorentini dome, octagonal and too attenuated, like a balloon in process of deflation; the S. Agnese in Agone dome, also raised but its verticality moderated by a pair of minaret-like towers; the dome of S. Carlo al Corso less ovoid than the two last; and that of S. Andrea della Valle, perhaps the most successful so far listed, and as regards outline a deliberate adaptation by Carlo Maderno of that of St Peter's. Still lesser domes can be spotted, dwarfed by high palaces and partly obscured by church façades according to the viewpoint. There are those of S. Carlo ai Catinari, of S. Maria di Loreto and SS. Nome di Maria, of the twin churches of S. Maria dei Miracoli and S. Maria in Montesanto, a seeming infinity of Roman domes, all creations of the baroque age, derived from and inspired by the overwhelming parent dome, St Peter's. That miracle of engineering and architecture could, it was agreed by Michelangelo's successors, never be excelled in grandeur or beauty. Never-

The obelisk in its original position on the south side of the basilica, adjoining the chapel of St Andrew; a drawing by Marten van Heemskerk

theless, a constellation of minor domes was deemed not to detract from, but rather to enhance its aloof majesty, as well as to do honour to the greatest artist of modern times, the man who conceived even if he did not live to give ultimate shape to the posthumous offspring of his stupendous invention.

Before taking leave of Pope Sixtus V, we must refer to an event which is a further demonstration of his insuperable ambitions and caused a flutter of admiration throughout Christendom. This was the removal of the great Egyptian obelisk to the middle of St Peter's Piazza. Ever since renaissance popes and architects first mooted the project of a new basilica, the incorporation of the obelisk in a worthy setting had been considered. Michelangelo declared the job of shifting it from its old site to be out of the question. This did not prevent Pope Gregory XIII giving further thought to its removal, which his successor had the supreme determination to achieve.

How long the obelisk had stood on its previous site to the south of the old basilica and on a line due east of the two round chapels of St Petronilla and St Andrew (both destroyed in the Renaissance) is, as I have already said, no longer certain. Until the recent excavations under St Peter's, it was supposed that the obelisk had marked the central point of the divisional wall, or *spina* of Caligula's Circus in which Nero's horrible massacre of Christians took place in A.D. 67. The discovery of a Roman cemetery under the foundations of Constantine's church now suggests that the circus was further away to the south; and that if the obelisk did once stand in the middle of the *spina*, it must have been moved at some unknown date to the site beside the basilica which it certainly occupied throughout the Middle Ages. The tremendous task of removing it in 1586, and indeed that of setting it up in A.D. 37 when first brought to Rome, make an intervening removal without any historical record most unlikely. Is it not therefore possible that instead of marking the centre of the *spina*, it stood in the middle of the circus' northern boundary? The elder Pliny in his *Natural History* refers to the obelisk's transportation from Egypt to Rome by order of the Emperor Gaius (Caligula) as an outstanding event. The barge that carried it had a huge mast of fir wood which four men's arms could not encircle. One hundred and twenty bushels of lentils were needed for ballast. Having fulfilled its purpose, the gigantic vessel was no longer wanted. Therefore, filled with stones and cement, it was sunk to form the foundations of the foremost quay of the new harbour at Ostia.

Pope Sixtus had not been on the throne four months before he erected in the middle of St Peter's Piazza a full-size wooden model in order to judge how the real obelisk would look on this prominent site. Having settled the exact spot, he made it known that a suitable agent was needed to do the removing. From all parts of Europe mathematicians, engineers and doctors of science flocked to consider the possibilities. More than five hundred architects are said to have submitted plans. Some of these were so preposterous as to cause much merriment among members of the Fabbrica. Resorts to magic and calls upon the Mother of God for miraculous intervention were put forward as well as several pseudo-scientific schemes of infantile ingenuity. Bartolomeo Ammannati assured the pope that given one year's reflection he was bound to find the solution, and begged him to wait. Sixtus, with an impatient gesture, merely waved the architect aside. When all the serious and silly proposals had been rejected as impracticable, Domenico Fontana, who was Della Porta's second in command, presented the pope with a little model crane of wood and an obelisk of lead. By gently turning a handle he raised and lowered the toy obelisk with ease. This simple method, he explained to His Holiness, was all he needed. Instantly convinced, Sixtus without further ado entrusted the undertaking to Fontana and commanded him to proceed at once. The unequivocal appointment aroused bitter opposition among the competitive savants and engineers.

Fontana may, in order to get the commission, have made light of the task. It is known that inwardly he viewed the whole affair with apprehension, which he cleverly disguised under an assumed air of self-confidence. Only to intimate companions did he disclose his belief that the pope was slightly mad. To lift a column more than eighty feet high, all of one piece, and weighing a million pounds, required superhuman effort. Fortunately Fontana's sense of self-importance came to his rescue. After all, he reflected, there was nothing he was incapable of achieving once he put his mind to it. He was a scholarly man, very precise, with a meticulous application to detail. Absurdly dignified, pedantic in speech and manner, he could not be defeated in argument and was maddeningly unruffled. In truth Fontana was unequalled as a technician, but as an artist second-rate. His strict observance of the scientific rules enabled him to carry out feats of engin-

Some of the fantastic schemes that were proposed for moving the obelisk *left*. Scaffolding is erected round the obelisk under Fontana's direction *right*

eering, and also to raise grandiose buildings of little grace or elegance. His Lateran Palace, vast, pompous, academic and dull, is a typical specimen of his architecture and the rather joyless generation which he represented.

The 30th April 1586 was the critical day on which Domenico Fontana's qualifications were put to the test. The architect had been careful to take precautions lest the dangerous enterprise should fail. He had a relay of post-horses ready harnessed on which to flee from Sixtus's anger if the worst should happen. The earth, which throughout the centuries had engulfed the obelisk at least half way up the shaft, had already been dug away, revealing the four enormous blocks of the same granite which Pliny had mentioned as forming the base. The needle itself, packed in straw mats and encased in wooden planks, was lashed by strong iron bands. At dawn Fontana led an army of eight hundred labourers to hear Mass in the open, while a hundred and forty carthorses chafed and stamped on the polished cobbles. With him were his brother and inseparable companion Giovanni, and his favourite assistant the thirty-year-old Carlo Maderno, who was never to forget this day. The whole of Rome was assembled to watch. Every window and every roof-top was crammed with spectators. After confessing and receiving the Blessed Sacrament, the army of workmen entered the enclosure set apart for them. Their leader

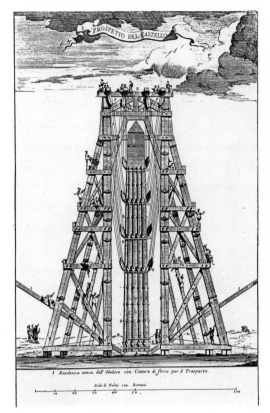

The obelisk, encased in a protective framework, is lifted off its base by thirty-five windlasses *left* and lowered on rollers *right*

mounted a raised rostrum from which to direct operations, as though he were about to conduct some monstrous orchestra. At two o'clock when all was ready Fontana raised his hand and the trumpets sounded the signal to begin. The enormous wooden machine which was to lift the obelisk with stout ropes was slowly set in motion by thirty-five windlasses, each worked by two horses and ten men. There was a sound of creaks and groans accompanied by the cracking of whips and the neighing of horses. Soon the bystanders noticed a perceptible wrench and quiver. Slowly but surely the great obelisk was lifted off the base on which it had rested for perhaps fifteen hundred years. At the twelfth turn, it had risen a foot or more into the air. The architect had so far triumphed. The obelisk was under his control. The spectators were jubilant. The guns in the Castle of S. Angelo fired a salute, the church bells of the city pealed forth and the workmen carried the self-satisfied little architect shoulder high around the enclosure.

The seemingly impossible had been achieved in that the granite monolith was hoisted. Still there were difficulties and perils ahead. On 17th May the obelisk was lowered horizontally to the ground and conveyed on rollers to its new destination. Then the pope announced that the exacting task of re-erection must wait until the heat of the summer was over. The day chosen was 14th September, a Wednesday, which Sixtus always

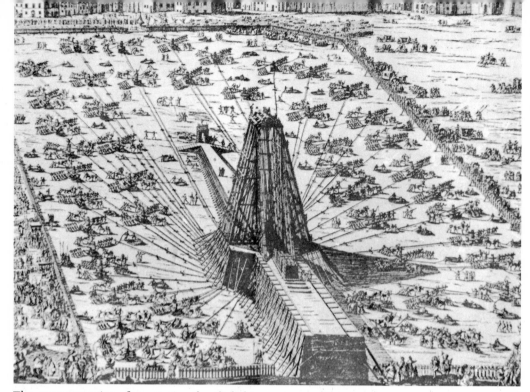

The great operation of re-erecting the obelisk

considered a lucky day, and the Feast of the Exaltation of the Cross. When the date came round, the eight hundred workmen again trooped at dawn to the nearby church of Santo Spirito, where they attended Mass on their knees. Fontana approached the pope and knelt to receive his blessing. A greater crowd than before had gathered to watch the scene. With bated breath in the deadly silence which had been enjoined by Sixtus on pain of instant execution the people stood in the sunshine of this early autumn day. A gallows had been erected as a warning to anyone daring to utter a sound. Again the trumpets blew. A bell was rung by Fontana and this time forty windlasses were turned by one hundred and forty horses. Thereupon 'the wheels', to quote an eyewitness, 'made such a noise that one might have thought the very earth was going to split and the sky above to open'. Fortunately no such thing happened, and the picturesque incident of a sailor from Liguria, who, seeing the ropes about to burn from the heat of the friction, risked his life by shouting, 'Water them!' may be apocryphal. Pope Sixtus is said to have pardoned the sailor's disobedience and asked what special favour he would like granted. The answer was the right for his home town of Bordighera to supply palms to Rome every Palm Sunday in perpetuity. Certainly the custom was observed for as long as the papal power lasted. Everything now proceeded smoothly with the lowering of the obelisk and an hour before sunset it was seen to sink happily on to the backs of four little couchant lions. Made of bronze, each of these delicious beasts wears a tiara over a flowing mane and has two bodies, of which the tails are amicably intertwined with its neighbour's and the claws clasped upon the pedestal below. The whole operation had been accomplished with only fifty-two movements of the windlasses.

On this occasion the exultation of the populace was uncontrollable. They sang and

The obelisk in its new position in the piazza of St Peter's

danced, drank and feasted, rang bells and let off fireworks until the early hours of the following morning. Meanwhile Fontana presided over a banquet given to the workmen. It consisted of bread, cheese, ham and two bottles of wine each, which do not seem excessive reward for so much labour. The architect was made a papal nobleman, given 70,000 scudi there and then and promised an annual pension of 2,000 scudi. The pope struck commemorative medals and received poems of congratulation in twenty languages. The event was recorded by the publication of a handsome folio with detailed plates showing how the stupendous transportation was carried out.[1]

The re-erection of the obelisk was considered a notable feat for several reasons. It was a triumph of the mind of man over a seemingly insoluble problem of engineering; and, the age being a scientific one, Fontana's machinery was appreciated as novel and ingenious. It marked a further stage in the gradual embellishment of the new basilica and its precincts. Lastly, it celebrated the triumph of the Faith of Christ, St Peter and the apostles over pagan superstition. The proximity of the obelisk to the old basilica had always been resented as something of a provocation, almost as a slight to the Christian religion. It had stood there like a false idol, as it were vaingloriously, on what was believed to be the centre of the accursed circus where the early Christians and St Peter had been put to death. Its sides, then as now, were graven with dedications to Augustus and Tiberius. On its summit was a bronze sphere believed to contain the ashes of Julius Caesar. When taken down, the sphere proved to be solid. Nevertheless, Sixtus had a bronze cross put in its place (in 1740, after repairs, a piece of the True Cross was

[1] Domenico Fontana, *Della Trasportazione dell'Obelisco Vaticano*, 1590.

inserted in one of the arms). Solemnly the pope had the heathen spirit of the obelisk exorcised. 'Impio cultu dicatum' he carved upon the base as a reminder of what the needle once represented, and 'Ecce Crux Domini fugite partes adversae' in proud defiance of Luther and the reformed Churches.

Fontana now became the pope's most privileged architect and was entrusted with the raising of three other obelisks at strategic focal points of the city. After Sixtus's death, however, the tables were turned on him. He was accused of having falsified the basilican building accounts. If not positively dismissed from the post of Assistant Architect to St Peter's, he was advised to retire. Greatly offended, he withdrew to Naples where he was received by the Spanish Viceroy with much acclaim. There he worked as regal architect and there, refusing ever to return to Rome, he died. In the Holy City which treated him first as a hero and then as a common peculator, he is chiefly remembered not for his several palaces and monumental buildings, but for the removal and re-erection of the great Egyptian obelisk in front of St Peter's façade. The operation captured the imagination of Christendom and was reflected over the next fifty years in countless town planning ventures in European cities, as well as in painting and literature. Even Shakespeare in his defiant sonnet addressed to Time may have had Fontana's classic achievement in mind when with typical English paradox he exclaimed:

'No, Time, thou shalt not boast that I do change.
Thy pyramids built up with newer might
To me are nothing novel, nothing strange;
They are but dressings of a former sight.'

When the great pope, whose unquestioned authority had suppressed all banditry and lawlessness in the Papal States and whose slightest frown had filled his subjects with awe, died in 1590 from a surfeit of melon accompanied by too much white wine mixed with snow water, the traditional rioting, pillaging, and looting broke out in the city with enhanced violence. With wonderful consistency, the Romans' proclivity to turn against their benefactors was once more asserted in this posthumous act of revulsion. The people dared not disobey Sixtus in his lifetime; so they snapped their fingers at him the moment the breath was out of his body.

It was the greatest pity that the reign of this zealous builder was so short and that the style of architecture which characterized it was not better. The love of overlaying surfaces with a plethora of polychrome marble and superfluous detail is sadly exemplified by the Cappella Sistina added by this pope to S. Maria Maggiore. The huge chapel, practically the size of a church, was spared neither expense nor loot from the pagan monuments of Rome. Sixtus, like many men of low origin raised to pinnacles of authority, believed good taste to derive from over-ornamentation and the Almighty's commendation to be won by the spoils of his enemies.

Sixtus V lived just long enough to see St Peter's dome completed, but for the lead covering, on 21st May 1590. In the following year the lantern was put in place by Gregory XIV, who reigned for only ten months. He had the grace to inscribe upon the rim of the eye under the lantern the concise Latin phrase, which may be translated: 'To the glory of St Peter and Pope Sixtus V in the fifth year of his pontificate, 1590.'

The obelisk rests upon four couchant lions, each with two bodies whose tails intertwine

The crowning cross was raised into place by Clement VIII. He had two caskets of lead filled: one with fragments of the True Cross and relics of St Andrew, St James the Great, and Popes St Clement, Callixtus and Sixtus; the other with seven Agnus Dei, which are medallions of the Holy Lamb made of a mixture of wax from the paschal candle and dust from the bones of martyrs. These precious objects were solemnly blessed, venerated and censed before being enclosed within the two arms of the cross. Between sunrise and sunset of one day, the cross was then lifted on pulleys from the ground and, amid the pealing of bells, hoisted into the position from which it has never been shifted. In 1594 Clement VIII also had the dome covered with lead and strips of gilt bronze laid along the edges of the sheets.

Clement VIII (1592–1605) was a Florentine of shining piety. He was painstaking, hard-working and far too indulgent of his nephews. Like most members of the Aldobrandini family, he was the friend of learning and piety. He was an intimate of Tasso. He hastened the work begun by Sixtus V on the Vatican Palace and resumed that on St Peter's Basilica. He got Della Porta, who was still official papal architect and much in his favour, to build the Cappella Clementina at the south-east angle of Michelangelo's Greek cross

An interior view of the lantern of the dome (see also p. 151)

plan, as a pendant to the Cappella Gregoriana at the north-east. Luckily Clement reigned for thirteen years, during which time he was able to put the finishing touches to the partially completed projects of his predecessors. He was just the right man for the job. He was not one to originate great ideas of his own, but his tidy, competent mind rejoiced in tying up the ends left undone by others.

Having erected the great cross over the lantern and covered the dome with lead, Clement turned his attention to the decoration of the inner dome. He confirmed Gregory XIV's engagement of the Roman artist Giuseppe Cesari, on whom he heaped honours and whom he made Cavaliere d'Arpino. For the spaces between the sixteen gilded stucco ribs d'Arpino designed cartoons for six rows of variously shaped compartments, which diminish in size as they approach the lantern. The Saviour, Our Lady, the apostles, saints and angels are represented. These adequate but uninspired paintings were translated into mosaics of which the colours are soft and dominated by powder blue and gold; but the significance of the subjects is lost in their great distance. Above them on the soffit of the lantern God the Father emerges from clouds, rather splendid but agonizing to look at from below. Under the drum and around the circular frieze Clement put in gold mosaic letters, four feet eight inches high, Christ's dedicatory words, which were to determine the divine tradition of papal sovereignty: 'Tu es Petrus et super hanc petram aedificabo ecclesiam meam et tibi dabo claves regni coelorum.'[1] For the great spandrels over each of the crossing piers d'Arpino enlisted two pupils, Cesari Nebbia and Giovanni del Vecchi, to compose cartoons. The four Evangelists are the result. They are gigantic and dull. The only comment any guide book has found to make upon them is that St Luke's pen is seven and a half feet in length.

Construction and decoration of the crossing had now reached a stage when something had to be done about the confession. In Pope Gregory XIII's reign, the pavement of the new basilica had been laid and the crypt below was already taking shape. It was no longer thought suitable to retain the meagre old presbytery and to leave exposed the twelfth-century altar of Callixtus II over the Apostle's tomb. Clement at once ordered the demolition of Constantine's apse and the removal of Bramante's protective walls round the old presbytery. Della Porta then made a new altar which enclosed without completely destroying that of Callixtus. For the purpose he used a table of white marble in one piece brought from the Forum of Nerva. This he raised on seven steps. According to an eyewitness[2] a fall of masonry during the construction of the new papal altar caused an unexpected crack to appear in the ground. Della Porta claimed to discern through it an altar older than Callixtus's and, what is more, the very cross of gold laid upon Peter's bronze sarcophagus by St Helena. The pope, who was at once notified, bustled to the site accompanied by three cardinals. By means of a torch held by the architect, the party were sure that they too saw these things. Clement and his companions were so awed by the spectacle that after a confabulation His Holiness forbade the sepulchre to be disturbed further and commanded the aperture to be filled with cement in his presence.

There are excellent reasons for doubting this picturesque story. In the first place, it is most unlikely that St Helena's gold cross and the bronze sarcophagus escaped the

---

[1] Thou art Peter, and upon this rock I will build my church; and I will give unto thee the keys of the kingdom of heaven.

[2] Francesco Torrigio, one of the chroniclers of St Peter's Basilica.

Saracen depredations of 846. If they did, and if they were truly seen by Della Porta and Pope Clement VIII, then they must have been rifled and destroyed since. In fact, no untoward events have taken place during the subsequent three and a half centuries up to our own day in which such a disaster could have befallen the sacred treasure of a sanctuary so hidden and well guarded. Furthermore, no mention of the cross and sarcophagus was made by Bernini when in the 1620s he dug the deep foundations for the baldacchino. Nor indeed were there any signs of them when Pope Pius XII's excavators reached the area below Callixtus's altar in the 1940s.

In 1594 Pope Clement VIII was able to celebrate his first Mass at the new high altar. Ever since this date the altar has been reserved for popes officiating in St Peter's on great festivals. Della Porta's next duty was to dig the horse-shoe shaped area below the new pavement level in front of the high altar. The purpose was to form the confession which exists today. From the confession he provided direct access to the niche of the Apostle's shrine. Covered with marble veneer, it is now known as the Niche of the Pallia where the scarf-like vestments (the pallia) are kept before being sent by the pope to newly-consecrated archbishops. Behind the shrine Della Porta constructed an underground chapel (the Cappella Clementina) approached from the circular corridor of the Grotte Nuove and connected with the Vatican Palace. It enabled the pope to resort to the holy of holies undisturbed for private prayer and meditation.

Della Porta lived long enough to fulfil most of Pope Clement's tidying-up process. He died only two years before his master at the age of sixty-nine. Even so, his death in 1602 was brought about prematurely by a disagreeable, if somewhat ludicrous, incident. Della Porta was a jolly man who liked good living. He had been staying with Cardinal Aldobrandini in the cardinal's sumptuous villa at Frascati. Disregarding the tragic warning in the death of his previous master, Pope Sixtus V, he had drunk too much wine and eaten too much of that fatal fruit, melon. On the homeward journey to Rome in his host's carriage, he was seized with violent intestinal pains. Being a man of much delicacy, he did not like to ask the cardinal to stop the carriage so that he might get out and relieve himself. Instead, he endured great agony. He was corpulent and plethoric and on reaching the Porta Giovanni he died of what the news sheets termed 'suffocation' owing to the jolting of the carriage. He was buried the very same day in the grave of his wife and son in the church of the Aracoeli.

With Della Porta's death came the final severance of the link between the office of St Peter's Chief Architect and Michelangelo. Della Porta had played an important rôle in that office. Originally a sculptor and maker of stucco reliefs, he had learned architecture under Vignola's tuition at St Peter's. And Vignola had worked with Michelangelo. It fell to Della Porta to put St Peter's dome, more or less in accordance with Michelangelo's design, upon the drum which the great master had left all but complete in 1564. In other respects, he deviated hardly at all from Michelangelo's projects for the basilica, which he helped fulfil by a great deal of decoration and the completion of the huge Gregorian and Clementine chapels. Cautious, scholarly and reflective, he was the last of that band of architects belonging to the short counter-reformation era which preceded the long era of the Baroque. Inevitably, his successors had very different ideas to his. Little did the conservative Pope Clement VIII realize what he was doing when he appointed Carlo Maderno in Della Porta's place.

The monument to Clementina Sobieski (see text p. 301)

MARIA CLEMENTINA M. BRI

...ANC. ET HIBERN. R...

7 Maderno's Nave

On Clement VIII's death the curtain finally came down on the Roman High Renaissance. The Michelangelo tradition was expended. The great master had been dead now for forty years. There was no one alive who even remembered him, and henceforth his message could conveniently be misinterpreted. Della Porta, to whom was committed the onerous and not altogether enviable duty of completing the dome, had already left the scene, his mission faithfully accomplished. The conservative Clement, who never so much as contemplated departing an inch from the great master's plan for St Peter's, was followed for a brief interval of less than one month by the last of the Medici popes, Leo XI (1605). This upright and strict pontiff, the intimate friend of St Philip Neri, was a child of the Counter-Reformation. And his reign was far too short to have any bearing upon the architecture of the basilica. His accession and the business of electing yet another pope merely prolonged the pause in building brought about by the death of Della Porta in 1602.

This pause had very important consequences. It gave time to the Fabbrica to take stock of the situation of St Peter's. The authority of the Congregazione della Fabbrica di San Pietro, which Clement VII established, had always been somewhat equivocal. Michelangelo, who was in constant disagreement with this body, would appeal to the popes to reverse whichever of its decisions he disliked. The popes, in their awe of the old artist, usually complied by over-ruling the Fabbrica, habitually composed of heterogeneous members drawn from different countries. This international composition was an obvious weakness. It made agreement upon important issues very difficult to achieve. Strong-minded popes like Sixtus V were inclined to brush aside its deliberations with impatience and impose their own decisions. The Roman Curia too had grown to resent the interference of a cosmopolitan committee in charge of what it now regarded as an essentially Roman place of worship. A preponderance of foreigners had been all very well in days when the structure of St Peter's was largely maintained by funds derived from the sale of indulgences overseas. Since this once lucrative source of revenue had dried up and the funds for maintenance were now found in Rome, the case was different. Clement VIII, aware of its shortcomings, reorganized the Fabbrica altogether. He suppressed the international body and constituted a new one under the more fulsome title, La Congregazione della Reverenda Fabbrica di San Pietro. The new Fabbrica was composed of a prefect, who was the Cardinal-Archpriest of St Peter's, several other cardinals, an economist and a few lay officials. In this guise, subject only to a few modifications brought about in the eighteenth century, the Fabbrica functions today. Perhaps the most important result of Clement VIII's reforms was the establishment of the Sampietrini, upon whom the whole physical welfare of the basilica depends.

The Sampietrini are a specialist body of maintenance men constantly on the spot. An illiterate mason called Zabaglia suggested to the Fabbrica in the year 1600 that the repairs

Maderno's nave. A view down the length of the church from the east gallery (see text p. 239)

Clement VIII *left* instituted the Sampietrini, one of whose functions is to illuminate the basilica on special occasions *right*

of the immense acreage of St Peter's ought no longer to be entrusted to casual labourers. With that body's consent, he trained thirty young workers to be experts in all the building and decorative crafts. Soon he had mustered an efficient force of masons, carpenters, painters, stuccoists, glaziers, gilders and plumbers. The young men married, founded families and brought up their sons in the trade. The Sampietrini have long been a devoted hereditary corps. They are a race apart, a large clan of dedicated men who have developed their own rules and customs. Almost from infancy they are taken in hand and trained in that craft to which they have a natural bent. Their workshops are hidden in the bowels of the basilica, from which they emerge like pigeons from nesting-boxes. St Peter's walls are riddled with cavernous chambers, approached by numerous narrow, twisting stairways, called 'snails', which give secret access to the most vertiginous platforms. The Sampietrini are as lithe and agile as acrobats. They soon learn to climb to any height, to run along cornices and roofs, to balance themselves on precipitous capitals, to squat on the heads of statues, to suspend themselves on ropes from jutting pediments and to scamper like squirrels over the dome and lantern. They think nothing of lowering themselves into the aisles from vaults a hundred feet above the pavement level. By these means they are able to inspect and repair the most inaccessible parts of the structure, to hang the great rolls of damask down pilasters for ceremonial celebrations, and, when required, to light the thousand oil lanterns on the dome up to the cross with incredible speed and precision. On rare occasions – St Peter's feast day is one of them – the Sampietrini are in their element and the spectators in their lasting debt. No other sight is more inspiring than the illuminations during a fine twilight. When the sun has gone down and the first stars begin to prick the violet canopy of the Roman sky, brilliant points of light appear at intervals upon the bulk of the great basilica. Then the points run together into strips until the clear outline is defined by a twinkling constellation of gold.

And this is not the end of the spectacle. Suddenly a magical thing happens. The diffused light from the oil lanterns is intensified by innumerable red plumes of curling fire. By indescribable means the expert Sampietrini – today there are hundreds of them – have lit their torches simultaneously. Crouched on various strategic parts of the colonnade, façade, lantern and even the arms of the cross, they have been waiting ready to strike. The first deep note of St Peter's solemn bell proclaims the night. And then a single snake of flame slithers over the dome and shoots a tongue from the top of the cross. At this signal each Sampietrino in one concerted movement strikes his set of torches. In a matter of seconds St Peter's appears to be a glowing furnace.

The election of Camillo Borghese as Paul V (1605–21) in May 1605 opened a new era in the history of Rome and, because Rome was still the fountain head of the arts in Europe, so too in the history of Western art. If the full maturity of the baroque style, the cradle of which was without question the Holy City, did not become apparent until the reign of Urban VIII, the infancy, to us who may look back upon the extraordinary phenomenon, is distinctly apparent in that of Paul V. This promise of marvels to come is seen less clearly in the architecture and painting of the reign than in the changed attitude of the Church, which was determined by the pontiff himself. Borghese's accomplishments may not have been more distinguished than those of many a previous renaissance pope. True he was very cultivated and loved learning for its own sake; and next to learning, art. His piety may not have excelled that of several counter-reformation popes, yet his ecclesiastical interests were pre-eminent. He was naturally industrious and rather taciturn. The presence of this tall, handsome man with hard lines round the mouth and strained gaze of intensely myopic eyes was forbidding. It did not suggest the happy hedonism which is so readily, and often mistakenly, associated with the great princely patrons of the baroque age. These qualities were on the other hand conspicuous enough in the Borghese cardinal nephews, of whom the affable sybarite Scipione was, as Bernini's bust of him testifies to perfection, the incarnate exemplar. Yet if nepotism, to the limitless extent of enriching his relations out of the papal exchequer, was Paul V's chief failing, family interference in matters of state was by no means permitted.

The image of the jolly Cardinal Scipione Borghese gives a far truer picture of the change that had come over the Catholic Church than that of the naturally dour pope. The baroque style, remember, was essentially ecclesiastical. The new phases in the Church's fortunes, which the baroque style reflected, admittedly did not allow any relaxation of dogma, or much easy complacency. The enemy still watchful at the gates was no less powerful and menacing than it had been during the reformation and counter-reformation phases of disaster and recovery. Heresy was a hungry and ever-present monster crouching ready to pounce. Anti-papal propaganda was everywhere rampant. The Venetian Republic was a nest of disaffection stirred up by the English envoy Sir Henry Wotton, one of the most insidious Protestant instruments that ever operated in a Catholic land. Nonetheless the attitude of the Church had changed. It set out to win, not to repel. Instead of a gloomy, rebarbative front, it assumed a milder, more cheerful aspect. The severe, disciplinary measures adopted by the Council of Trent had long ago done their work. The somewhat preposterous and philistine directives to artists as to what they should and should not create were now overlooked. Christian art no longer needed to exclude pagan connotations, nor to forbid the representation of everyday, commonplace incidents. The homely cat and dog were allowed to creep back into the forefront of paintings of the Annunciation. Dwarfs and buffoons once more played incidental parts in Last Suppers, and humble wild flowers were permitted to grow at the foot of the Cross on Calvary. The exteriors, even of quite unimportant churches, were designed to impress and delight the populace with a grandeur which was often make-believe. The interiors became stage settings in which counterfeit perspectives and ingenious lighting effects were focused upon sculptural scenes of the most exotic, and sometimes erotic (if sublimated) kind. Tremendous emphasis was put upon ceremonial and pageantry. Churches became theatres as well as houses of prayer. They were intended to dazzle as much as to edify the simple.

There was much wisdom in this novel step taken by the Church. In concentrating upon the blessings to be reaped from observing the Christian dogmas, rather than the penalties to be incurred through disregarding them, the Church successfully diverted souls from the stark and narrow paths of Protestantism. Above all, it sought to demonstrate the glory and benefit of the Sacraments in the most attractive manner of which commissioned artists were capable. There is no doubt that opportunity gives birth to talent and genius. The policy, adopted by Paul V and followed by his successors, of re-establishing the divine authority and emphasizing the mystique of the Catholic Faith by means of art caused a trail of the brightest meteors across the baroque sky, in Caravaggio and Cortona, Bernini and Borromini.

Paul V was a great builder more out of political motive than love of architecture or innate taste. In the latter quality he seems to have been conspicuously lacking, to judge by the Borghese Chapel in S. Maria Maggiore, which he embarked upon at the beginning of his reign. It is an over-decorated, highly concentrated medley of polychrome marbles, still in the costive manner of the Roman late *cinquecento*. The style of the chapel shows no sign of the free rhythm and flow of the architecture soon to emerge. Paul was also a faithful restorer of churches and the creator of several monumental fountains about the city. He recalled that under the Emperor Trajan Rome boasted no less than thirteen hundred fountains fed by eleven aqueducts crossing the Campagna. The Acqua Paola on the Janiculum Hill, with its streams gushing from five triumphal arches, is the grandest and best known of the several living waters which he harnessed from Lake Bracciano and the springs of the distant hills. He took the colossal pine-cone from the domed canopy of the fifth-century cantharus in Constantine's atrium, and placed it on its present platform within the hemicycle of the court of this name. As though in expiation of this action he got Carlo Maderno to construct on the north side of St Peter's Piazza the splendid fountain which later in the century was practically rebuilt by Bernini and duplicated on the south side by Carlo Fontana. A powerful plume of water is made to shoot into the air and descend upon a mushroom ledge, thence into a wider upturned basin of Egyptian granite, and again into a hexagonal pool. Upon the veil of spray from the falling shower the even-

After the completion of the dome the nave of the old church and the buildings facing the piazza still survived for a time; a painting by L. de Caulery

ing sun paints a perennial rainbow. Of the twin fountains the northern is better preserved because more sheltered from the wind. Queen Christina of Sweden on her first entry to Rome was struck dumb by astonishment at its beauty. She supposed it had been specially turned on for her benefit, and begged the pope, after she had glutted her admiration, to turn it off in order to prevent a waste of water.

Paul V was barely elected before he confirmed the privileges and constitution of the Fabbrica, adding to the Congregation eight cardinals whom Leo XI just had time to create during his twenty-seven day reign. For two years this august body deliberated how it was to proceed with the building of the basilica and whom it was to employ. At the time, the unfinished new building was still separated from the old by the divisional wall erected in 1538. In front of the medieval church a preposterous jumble of Gothic and Classical appendages, quite unrelated to each other, remained: on the south side the palace of the archpriest and on the north the three-storeyed benediction loggia and the campanile. During the Fabbrica's deliberations, what was left of the old basilica continued to deteriorate. In September 1605 during a storm a large block of marble from a cornice crashed to the pavement close to the altar of the Madonna della Colonna where Mass was being said. By a miracle none of the worshippers was injured. But there was panic and the people were seriously alarmed. The incident determined the Fabbrica to demolish every part and appendage of the old basilica still standing. The pope felt obliged to agree. He stipulated, however, that all the relics of the saints must be moved to safety and, whenever possible, the old monuments be preserved in the crypt, or Grotte Vecchie, constructed for the purpose between the pavements of the old and new basilicas. Certain works of art found their way to other churches, like the eighth-century mosaic of the Adoration of the Magi which was set up in S. Maria in Cosmedin, and even to private chapels. The pope also insisted that records should be taken of any monuments that had to be destroyed. Accordingly, two canons were deputed to superintend the openings of tombs and the translation of remains. The work was done with the utmost reverence and solemnity. The archivist of St Peter's, Iacopo Grimaldi, an enthusiastic antiquarian, made an inventory and some invaluable sketches of the monuments as they were being dismantled. Far more care was taken now than by Julius II and Bramante a hundred years previously, when the ancient treasures were smashed to pieces without the slightest compunction, and without record. What Paul V salvaged was a fraction of the works of art lost under Julius II.

The decision to complete the demolition was not received without some opposition. The learned Cardinal Baronius, who was Vatican librarian and the Church's greatest living historian, was loud in his condemnation. He bitterly denounced the impiety of sweeping away a building which enshrined the history of thirteen hundred Christian years. Needless to say, his was a voice crying unheeded in the wilderness. The work of demolition was undertaken with feverish haste by night as well as by day as though to forestall possible last minute regret and counter-decision. Indeed, when the turn of the campanile came, the structure was loosened at the base in such a way that the tower was made to collapse in an avalanche of rubble.

Before hands were laid upon the first tile of the old church various ceremonies were performed according to the ritual agreed upon. There was something tragic about the solemnity which attended the dismantling of the doomed basilica. On 28th September 1605 the archpriest transferred the Blessed Sacrament into the Cappella Gregoriana of the new building. All the cathedral canons took part in the procession. Next, the chapels were deprived of their consecration like poor old clergymen divested of their priesthood. Their relics were removed and their altars taken down. The tombs of the saints were opened and the corpses disinterred. With much pomp the ghastly remains, some bursting from decayed coffins and shrouds, saw the first light of day after a whole millenium. St Veronica's handkerchief, St Andrew's head, the holy lance, the fragments of the True Cross were likewise removed from their ancient resting places, and reverently carried away.

On 18th February 1606, Ash Wednesday, the work of demolition of the old church began. A squad of labourers first attacked that part of the roof which adjoined the front. They took down the marble cross which crowned the apex, the venerable cross put in position by Pope Sylvester and the Emperor Constantine as the symbol of Christ's absolute triumph over paganism. On the base the workmen read the one word carved in Greek letters: Agrippina. So the base of the statue of the infamous Nero's mother had for centuries been carrying the cross of Christ. Next, the tiles, several of them dating from the reign of Theoderic the Great, a few even from Constantine's, were hurled to the ground. Then the beams of oak, once brought from the Abruzzi forests by order of

Gregory the Great were either hacked to pieces by the axes, or, so strong were some of them, re-used in building the Borghese Palace.

On 26th March the picks assaulted the walls, quickly razing them down to the foundations. One by one Constantine's columns of the nave were lowered, the most precious, a couple of black African marble and the largest monoliths of the sort in existence, being kept for re-erection in the new portico entrance. On the capital of one was carved the head of the Emperor Hadrian. It came originally from his mausoleum. In a clumsy attempt at preservation, a workman broke it. On 15th November the last sung Mass took place in Rossellino's choir, the Tribuna di San Piero, in the presence of a vast congregation. Then it too was pulled down. The bronze tomb of Sixtus IV was opened and the body of that pope disclosed. It was found clad in a chasuble of gold brocade and the pallium. The head wore a mitre and the feet sandals embroidered with a cross. From the finger a splendid ring was taken to the Treasury. Likewise the coffin of Sixtus's nephew, Julius II, was opened, and the remains, which had been desecrated by the Constable of Bourbon's troops, were reinterred in a new grave beside the bones of his uncle.

Long before the last vestige of the medieval basilica had disappeared, the Fabbrica was engaged in a heated discussion how the new one was to be finished. Indeed, ever since Paul V's election the question had been debated. The pope professed that he wished to abide by Michelangelo's scheme. So too at first did the Architect in Chief, Carlo Maderno, whom Clement VIII had appointed to succeed Giacomo Della Porta in 1602. Maderno, in claiming to keep to the Greek cross plan, nevertheless wanted to break the harmony of Michelangelo's contour by flanking it with numerous projecting chapels – a proposal which received a good deal of criticism. The prevailing opinion in the Congregation of the Fabbrica however was that the space occupied by the old basilica, as well as by those ancillary buildings, baptistry, sacristy, and so forth, not hitherto under one roof, must be entirely covered by the new. It was a conscience-saving view, a way of making amends for sacrificing Constantine's historic basilica. The Fabbrica felt that so long as the whole sacred area was embraced by a new consecrated church, all would be forgiven by the shades of those saints and martyrs who had contributed to the making of the historic building which they were about to sweep away. A secondary, but hardly less cogent reason was the belief, which had gained ground during the Counter-Reformation, that the Greek cross plan was a pagan innovation but the Latin cross plan a tradition of the Christian Church in that it represented the crucified body of the Saviour.

Early in 1607 Paul V took it upon himself to summon a concourse of ten eminent architects to advise the Fabbrica how to proceed. Amongst them, Maderno sat as the pope's nominee. The outcome was a recommendation of the Latin cross solution. The overriding argument on this occasion was the necessity of more space to accommodate under cover the multitudes assembled for functions at which the Pope as head of the Church officiates. The recommendation received practically unanimous endorsement by the cardinals. Cardinal Maffeo Barberini, the future Pope Urban VIII, a man of far greater artistic discernment than any other member of the Curia, was the single dissentient. Paul V, impressed by the majority view, gave way. Thereafter, he never swerved from his decision. How far Maderno honestly disapproved cannot be ascertained. He has always been held the chief protagonist of the Latin cross plan, because he carried it out. In fairness to him, a letter which he wrote on 30th May 1613 should be remembered. It bears out that the decision was forced upon him by the pope and cardinals and that he accepted it with reluctance. There is irony in the fact that for three and a half centuries he has borne most of the blame.

Whether reluctant or willing, Maderno was commanded to draw up plans for a prolongation eastwards of Michelangelo's nave. In great haste he complied, and in no less haste his plans were adopted by the Fabbrica.

Carlo Maderno was a nephew of Domenico Fontana. He had been apprenticed in youth to a stuccoist. He arrived in Rome from his native Lake of Lugano about 1580. On the appointment by Sixtus V of his uncle as Architect in Chief to St Peter's, opportunities came to him. He was then in his early thirties. He helped Domenico in the raising of the various obelisks about the city. When his uncle fell into disgrace in Clement VIII's reign, Maderno continued to work under the brother Giovanni Fontana, who stayed on as architect to the Fabbrica. Giovanni was a specialist in fountains and the nephew copied his style and imbibed his spirit. Giovanni retired in 1607, which happened to be the opportune year for Maderno to spring to the fore. The nephew was already much in favour with Paul V, who had watched with approval the development of his distinctive style.

Maderno had shown originality in treating the façades of churches. At S. Giacomo degli Incurabili, the upper stage, within great scrolls made to embrace two orders and a central loggia under a shell-headed niche, was considered a startling and beautiful innovation. So too was the façade of S. Susanna (1603) with a lower order of columns half embedded in the wall surface, a flimsy pilaster at each corner and a balustrade made to run up and down the pediment. Maderno was deliberately transposing weak and strong elements, and making experiments hitherto untried even by Michelangelo. Such daring solecisms were unconventional, to say the least. They certainly lent his façades a new rhythm, which was revolutionary and baroque. Likewise his additions to the Palazzo Mattei introduced animated surfaces of bas-reliefs, busts within roundels and perspective arches. These features shocked the diehard critics, who accepted the lifeless counter-reformation classicism as the only standard of correct architecture. Pope Paul, on the other hand, was thrilled by them.

On 8th March 1607 work was begun on digging the foundations of the nave of St Peter's in the presence of the Governor of Rome and a gathering of architects. On 7th May the cardinal-archpriest laid the first stone which the pope had previously sanctified. By the summer a wooden model of Maderno's completed scheme was available for inspection. It received Paul V's unstinted approval. By now the building activity was bewildering. Relays of carts were dragging loads of tufa from the quarries near Porta Portense. The carriage of travertine from Tivoli was such that the Santo Spirito road to the Vatican was worn into deep ruts. The waggons were frequently overturned. Whole tree trunks from the hillsides were brought for the scaffolding. Seven hundred labourers were permanently employed. When we realize that in the following year the façade was actually begun to the accompaniment of a pealing of bells, and that in 1612 plaster models of the colossal statues were set on the parapet to test their appearance and scale, the speed of the work seems almost incredible. By December 1614 the stucco vaulting of the nave was completely decorated with roses, and in 1615 the divisional wall in the nave taken down. By Palm Sunday the last vestiges of rubble had been carted away. When revealed, the overall length of the new basilica was $211\frac{1}{2}$ metres, or thirteen metres more

A side elevation of St Peter's, showing the extension of the nave undertaken by Maderno. (The cupolas to the west of the dome were, in fact, never built)

than the combined length of Constantine's basilica and atrium. Whereas the western apse of the old church had just embraced the site of the present baldacchino, the east entrances stood on an imaginary line drawn between the two existing water stoups of Maderno's nave.

In fact Maderno extended eastwards the single bay of Michelangelo's arm by three more, namely those arches between coupled pilasters which give access to the aisles. In the nave ceiling the break can be seen where Maderno's extension begins. The aisles and the chapels they lead to are also his. The aisles are very satisfactory. Immensely high openings, in the form of giant portals under segmental heads on Cottanello marble columns, separate the three bays. Over each portal head a blind window is tightly jammed in a thoroughly mannerist fashion. The windows are made of boards painted with counterfeit panes. Overhead, each compartment is lit by an oval cupola on a drum divided into separate tabernacles holding statues of angels. The soffit of each dome is decorated with scenes in mosaic. These little cupolas are among the most beautiful of Maderno's architecture. The same cannot be said of the two large rectangular chapels of the Blessed Sacrament and Choir, both approached from the aisles. The first, to which additions were made by Bernini (the lovely gilt bronze ciborium on the altar inspired by

The interior, showing the nave of St Peter's in its original form before the baroque additions; an anonymous painting of the Expulsion of Heliodorus from the Temple (c. 1616–26)

Bramante's Tempietto), and Borromini (notably the grilled screen) contains so many individual works of art that we must try and overlook the excess of decoration. The second, devoid of individual works of high merit, was made merely ornate and ugly by the Borghese pope's successor, Gregory XV, and is a medley of mud and mustard. Maderno should not be held responsible for the present appearance of either chapel.

Francesco Milizia[1] writing in 1768 when the baroque style was at the nadir of depreciation was extremely critical of all Maderno's architecture at St Peter's. The nave and aisles come in for some very severe strictures. Firstly, Milizia complained that Maderno's extension of the nave was not in a straight line but inclined slightly to the south. This is certainly true, and how many people notice it? 'He appears to have lost', Milizia wrote unfairly, 'whatever knowledge he might have possessed, even that of drawing a straight line.' Maderno indeed made the kink deliberate, and deserves high praise for having done so. He thus rectified a fault of Sixtus V and Domenico Fontana, who had not set the obelisk axially with Michelangelo's east arm of the church. Secondly, Milizia noted that Maderno's three nave bays were slightly narrower than Michelangelo's single bay. This also is an indisputable fact. Again, how many people notice it? Maderno purposely made the disparity in order to distinguish between Michelangelo's Greek cross unit and his own addition. The difference was a drawing-board one, and it can offend nobody. Thirdly, Milizia stated that Maderno's aisles were 'not wider than one of the many

[1] *Lives of the Celebrated Architects*, 1768, trs. 1826.

altars which are in them', which is just not true. No further exculpation therefore is called for. And fourthly, 'Even the elliptical cupolas', he went on, 'are not exempt from error being placed on four arches, of which two are wider than the others, so as to appear inadequate to support cupolas.' If the pointed ends of the elliptical cupolas had been supported on the wider arches and not, as they are, on the narrower, there might have been some substance in this complaint. As things are it is hard to see to what exactly Milizia took exception. I have recounted these somewhat frivolous complaints made by a distinguished architectural critic merely as an example of the total inability of the neo-classical age to detect merit in the baroque choice of evolving forms and tensions in architecture.

Wölfflin,[1] on the other hand, saw in the longitudinal nave of St Peter's the triumph of the baroque conception of 'space directed towards infinity'. The earliest attempt at this effect had been made by Vignola in the Gesù. Maderno consummated it. No longer was the old renaissance aim to achieve fixed spatial proportions acceptable to architects. Now the objective was to create the illusion of infinite distance and to spot-light the holy of holies by means of the dome. Gradations of light, supplied by the unconventional windows in the nave vault, and shadow, where there are no windows, are calculated to draw the pilgrim to the Apostle's shrine further and further down the long vista, barrel-vaulted to suggest the illimitable sky. On either side of the nave unfathomable depths of darkness within aisles and side chapels accentuate the silent mystery of his fearful passage towards the longed-for goal. This sense of drama is indeed experienced within St Peter's, if Maderno's intentions are properly understood.

When we consider the actual façade we find it difficult not to be censorious of both Maderno, who was responsible for its design, and the Fabbrica which chose it. Even the most impartial critics are agreed that it is a mistake. Some are of the opinion that it is a disaster. At all events the failure was due to two things, hurry and muddle. Paul V was so desperately anxious to proceed with the building that he chivvied the Fabbrica into accepting a design without careful enough forethought. Of the ten architects who had submitted designs for the façade in 1607 Maderno was chosen because he had, so to speak, inherited the post of Capomaestro of St Peter's from the Fontana brothers, and also because he showed some respect for Michelangelo's existing fabric. In a paradoxical sense he showed too much respect, which led to his design being neither Michelangelo's nor truly his own. Since Maderno's prolonged nave was a basic infringement of Michelangelo's plan for the new basilica, he was obliged to drop the great architect's scheme of a Pantheon-like portico of double columns, because it would have over-emphasized the already inordinate length. Instead he allowed his façade to be conditioned by Michelangelo's lateral elevations, but with a difference greatly to its detriment as I shall try to show.

A dispassionate view reveals at once that the façade is too congested, too over-weighted and too broad. Windows, mezzanine openings and balconies are crammed between the columns and endowed with heavy detail. The most objectionable feature is the deep and heavy attic storey. Maderno's self-vindication would doubtless be that it is a continuation of Michelangelo's pre-existing attic. It is true that where Maderno has continued the

[1] *Renaissance and Baroque*, 1888, trs. 1964.

Maderno originally intended the façade to be flanked by bell towers *above*; but the front remains without any vertical features to this day *below* (see also pp. 104–5)

original attic along the side elevations of the nave he has been successful, because he reproduced Michelangelo's detail exactly. On the façade attic he has made alterations to the openings which go a long way to detract from the design. These alterations are the split pediments of the central openings and the entablatures of the end openings, which he has accordingly thrust into his cornice as though they are supporting it. Maderno would in fact have done better to follow Michelangelo's attic faithfully. In 1923 a young Roman architect, Florestano di Fausto, put forward a serious proposal to slice off the attic altogether, merely leaving the end bays with Valadier's beautiful cresting over the clock faces. The dome, he claimed, would thereby be visible from the Borgo and most of the piazza. Fausto evidently disregarded the fact that the nave roof would have projected above the pediment, unless it were somehow concealed. His bold suggestion was, needless to say, rejected.

In fairness to Maderno we must remember that the end bays, which project beyond the aisles, were not intended by him to be part of the façade. After the façade was begun the Fabbrica decided in 1612 that bell towers would look well at either end. The substructure of these, never properly completed, now forms the last bay of each end. Maderno had originally meant to build a detached clock tower near the site of the present entrance to the Scala Regia. He left a design which shows a graceful baroque affair with a cupola of scrolled supports to the lantern. The detached clock tower never got further than paper and the 1612 pair of towers no higher than their bases because the difficulty – to say nothing of the expense – encountered in digging the deep foundations required was deliberately shirked. The architect admitted only just in time that the bases already built would not be firm enough to carry more than their own weight. Paul V took fright and positively forbade continuance of the towers. And here Maderno is to blame for not first ascertaining that the muddy soil on this part of the Vatican Hill could not carry high structures without very careful preliminary drainage. The pair of towers was to have flanked the façade, without forming part of it. They would have given the proportion, as well as the verticality, which the composition now lacks. How exactly the shortened façade would have been treated at either end is not known.

Maderno also planned a detached clock tower over the site later occupied by the entrance to the Scala Regia *left*. All work on the towers was halted by Paul V, a portrait by Guido Reni *right*

The portico; a water colour by Louis Haghe, 1875 (see also p. 133)

The faults of the lumpish façade we now have are so glaring that Milizia dismisses Maderno with the savage remark, 'that [here] he studied to do his worst'. Recent critics[1] of the architect have been more charitable. They rather incline to excuse him from full responsibility for the finished façade because of the numerous problems he had to encounter. These indeed were formidable. Nevertheless, a more imaginative and less heavy-handed architect would have found some happier way of resolving them. A contemporary[2] observed that Maderno was not partial to painting and too partial to stucco work. That there was nothing of the painter in him is apparent in the total want of pictorial quality in his architecture. Like stucco work, on the contrary, it is plastic and rounded; but like that material, when handled by the most proficient master lacking genius, it can be both colourless and rather dull.

Maderno was prouder of the portico, or vestibule of the basilica than any of his constructions. He had its authorship specifically mentioned on his tomb. It is certainly an impressive entrance with its five great doorways to the church, the three central ones framed by pairs of antique pillars, and with its end vistas, through screens of Ionic columns, of Constantine and Charlemagne's equestrian statues, both of course added at later dates. The central bronze door by the fifteenth-century Florentine, Filarete, was saved from the old basilica. The architect was obliged to add strips of bronze to the top and bottom

[1] Notably Armando Schiavo and Antonio Muñoz (see Bibliography).
[2] G. Baglione, *Le Vite de' Pittori, Scultori et Architetti*, 1642.

The confession. One of the oil lamps that surround it *above left*. The doors to the Niche of the Pallia *above right*. Pilgrims on St Peter's day, 1867; a water colour by Louis Haghe *below*

in order to heighten it. Between the doors three venerable inscriptions on marble were likewise saved and re-erected. They are the Jubilee bull of Boniface VIII granting plenary indulgence to the pilgrims of 1300, Charlemagne's funeral inscription for Pope Adrian I, and an act of donation dated 720 of some olive gardens for the upkeep of lamps before the Apostle's shrine.

The great tunnel vault of the portico was stuccoed by G. B. Ricci to Maderno's design, the central panels displaying the Borghese pope's coat of arms and recounting scenes in the life of St Peter. The ribs and arabesque reliefs are a dull gold, or rather mustard (I suspect nineteenth-century repaint) upon an exiguous white ground. The plethora of gold detail is easily assimilated into the vault owing to the great height of the portico. In a lunette over the central opening into the portico is Giotto's heavily restored mosaic, the Navicella, or St Peter walking on the Sea of Galilee. This famous but mutilated mosaic survived the depredations of successive renaissance popes, not on account of its artistic interest, but the affirmation of papal dogma which it represents. The Navicella was re-affixed in its present situation by strict command of Paul V, who had anxiously watched it being dismantled from the Archpriest's Palace adjoining the old forecourt.

Maderno's last work for the basilica was probably the horse-shoe shaped confession under the dome, which Della Porta had begun digging in front of Clement VIII's high altar. The purpose of the confession was to give access to cardinals and privileged persons from the church to St Peter's resting place. The marble balustrade, on which ninety-five oil lamps of gilded bronze with fronded stems are kept perpetually flickering, and the double ramped staircase are Maderno's. The steps were made from parts of the architrave of the old basilica, and doubtless still retain Constantinian moulding on the undersides. They descend to the level of the existing crypt where Canova's oversize figure of Pius VI kneels before the perforated bronze door of the Niche of the Pallia. The vault of the niche is lined with mosaics by Ricci. Paul V made Maderno lavish upon floor and walls of the confession an inordinate amount of precious marble intarsia, still in the style of the late cinquecento, which the pope mistakenly believed did exceptional honour to the simple fisherman from Galilee.

Maderno did not retire from the post of Chief Architect before his death in 1629 at the age of seventy-three. But long before this date he became incapacitated by illness. He suffered so severely from kidney trouble and stones that he was barely able to work, and was always accompanied by a close stool. He was a patient, good-natured man, and popular with all who had dealings with him.

The mosaic in the Choir Chapel (see text p. 318)

8 The High Baroque and Bernini

The death of Paul V and the retirement of Maderno saw the end of the early phase of the Roman Baroque. The reign of the Ludovisi pope from Bologna, Gregory XV (1621–3), was too short to make much mark upon the building of St Peter's. Gregory was the patron and the friend of his compatriot, Domenichino, whose debts he paid. He was gentle and good, but by the time of his election sickly. The political success of his reign was due to the skill and diplomacy of the cardinal nephew Ludovico Ludovisi, to whom the pope handed over the reins of government with the words, 'Datemi da mangiare e al resto pensate voi!' Cardinal Ludovisi, in addition to being an able administrator, was an avid collector of works of art and the builder of S. Ignazio for the Jesuits. The forceful cardinal issued to the nuncios overseas instructions drafted by the poet Agucchi in emphatic and fiery language, often in swinging cadences, hitherto unknown in papal documents which are habitually couched in the driest phraseology. Agucchi's are nothing if not flamboyantly baroque.

Gregory XV was succeeded by Urban VIII (1623–44), perhaps the greatest of the baroque popes, during whose reign St Peter's assumed much of its present character. Cardinal Maffeo Barberini was fifty-six at the time of his election. A man of spotless virtue, he was immensely clever. His portraits show a strong head and lofty forehead. He had thick black hair, streaked with grey, a square-cut beard, and shrewd piercing blue eyes. He trusted no man's opinion but his own; and in spite of shameless nepotism retained absolute government in his own hands. Although he brooked no contradictions, his manners were engaging, and he was always gentle with his servants. A contemporary historian wrote of him, 'Princeps potius videri voluit quam pontifex, rector quam pastor' – he wished to seem a prince rather than a pope, a ruler rather than a priest. Indeed there was little milk and water spirituality in the make-up of this masterful prince of the Church.

It was well for the Faith that Urban was a man of determination, for the political difficulties of his reign were daunting. His pontificate coincided with the worst horrors of the Thirty Years' War in Germany. It also witnessed the long unedifying process of France and Spain's jockeying for power in Europe. France's lack of scruple in international relations set a horrible example to the nations which has been followed ever since. Her aggressive chauvinism, disguised under Louis XIV's special brand of royal absolutism, was to be repeated by the dictatorships of later centuries. Cardinal Richelieu's military interventions in Italy and alliance with the Protestant powers flouted all pretence of loyalty to the Church, of which the French kings boasted the title 'Most Christian'. With tact and firmness Urban parried the French cardinal's assaults in a ceaseless endeavour to preserve peace. With commendable restraint he likewise submitted to unprecedented insolence from Cardinal Borgia, emissary of the Spanish monarch, who

Bernini's baldacchino (see text p. 250)

247

endeavoured to treat the pope as a catspaw in his resistance to Louis XIV's territorial claims in Europe. At a consistory session Urban was obliged on one occasion to yell at Cardinal Borgia, 'Taceas aut exi!' – shut up or get out! An Italian tried to lead the Spaniard from the pope's presence. In the scuffle that ensued, one cardinal broke the spectacles of another; a Spanish cardinal stamped on the biretta of a French cardinal. Again, if the pope was not combatting the pitiless, unforgiving doctrine of the Jansenist heresy, which denied to man all possibility of exercising his own salvation, then he was attempting to relieve the lot of the English Catholics under the Stuarts; or to regain to the Papal States that Naboth's vineyard, the fief of Castro, dishonestly appropriated by the Farnese family. There was no end to his political vexations.

Urban's real interests were, notwithstanding, music and the arts, in that order. He himself was a poet. During the worst crises of his pontificate, he would still read and even write verse. His Latin poems were perhaps his best. They were translated into several languages. He urged his fellow poets to treat of Christian rather than classical subjects. He patronized composers and made Allegri a member of the papal choir. The composer's Miserere for nine voices was written specially for St Peter's, and so jealously conserved that no pope would ever allow it to be published. Yet Mozart, after a single hearing in Holy Week of 1771, went home and scored it note by note on paper. After listening to a Mass in forty-eight parts by Agostini in the basilica, Pope Urban, greatly impressed, rose to his feet and bowed to the composer who was present. If proof of his love of the arts were needed, the list of the painters and decorators he employed would be sufficient. Every year he launched some new enterprise and the work of beautifying the basilica never slackened throughout his reign. His pursuit of truth was as great a passion as that of beauty, and explains his close friendship and correspondence with Galileo. When the Inquisition made the Church a laughing stock by denouncing the Copernican system and condemning Galileo to indefinite imprisonment, Urban commuted the sentence passed upon his old friend to one of retirement.

This pope was never happier than when he could escape to the solitude and tranquility of Castel Gandolfo to enjoy the occasional society of persons of his own mental calibre. But it was not often he was able to leave behind him the bustle and business of Rome, where the noise induced such hypochondria that in order to sleep he had the birds killed in the Vatican Garden.

Urban has earned our particular gratitude for his contribution to the new St Peter's. Many of this pope's predecessors had, as we have seen, abundant zeal in carrying on the rebuilding of the basilica. Several achieved remarkable progress within far shorter reigns than his. But none had surer judgment or better taste in the arts than he. The pity is that by the time Urban was elected the bulk of the church was already in being. Let us recall that when the Fabbrica was deliberating in 1607 how to complete the plan left by Michelangelo, Maffeo Barberini was the only cardinal strenuously to oppose the lengthening of the nave. His opposition went unheeded, with the result that the principal view of St Peter's is Maderno's regrettable façade, whose shortcomings no subsequent architect has been able to redress. It happened that before Maderno was dead an architect of stupendous genius appeared on the scene at the instigation of Pope Urban. With amazing dexterity, he was able to modify to some extent the overbearing and crushing effect which the façade makes upon Michelangelo's fabric. Had he only been given a free hand, he would have corrected it altogether.

Urban VIII *left* appointed Bernini *right* as Architect to St Peter's

In 1626 Pope Urban called upon Gian Lorenzo Bernini to begin the great baldacchino over the papal altar. In 1629 he appointed him Architect to St Peter's in succession to Maderno. Thereafter, for at least forty years, the greatest of the baroque architects was engaged upon the basilica's embellishment.

The partnership of Urban VIII and Bernini is the classic relation between patron and artist. It transcended, not certainly in renown but in success, that between Julius II and Michelangelo. As in the earlier partnership, two exceedingly able minds and forceful personalities were involved. But, by contrast, master and man remained united in intention and idea. Pope Urban had loved and cherished Bernini ever since he had been a boy sculptor in his father, Pietro Bernini's, studio. Gian Lorenzo used to quote and refer to the pope, long after he was dead, with touching affection and gratitude for having, as cardinal, launched him on his career. Bernini's early reputation throughout Europe was, of course, owing to no man's backing but to his own genius which instantly struck all who met him. Contemporaries described his temperament of fire and the eagle look of his face, particularly the eyes. His eyebrows were low and bushy, his forehead high and somewhat sunken in the middle. His thick, wavy hair was in his youth black, in his old age quite white. Even in his advanced years he kept his spare, slim figure, which was of middle height, and walked deliberately and rapidly. His understanding, wrote one observer,[1] was of the most splendid sort with which nature endows few men, because

[1] Chantelou, *Journal du Voyage en France du Cavalier Bernin en 1665.*

without having greatly studied he yet seemed to grasp readily all that the sciences taught. He had a wonderful memory, a quick and vivid imagination, and a sharp and sound judgment.

Bernini was, like Michelangelo, a titanic being, subject to his own laws and demeanour. The dictates of conventional thought and conduct had little meaning for him. Pope Urban had the perspicacity to observe and accept this. The artist was an alarming person, at once warm and irritable, humble and haughty. His nature was fundamentally charitable and not given to slander and backbiting. He did not carp at his rivals. He was profoundly Christian. His whole art was conditioned by his religion, of which it was the outward and visible expression. His architecture and sculpture were for the glory of God; his works at St Peter's in honour of the Prince of the Apostles. None of his performances was, in his opinion, good enough return for the benefits he owed to his maker. An eyewitness recorded watching the architect at the height of his fame drive through the Piazza Navona. On passing by his incomparable fountains of the Four Rivers and the Moor, Bernini hastily raised the window shutters of his carriage so as not to be reminded of their shortcomings.

As a monk dedicates his whole being to God, so Bernini devoted every moment of his life to his art. He would work for seven hours on end without pausing to take food or drink. Abstracted, he would refuse to talk, and when pressed to attend to some irrelevant business would reply brusquely: 'Do not touch me! I am in love.' The most eminent visitors were obliged to wait and watch, which they were content to do, until he was ready to receive them. When Queen Christina of Sweden was at last admitted to his studio she fingered his workman's overall, murmuring, 'It is more precious than purple.'

Today, Bernini is given his proper place in the hierarchy of the world's great architects. He has had to wait for it. Even so, the profound classicality of his art is not always appreciated by modern historians. For instance Vincenzo Golzio[1] identifies the style of his architecture with that of the poetry of his near contemporary Marino. But the verse of that jovial Neapolitan reprobate was worldly, affected and abounding in conceits. It was the very antithesis of Bernini's spiritual, disciplined and ordered constructions. For one secret of Bernini's baroque is its foundation upon traditional sources, and its derivation from the Roman antique. Golzio displays complete misunderstanding of his architecture in protesting that when Bernini turns from fantasy to reason he becomes the incarnation of corruption!

The baldacchino occupied Bernini from 1626 to 1633. The vast undertaking was fraught with difficulties that would have daunted a lesser man. The canopy and four supporting columns are of bronze. The guide books love to tell us how the metal from which the baldacchino was fashioned was ripped off the beams of the Pantheon portico and the covering of the dome, what was left over being made into cannons for the Castle of S. Angelo. The action gave rise to the pasquinade freely quoted by Pope Urban's critical subjects: 'Quod non fecerunt barbari, fecerunt barberini.' That the pope stripped the Pantheon of its bronze is certain: that his architect used it for the baldacchino has not yet been proved.

The weight of the structure is tremendous. It necessitated the digging of very deep

[1] *Il Seicento e il Settecento*, 1950.

and rather massive foundations around the site of the Apostle's resting place far below the pavement level of Constantine's basilica. There can be no doubt that Bernini was obliged to destroy hitherto undisturbed graves and relics dating from the first Christian centuries in what was held to be the most sacred precincts of St Peter's. The architect had the effrontery to disturb soil that no previous generation of Romans, not even Goths and Vandals, and only one generation of infidel Saracens had dared to tamper with. It is hardly surprising that he met with bitter opposition from devout and superstitious persons, as well as from experts who, with some reason, feared for the safety of the renaissance church overhead. It so happened that a chain of misadventures, and moreover deaths, accompanied the operations. The custodian in charge of the high altar and the precious locality below died suddenly one morning. His deputy and confidant likewise died the same afternoon. Within a few days, the custodian's secretary died mysteriously. Then his servant, who may or may not have been party to these deaths, was accused of homicide and condemned to be hanged. As though these tragedies were not sufficient indication of St Peter's displeasure, the pope himself fell seriously ill. He recovered. But by now the workmen had thrown down their tools in holy terror and refused to proceed with the excavations. The Roman people, equally superstitious, organized protest marches in sympathy with the workmen and the city was almost in riot. Needless to say, Bernini, who never once forfeited Urban's confidence and support, even when the pope was on his sickbed, ignored the critics and eventually overcame the scruples and objections of the workmen by dint of offering extra wages. It is only fair to stress that the work was carried out from beginning to end with the utmost reverence, and the remains of dislodged graves, sarcophagi and relics were decently removed into storage.

When we realize that the height of the baldacchino – again the guide books are adamant on this fact, which it is almost impossible to believe on the site – corresponds with that of the Farnese Palace, we marvel at Bernini's engineering skill. There have never, in over three hundred years, been qualms about its stability. It stands, this absolutely vast and fantastic object, so high that its effect is to diminish the distance of the dome above it. Bernini of course intended this very illusion, which is one evidence of his genius. Another is the innovation of the design, which allows views through it from all directions and obscures nothing beyond. The baldacchino is enchantingly deceptive. It imitates one of those processional canopies made of wood, draperies and tassels which choir boys carry around Catholic churches over some sacred vessel for veneration. Though made of bronze and as high as the greatest palace of the Roman Renaissance, it seems so light that a puff of wind might make the supports tremble and the pelmets and tassels of the canopy rustle. The spiral form of the four columns contributes to the illusion of frailty.

The twisted columns were of course meant to recall those famous ones which for over a thousand years had formed a screen before the shrine in the medieval basilica. They recall but do not reproduce them. Whereas the ancient *solomónicas*,[1] as they are termed in Spain, are in four parts alternately fluted and decorated, the baldacchino columns are in three, of which the lower only is fluted. The decorated parts are covered with trailing olive foliage, not vine branches as on the *solomónicas* which date from classical

[1] Because they were believed originally to come from Solomon's temple.

The baldacchino is one of the masterpieces of baroque art (see also p. 246)

times. Among the leaves *putti*, or naked children, play and reach intrepidly towards swarming bees, the Barberini pope's insignia. The Flemish sculptor, Duquesnoy, was responsible for the very secular air of the *putti*, whose round, plump little bodies are touchingly lifelike. The four columns rest on stalwart plinths made of white marble panelled with *verde antique*. The plinths bear Urban's escutcheon of bees, above seven of which the face of one of the pope's nieces is carved during the different months of her pregnancy. Anxiety, fear, agony, ecstacy and other appropriate moods are represented. Finally, the small head of a newly born baby boy appears on the eighth plinth. Nicely pagan too are the sun heads on the frieze of the canopy and the capitals, for the classical-trained sculptor never hesitated to mingle profane with sacred motifs. And on the soffit of the great tester he displayed the Holy Dove from whom rays of glory are shed. The whole is crowned with a coronal formed of inverted scrolls rising from each angle and meeting at a central apex to support the cross, on to the ball of which bees have again been permitted to crawl.

The baldacchino, which is not set centrally under the dome but a little to the west (it exactly replaces the medieval canopies over the Apostle's tomb within the chord of Constantine's apse), went a long way to resolve the break between Michelangelo's zone

The statue of St Longinus *left* and the loggia of the relic of the lance above it *right*

of the new basilica and Maderno's extension. It is a combination of architecture and sculpture. It is a monument of change from the simplicity of early Christianity to the ostentation of the triumphant Church after it had undergone the travails of the Reformation.

With Bernini's design for the baldacchino, plans for giving a new look to the four great piers supporting the dome were accepted. They involved the construction in each pier facing the papal altar of a gigantic niche, with a loggia over it. The niches were to be occupied by statues of the four sacred figures whose relics were, after the Apostle's, the chief treasure of St Peter's. The relics were to be placed in the loggias over the statues of their respective owners. Work was begun on the niches in 1628 and on the loggias in 1633. Some harrowing circumstances attended the erection of two of the statues.

The north-east pier is devoted to St Longinus, whose statue is the only one of the four by Bernini. It is probably the best. Bernini took infinite pains over it. He made innumerable rapid sketches and twenty-two small terra cotta models as well as one the size of the finished statue. The figure is vigorous and devotional. In his right hand, the soldier saint holds the sacred lance which had pierced Our Lord's side; with his left, he indicates reverent amazement at what he has just done. The expression of the head is one of pious acceptance of the will of God. The sculptor has made the folds of the robe radiate and swirl from a point under the left arm. They lead the eye towards the holy lance.

St Helena's statue in the north-west pier is by Andrea Bolgi. Bolgi who was about the most pedestrian of Bernini's pupils spent the greater part of ten years on this dismal statue. His St Helena is stiff and seems to be apologizing for the Holy Cross and nails which she is holding deprecatingly in her left hand. Or is she merely bored?

St Veronica by Francesco Mochi, in the south-west pier, is at least lively. Passeri[1] has observed that if the word 'statue' is derived from the Latin verb *statuere* (to cause to stand), then this figure is not statuary, since it depicts the lightning moment of someone in motion. Mochi clearly had in mind the antique figure of Niobe, which the stance of St Veronica somewhat resembles. But he has given to his figure far more movement than the bereft Theban mother, charged with pathos though she be. St Veronica is shouting to attract attention, almost tearing the veil with the sacred imprint in her uncontrollable ecstacy. The emotion registered is superb, though one could dispense with the gentility of a crooked finger and thumb. Mochi was a highly nervous artist and jealousy of Bernini's superiority drove him to utter despair and final breakdown.

Duquesnoy's St Andrew in the south-east pier is loaded with pathos. The expression of ecstatic martyrdom is typically baroque. Although the face is deeply anguished, the figure remains academic-classical, adapted, as Rudolph Wittkower points out,[2] from ancient statues of Jupiter. The sculptor has merely clothed the heroic body with robes of which the folds repeat the diagonal contours of the background cross. Duquesnoy, being a foreigner, suffered from the jealousy and malice of his Italian colleagues. His great plaster model of St Andrew was deliberately broken in pieces. He had to begin all over again. Then after three years' further work the niche, for which he had designed it to receive a particular light, was denied him. The cruel injustice is said to have brought about his death. But ironical fate decided that the terrible disappointment was to be redressed, for the niche which the sculptor wanted was given to the statue posthumously.

More successful than the statues in their colossal niches are the loggias over them. Bernini re-used eight of the twelve historic twisted columns, which since the reigns of Gregory I and III had served to screen the Apostle's shrine in the old basilica. These ancient and highly revered columns, now set in pairs, still stand sentinel above St Peter's grave but in front of the treasured relics within the piers. Through binoculars the flutes and vine ornament are seen to be much worn and broken. Here are visible the scars of innumerable incidents of past violence, including no doubt the sacrilegious depredations by the Saracens in 854 and the sack by the imperial forces under the Constable of Bourbon in 1528. The *solomónicas*, or twisted columns, support concave pediments so as to form tabernacles. These frame panels of *verde antique* on which angels in beautiful white marble relief are portrayed carrying the relics. Bronze grilled doors, with gold bees swarming upon the overthrows, lead to the recesses where the actual relics are kept, and from which on anniversaries they are taken to the loggias for veneration by the faithful.[3]

[1] G. B. Passeri, *Vite dé Pittori*, 1772.
[2] *Art and Architecture in Italy 1600–1750*, 1958.
[3] Pope Paul VI gave St Andrew's head back to the Greeks in 1965.

The Blessed Sacrament Chapel (see text p. 285)

In 1637 Pope Urban adopted a scheme by Bernini to achieve what Maderno had failed to do, namely erect bell towers at either end of the façade. The project was doomed to failure and brought upon the architect the greatest humiliation and distress of his career. Ever since Maderno's towers were countermanded in 1612 by Paul V, who feared for the safety of the nave, men had pondered how the appearance of the over-wide façade could be improved. The problem was frequently turning over in Bernini's mind. He thought he would resolve it by raising a pair of towers on the bases left by Maderno. Here he made a great mistake. His towers were to be of three stages and higher than those projected by Maderno. What reasons did Bernini have for supposing that Maderno's inadequate foundations would support his heavier, more ambitious towers? If he ever had any anxieties they were soon allayed by the assurance of two old masons who had worked under Maderno that all would have been perfectly well, if only Pope Paul had not taken fright and had allowed his architect to proceed. With his usual confidence Bernini set to work in 1638. The following year building was in full swing. The south tower was carried 171 feet above the attic of the façade. By 29th June (the Festival of St Peter) 1641, the two stages were completed, and a wood and canvas model of the top stage, carefully painted, was put in place at the architect's own expense. The public could now see what the finished thing would look like. They approved it jubilantly. The occasion was celebrated by fireworks and bonfires in the Borgo. For a month the temporary structure remained, while the architect basked in adulation and praise.[1] Then suddenly alarming cracks appeared in the second stage and, worse still, in the façade itself. The third and wooden stage began to topple. The Fabbrica was terrified, and ordered the tower to be dismantled at once. Everyone now turned against the architect. Even Pope Urban berated him. The bitterest sequel of all was the Fabbrica's invitation to other architects to design alternative towers. Bernini took to his bed and became positively ill from disappointment and hurt pride.

What had happened? Had Bernini been merely over-confident that he must succeed on the very ground, indeed the very foundations on which Maderno had come to grief? It certainly seem so. He was one of those people who believe that where others may fail they will always be victorious. From the start he ignored the fact that his load was to be far heavier than Maderno's. St Peter's account books disclose quite clearly that while the building was in progress the design of the second stage of the south tower was repeatedly undergoing changes. Certainly the architect and the Fabbrica were not of one mind. Our inference therefore is that as soon as Bernini got from that body an agreement, he proceeded too hastily for fear lest it might change its mind once more.

Only one wash drawing by Bernini is extant to show the south tower as actually built.[2] The north tower was certainly begun, and most of the architectural members for it were carved, because records of payment for these features appear in the account books. The design of both bears little resemblance to the architect's subsequent essays of the sort on paper. The plan was oval. Although the ill-fated south tower existed so short a time it was not without influence upon contemporary architecture.[3] Borromini's oval towers

---

[1] Paul A. Underwood (*Art Bulletin*, xxi, no. 3, September 1939) maintains that the top stage of the tower was not a temporary structure, but a finished thing in three pieces made of wood in order to lighten the weight.
[2] It is in the Palazzo Chigi at Ariccia.
[3] After final dismantling by order of Pope Urban's successor in 1646, the columns of the Corinthian order were

One of the angels in the Blessed Sacrament Chapel (see text p. 285)

Statues in the niches around the high altar: St Veronica *left* and St Andrew *right*

of S. Agnese in Agone and Wren's west towers of St Paul's in London, although square in plan, were decidedly affected by the grouping of Bernini's angle piers and the general shape of his upper stage.

After recovering from the terrible humiliation of 1641 Bernini, never daunted for long, returned to the bell tower problem. About 1650 he prepared a drawing for a pair of towers, this time to be entirely detached from the façade, which would not thereby be endangered by any lateral pull. The façade would have been considerably shortened, for both penultimate bays – those containing the blind tabernacles, mezzanine openings and niches – were to disappear. The flanking towers on the existing bases would have stood forth on their own. They were to be composed of two stages of open arcades and a third crowned by a compelling cage of inverted scrolls made to resemble the canopy of the baldacchino. The front of St Peter's would by this means have presented a beautiful composition of rich and shadowed groups. But Pope Innocent X, now on the throne, was no friend to Bernini, and would not sanction the structural changes involved. Thus the best devised improvement to the new St Peter's, one which would have made the

re-used in the porticos of the twin churches in the Piazza del Popolo.

church front the most striking, instead of the dullest in Christendom, was thrown away for ever. If only Urban had lived a little longer to recover from the fiasco of 1641, he would surely have appreciated the merits of Bernini's splendid revised scheme, and might well have adopted it.

At the time of this pope's death in 1644, Bernini was still working upon his friend and master's tomb. Unlike Michelangelo's tomb for Julius II, Bernini's for Urban VIII was ultimately carried out according to plan. It was of course nothing like as ambitious as the other's. Urban commissioned the monument in 1627. It was finished in 1647.

Urban was not the man to hesitate in choosing the most conspicuous site available in the basilica for his own memorial. He took the niche on the right-hand side of the western apse, where Bernini was later to construct the cattedra, now the focal cynosure of the whole interior. At the same time he had removed to the balancing niche on the left side of the apse the tomb of Paul III, to which he intended his to be a sort of superior pendant. In fact, the outstanding quality of Bernini's monument was meant to be no slight

Bernini's design for bell towers on the façade *left*; work on these was cancelled when one tower was only partly completed, as shown in this seventeenth-century engraving *right*

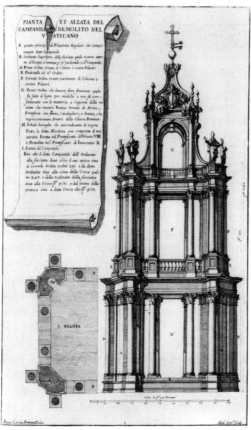
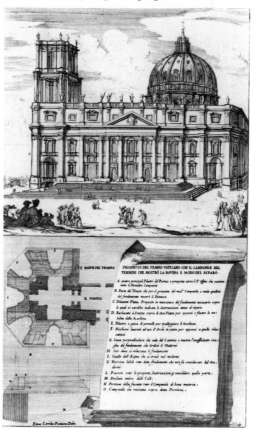

The monuments of Paul III *left* and Urban VIII *right*

reproach to the earlier one which had been sculptured by Guglielmo Della Porta under Michelangelo's direction. Paul III's monument, in spite of the ridiculous stance and pose of the two allegorical figures, is still one of the best in St Peter's. The pope's seated effigy combines pathos and nobility. Unfortunately, the composition of the monument is incomplete. Della Porta resented the advice of Michelangelo, to whom he owed his advancement, and turned against him. Michelangelo thereupon refused to allow the monument to be sited in the apse, insisting upon it being put against one of the piers. It was subsequently shifted into other positions. In the process it lost the allegorical statues of Abundance and Peace. Only those of Justice and Prudence survived. The former, a naked representation of Paul III's seductive sister, Giulia Farnese, was given a metal tunic by Pope Innocent X; the latter, an old hag in the likeness of the pope's mother looking at herself in a glass, was suffered to remain nude down to the navel.

With great skill then and no little stratagem, Urban VIII and Bernini set out to eclipse one of the great renaissance tombs with which the immortal name of Michelangelo was associated by cunningly arranged proximity and contrast. Bernini reverted to the use of a scroll top sarcophagus, first introduced by Michelangelo on the Medicean tombs and followed by Guglielmo Della Porta on Paul III's tomb opposite. This was a bold enough move since such motifs had in the meantime become quite outmoded in sepulchral sculpture. The two allegorical figures of Charity and Justice, which he took as appropriate symbols of Pope Urban's character, are far more naturally related to the central effigy than the corresponding attendants upon the earlier monument. Made to lean against the sarcophagus, they form essential contributions to the pyramidal theme and are part and parcel of the composition, instead of isolated appendages. In themselves they are extremely moving and tender, particularly Charity with her expression of maternal solicitude, and the mischievous *putto* nestling between the sarcophagus and the folds of Justice's skirt.

In his use of different coloured materials, Bernini inaugurates a departure from tradition. It is his means of contrasting foregrounds with backgrounds, and of emphasizing central features. Here Charity and Justice in white marble stand forward from the dark marble sarcophagus, only partly gilt, and the towering bronze effigy of the seated pope. Maffeo Barberini, wearing the triple tiara, his right benedictory hand emerging from a laced sleeve of the alb, is truly an awe-inspiring, Jehovah-like figure of intense majesty. Here is no impersonal representation of a pope, but the portrait of a very positive and powerful individual. He is made to appear triumphant over life and death. Indeed, death is introduced below his feet in the form of a winged skeleton rising from the sarcophagus. The ghastly object holds with one grizzly hand a scroll of parchment on which with the other he writes the name and title of the deceased pontiff. His head and face are partly concealed by a cap.

Was Bernini the first sculptor to introduce active skeletons on tombs? On medieval monuments cadavers, or recumbent skeletons of the deceased, were commonly met with; and skulls and crossbones were even more popular *memento mori* because easier and cheaper to produce. The Death on Urban's monument was, according to Wittkower,[1] planned as early as 1630 when the pope was in the full vigour of life, although it was not sculptured until 1644. On the other hand, Bernini's first fully fledged Death appeared in S. Lorenzo in Damaso as a device holding the oval medallion of Alessandro Valtrini in 1639. In this very year a Mass in the Gesù church was sung for the repose of the souls of the Jesuits' benefactors.[2] The congregation were greatly awed by the funereal decorations and mechanical devices set up for the occasion by the Fathers. Conspicuous among them were menacing skeletons made to perform various activities. One seized hold of Adam and Eve at the moment of picking the forbidden fruit. Another reigned as supreme mistress of the world. Four waved aloft triumphantly the symbols of earthly power. Bernini was very probably present at the Mass and an observant eyewitness of these necrological symbols. He had been brought up by the Jesuits and nurtured on Loyola's *Spiritual Exercises*. All his life long he remained faithful to the book's exhortations to subdue the flesh, and was obsessed with the trappings and the inevitable physical transmutations of death.

Cardinal Pamfili's election as Innocent X (1644–55) in a great hurry during the September heats of 1644 boded no good to Bernini. The cautious, suspicious pope was not disposed to take his predecessor's cherished architect to his bosom. For a long time, he remained aloof and withheld commissions. Innocent was a cold and grave man. Tall and thin, he was uncommonly ugly, with a green complexion, small eyes and large feet. His famous portrait by Velasquez elicited from the subject when he examined it the terse comment, 'Troppo vero'. Although he mistrusted everyone, he allowed himself to be completely

---

[1] *Gian Lorenzo Bernini*, 1955.
[2] E. Mâle, *L'Art Réligieux du XVIIe Siècle*, 1951.

dominated by his sister-in-law, Donna Olimpia Maidalchini, who was clever and ambitious. She spent hours each day dictating to the pope what he should do. In consequence, she was courted by all who wished to gain access to Innocent's ear, for without
first winning the favour of this meddlesome woman it was difficult to make headway
with him. Their best hope of success was by gifts, for she was extremely avaricious.

Innocent had no liking for literature. He had, however, a sound taste in the arts, with
this one reservation: he indulged in a neurotic fear of the nude. Though in most respects
illiberal, he distributed fig-leaves and breast-plates gratis. No statue in the Vatican precincts was spared superfluous metal or plaster garments. He even persuaded Pietro da
Cortona to paint swaddling clothes over his favourite picture by Guercino of the Child
Jesus.

Innocent X was a true baroque pontiff in that he commissioned much building by
leading architects of the day. Of these he preferred Borromini, Rainaldi and Grimaldi.
Of sculptors he favoured Algardi whom he employed to carve the enormous relief in the
Cappella Madonna della Colonna of Attila's meeting with Leo the Great. In this realistic
work of art Attila looks seriously alarmed while he puts his hand before his face to avert
the menacing vision of the apostles Peter and Paul descending from the clouds with
brandished swords. Algardi used subtle gradations of depth in carving to indicate
closeness and distance of figures from the spectator.

Innocent's hostility to Bernini was finally overcome by unfeigned delight in the great
master's design for the fountain of the Four Rivers to face the Palazzo Pamfili in the
Piazza Navona. In fact the design was sprung upon the pope during a visit to his family
palace by an admirer of Bernini. It came as a complete surprise. Innocent was at once

Innocent X, by Velasquez *left*, commissioned the relief of Leo the Great and Attila *right*

captivated by the exquisite naturalism and poetry of this engaging composition. He even preferred it to a design by Borromini who thought he had already won the commission. From that moment onwards, Bernini was again in papal favour. He was given the tasks of completing the marble decoration of the Gregorian and Clementine chapels as well as the nave and aisles of St Peter's; and of sculpturing the equestrian statue of the Emperor Constantine.

The decoration of the nave of the new basilica was first put in hand very soon after Michelangelo's Greek cross structure was finished. Before the dome was on, Gregory XIII (1572–85) had begun encrusting the lesser order of pilasters – that is to say those carrying the arches within the giant pilasters – of the then short nave with geometrical panels of variegated marbles. The process was continued by his successors into the tribune, transept and chapels adjoining. Until Innocent's reign, the incrustations remained sunk, or flat, and multi-coloured. For late *cinquecento* decoration, they were fairly innocuous, although rich. Bernini substituted a different form of decoration altogether. He designed for each pilaster three-dimensional reliefs of *putti* holding three medallions, all in glistening Carrara against a Siena marble ground. Within the top and bottom medallions, which are oval, he had carved the heads of the first thirty-eight popes; within the middle vertical panels, tiara, keys, bible and swords. The portraits and insignia were an echo of the counter-reformation answer to the Protestant attack against the papal supremacy. The Pamfili dove and olive branch visible at the extremities of each pilaster, were meant to be a perpetual reminder of Pope Innocent's munificence. The greatest care was taken to get the scale of the medallions right. Painted canvas models were set up and left for

Reliefs of early popes on the nave pilasters: Lucius I *left* and Marcus *right* (see also p. 265)

several weeks' inspection by the pope and Fabbrica. After their approval, Bernini employed an army of thirty-nine sculptors and masons who with incredible industry carried out the carving between 1647 and the end of 1648. Of this band, the leader was Antonio Raggi, who later became Bernini's most trusted carver and faithful disciple, and was in his own right a master sculptor of inventiveness and skill.

Examined in detail, Bernini's nave medallions appear far more interesting and beautiful than the conventional polychrome marble panels on Michelangelo's structure. The *putti*, the heads of popes, the insignia and the sheaves of foliage are in themselves exquisite works of sculpture. But, it must be admitted, the medallions in mass appear too prominent and repetitive. They cease to be decoration and clamour for individual recognition, which in a building the size of St Peter's is hardly tenable. Instead, they are disturbing in that they accentuate the over-ornate panels of the nave roof and arches of the arcades. We come to wish they were not there in a longing for greater simplicity.

At about this time too the stucco allegories were placed in the spandrels of the nave arcades. They were not modelled but only supervised by Bernini. These reclining ladies are collectively striking. They are also individually remarkable. Each is accompanied by an attribute, picked out in gold – the lamp of vigilance, the pine-cone of benignity, the elephant of docility, and so forth. One virtue has attached to her foot a globe – is it the ball of humility? – which overhangs the nave in a somewhat alarming fashion.

Bernini's contributions to the nave included the substitution of thirty-two of Maderno's columns by new ones in red and white veined Cottanello marble, and the sumptuous marble pavement.

Between the giant pilasters of the nave, and of the transept, are two stages of niches with frilly shell-heads. These form part of Bernini's decoration and now carry out his intention. They are occupied by thirty-nine statues of founders and foundresses of religious orders, which vary considerably in merit. The earliest and one of the best by Pierre Legros the younger of St Dominic was erected in 1706, the last and one of the worst by A. Berti of St Louise de Marillac in 1953. It is run fairly close in the race for insipidity by Pietro Canonica's St John Bosco, looking like an infatuated village schoolmaster with his arm round two little waifs. Stendhal[1] remarked of the nave statues that 'elles présentent des mouvements assez ridicules, mais on ne les regarde pas; et, comme elles sont bien placées, elles contribuent à l'ornement'. It is true that this colossal collection of colossal statuary is usually passed over as part of the wallscape. But it deserves, if not minute, certainly selective attention, as representing for the most part baroque sculptors of the eighteenth century working in the Bernini tradition. St Teresa by Filippo della Valle and St Vincent de Paul by Pietro Bracci are above average merit; whereas St Bruno spurning the offer by a winged cherub of a bishop's mitre, by Renato Michelangelo Slodtz, is a statue of dramatic devotionalism, already imbued with the elegance of Parisian rococo.

Although Innocent X commissioned the equestrian statue of the Emperor Constantine, it did not get further than a state of blockage in the rough marble during the Pamfili pope's lifetime. His successor, accompanied by Queen Christina of Sweden, watched Bernini chiselling the marble in the summer of 1662. On All Saints' Day 1671 the finished

[1] Stendhal (Henri Beyle), *Promenades dans Rome*, 1826–7.

The relief of Damasus I on one of the nave pilasters (see text p. 263)

sculpture was unveiled on its present site midway up the Scala Regia. There it may be seen by those about to enter the basilica, if the great door at the north end of the portico happens to be open. This unfortunately is not always the case, and there is no guessing the whim of the janitor responsible. The perspective setting admirably suits the dramatic subject. Bernini seized the very moment when Constantine was struck by the awful vision of the *labarum* in the sky. The terrified horse rears and the rider, his hand stretched outwards, lifts up a face on which an expression of mute belief is carved. Bernini went to great pains to reproduce the young emperor's features correctly from historical descriptions. They are regular and handsome. The head is slightly underjawed, and distinctly imperial. Tremendous tension is expressed by the horse's protruding eyes, the swollen muscles of its legs and the veins of its belly. As a background to horse and rider, which are in neutral marble, the lower part of an immense curtain of fringed damask has been devised in polychrome marble. The curtain is in the act of billowing as though stirred by a supernatural wind coming from the west, a divine afflatus of understanding. Lucky is the visitor who catches a glimpse of the statue when a shaft of morning sun through the open arcade of the portico enhances the palpitating movement of the composition. This wonderful specimen of pictorial sculpture with its sparing use of colour was to have widespread influence upon German and Austrian carvers of the following century.

The revolting cynicism of Cardinal Mazarin in supporting the Protestant powers and humiliating the Catholic states of Germany (not to mention his protection of the disgraced nephews of Urban VIII), the terms of the Peace of Westphalia whereby the Holy Roman Empire was forced to recognize the Evangelical and Calvinist Churches and religion was made subservient to the territorial ambition of princes, the war between France and Spain, and the growing popularity of Jansenism among the aristocracy of France and Flanders, all contributed to the misery of Pope Innocent's declining years. Donna Olimpia's meddling and greed only added to his worries. When the pope died in 1655 this hard-bitten woman who owed her fortune to the indulgence of her brother-in-law would neither pay for the customary lead coffin nor even for the funeral rites. On his deathbed Innocent received no attentions from his family. The corpse, with eyes left open and tongue out, was dumped on a slab in a mouldy corner of the sacristy. A workman happening to pass by lit and put out of pity one wax candle at its head.

Apart from the astonishing speed of decorating the nave, work elsewhere in the basilica slackened during Innocent X's reign. During that of his predecessor, Urban VIII, each year had witnessed the beginning of some new enterprise. During that of his successor, the tempo revived immediately. On the very day of his election Alexander VII (1655–67) sent for Bernini and ordered him to draw up a scheme for the great colonnades in front of the basilica. This pope was the consistent friend of Bernini. Never for a moment was he, like Innocent X, hesitant over continuing the great artist's services. On the contrary, he was an even greater benefactor than Urban VIII in so far as the number and magnitude of his commissions are concerned. In a sense, he was an even better patron, for unlike the Barberini pope he did not claim to be an authority on architecture, nor did he assert his own opinions. From the first, he recognized Bernini to be a man of unparalleled genius. He merely wished to give him every licence to produce as many masterpieces as circumstances, time and money would allow. His wish was certainly

One of the Doctors of the Church that stand beside the cattedra (see text p. 279)

Statues of founders of orders are placed in niches: St Bruno *left* and St Benedict *right*

fulfilled. In addition to important contributions to St Peter's[1] and the Vatican Palace, he got Bernini to build the churches of Castel Gandolfo and Ariccia, and the Chigi chapels in S. Maria del Popolo and the cathedral at Siena; also to model his enthroned effigy in the last. His affection for Bernini was only matched by Queen Christina's. He delighted to visit and chat with him at his house, at his studio and in the foundry where he might be casting. He delegated to him, as the most distinguished of his subjects, the duty of receiving Christina on her first entry to Rome, and accompanying her with a procession of torches to the Vatican.

Fabio Chigi was a member of the rich banking family from Siena. At the time of his election, which took eighty days, he was fifty-six years old. He was a delicate patrician,

[1] The deep crimson damask hangings with gold fringes, still used for covering the pilasters inside the basilica on festival days, were given by Pope Alexander VII.

Bernini's statue of Constantine *left* stands on the Scala Regia *right* (see also p. 284)

with a narrow, finely chiselled face – but sallow complexion – and high forehead. He was ascetic and devout, ever mindful of the transitoriness of this life. He kept his coffin in his bedroom and a skull carved by Bernini on his writing-table. He avoided nepotism, was always available to petitioners, particularly the humble or those fallen into trouble or disgrace. He was above all an intellectual, determined to advance the cause of learning. With this end in view he completed the buildings of the Sapienza, the ancient Roman university, where he commissioned Borromini to design the eccentric chapel of S. Ivo. He established the Libreria Alessandrina. He was also something of a poet. He so loved poetry that busy as he always was he would sacrifice the siesta hour in the hottest months to read and discuss it with his friends. Only in this way, he said, could he temporarily forget the political troubles caused him by Louis XIV's government, and be truly happy. His reign was the golden age of the Roman Baroque in learning and the arts. It saw its apogee, and heard its swansong.

Alexander VII *left* commissioned Bernini to design the colonnades encircling St Peter's piazza *right*. The original intention was to enclose the entire piazza, as shown in a papal medal *above*

The scheme of the great colonnades in the forefront of St Peter's must have been in the mind of Alexander VII before he became pope, as it certainly was in Bernini's. After much deliberation by artist, pope and Fabbrica as to what final form the scheme was to take, the first stone was laid in 1657 and work begun in earnest two years later. The colonnades as we have them were finished in 1666.

There were a number of conventional factors which Bernini was obliged to observe in undertaking the formidable task, quite apart from his intention to improve the approach to St Peter's. First of all the old entrance to the Vatican Palace on a site 400 feet north-east of the portico had to be retained, and a covered processional way provided for state visits to the Pope in bad weather. This necessitated incorporating within the scheme the space immediately in front of the façade, known as the *piazza retta*. The loggia for the time honoured papal blessings *urbi et orbi*, which exists over the central entrance, had to be kept within view of the greatest possible number of people. So too the Pope's private window in a contrary direction high up in Fontana's cliff-like palace to the north must always be visible in case the Holy Father wished to appear to his people in emer-

The piazza of St Peter's; an engraving by Piranesi, 1770 (see also pp. 294–5)

gency. For these purposes, a vast space was required in which to gather the faithful at Eastertime and on other important occasions, 'a ricevere maternamente', to quote the words of Bernini himself, 'i cattolici per confermarli nella credenza, l'heretici per reunirli alla Chiesa e gli infedeli per illuminarli alla vera Fede'.[1] A symbolic welcome therefore was to be implied in the form of the colonnade designed to enclose the large piazza. There exists an early sketch by Bernini of St Peter's dome made to represent the head, and the curved sides of the piazza the arms, of the Almighty clasping the faithful in a huge embrace.

As though these prerequisites were not sufficiently demanding, there was another physical factor to be taken into account, namely the setting of the great obelisk. It could not be shifted again and must of necessity somehow be made a focal feature of the scheme. Mercifully, Maderno had already made it axial with the basilica by ingeniously tilting his façade several degrees out of the right angle with the nave. Bernini was not therefore confronted with an obstacle on an asymmetrical site. The obelisk was in fact what determined the hub of the new piazza. It dictated the distance of that hub's projection from the basilica. Everything fell into place owing to Bernini's extraordinary vision and genius in finding a solution to the most intractable problems.

[1] To receive in a maternal gesture Catholics in order to confirm their belief, heretics in order to reunite them with the Church, and infidels in order to reveal to them the true Faith.

The view from the dome looking down into the piazza (see also p. 106)

The corridors flanking the approach to St Peter's which connect the basilica with the piazza

Having accepted these obligatory conditions, Bernini concentrated on the aesthetic implications of the scheme. There was the overriding need to correct the too apparent width of Maderno's façade caused by the existing bases of the flanking towers which never materialized. The only means available to him for achieving this was by optical illusion. So with the greatest ingenuity he proposed to connect the colonnades to the basilica with corridors which, instead of contracting as they approached the façade, splayed outwards. In this way, the basilica appears to be brought forward and the height of the façade accentuated at the expense of the width. The success of the deception is gauged by the surprisingly long time it takes to walk to the portico from the colonnades, a distance far greater than the visitor standing in the piazza imagines it to be.

Originally Bernini proposed to enclose his oval piazza with colonnades of two storeys with Palladian openings in each. Fortunately these double colonnades, for which drawings exist, were considered too high and were abandoned. Heated arguments over the precise form the colonnades should take ensued within the Fabbrica. At one stage opinions and even alternative suggestions from outside architects were invited, much to Bernini's chagrin. It had always been his wish to enclose the east side of, or entrance to the piazza with a *propylon*, or gateway, of which the foundations are said to have been actually laid. The gateway is shown on several contemporary medals and in prints.

Bernini's object was to interpret the *quadriporticus* of the Constantinian basilica and the atrium behind it, and to protect, as it were symbolically, the faithful congregated within the sacred precincts from the hostile outside world. In 1667 he changed his mind to the extent of wishing to move the 'third arm' as he called it, or gateway, eastwards into the Borgo so as to provide that introductory space he was so fond of, a space from which the visitor could better comprehend the oval of the piazza just as though he were standing outside, and not within it. But on the death of Pope Alexander the gateway conception was defeated by the Fabbrica on the grounds of unwarrantable expense.

In fashioning his piazza and colonnades Bernini wished to complete the new approach to St Peter's by improving the Borgo, which is that part of the city between the Vatican and the Tiber. He did not envisage a straight, wide thoroughfare of the sort brought into being by the makers of the present Via della Conciliazione in 1937. His idea was to provide a long central spine of buildings, or gallery, running axially between the proposed gateway to the S. Angelo bridge, with two parallel narrow streets along either side of it.

Not all of Bernini's schemes then came to fruition. But, thanks to Pope Alexander's unfailing support, the greater part that mattered was carried out. St Peter's Piazza and colonnades amount to one of the most successful compositions of the baroque age. A measure of their success is the unusual fact that they have never been adversely criticized even in the late eighteenth, or in the nineteenth century when baroque art reached its lowest ebb in the esteem of connoisseurs. Stendhal, who despised Bernini, was constrained to admit that the piazza was the most beautiful in the world. He remarked upon the astonishing impact it made on the visitor suddenly debouching from one of the narrow streets of the Borgo, and he condemned the folly and vulgarity of Napoleon, who threatened to demolish the central houses of the Borgo, which is exactly what Mussolini

Gigantic statues line the top of the colonnades

Details of statues on the colonnades

was to perpetrate more than a hundred years later. The great open space was a revelation, he said, which literally took the breath away. There on the right towered, as it still towers, the noble asymmetry of the Vatican Palace as though carved out of an immense pink rock face. It is dominated by the Pope's apartments, projecting like the prow of Peter's barque. It is an extraordinarily happy juxtaposition of irregular groups of individually correct architecture, just avoiding the ridiculous in the kitchen clock over the Raphael Gallery and the homely in the earthenware pots of cypress, orange and oleander on the flat roof above the Scala Regia. To the south the umbrella pines and the curved College of the Propaganda Fide follow the contours of the Janiculum heights. And ahead, always present, is the overbearing façade, much modified by the grand sweep of the elliptical colonnades. Alas, that the revised scheme of Rome's greatest baroque architect wholly to correct Maderno's heavy design by means of towers was never implemented!

There had been nothing like Bernini's free-standing, elliptical colonnades in any previous architecture of modern times, either for originality of plan, or beauty. What matter that the master committed a solecism in putting an Ionic entablature upon Doric columns! The very unorthodox treatment gives a peculiar strength to the colonnades and helps to emphasize by contrast the verticality of the slender Corinthian columns of the façade. The fact that there is no solid background to the colonnades, and that the stout columns forming nave and aisles are totally disengaged suggests a constant forest of movement to the visitor in the piazza every time he shifts as much as from one foot

A view of St Peter's and the piazza from the Janiculum; an engraving of about 1775

Caprarola

Montereoio

Monte Mario

La Storta

Monte Ma

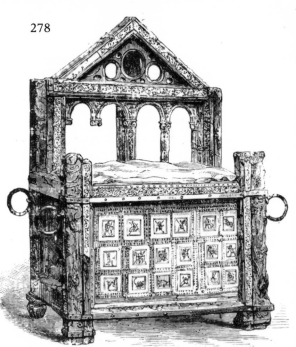

The ancient chair *left*, believed to have been used by St Peter, that is enshrined within the cattedra *right* (see also p. 182)

to the other. Walking up the colonnades causes him an ever varying pleasure. Because of the curve he experiences at first an acute feeling of tension as to what may lie ahead. The suavity, rhythm and simplicity of the colonnades soon dispel anxiety and induce nothing but ease. It seems a pity that lately the plain nave vaults have been degraded by the introduction between the old hanging lanterns of cheap basin lights made of tin.

The northern colonnade leads of course to the ceremonial entrance of the Vatican Palace. If the great, green bronze doors, which Pope Paul V presented, happen to be open, the Swiss Guards on duty may (or may not) allow you to step inside and look up the long, astonishing perspective of the Scala Regia. This dream staircase was the work of Bernini between 1663 and 1666. Over the inner arch where the steps are already rising, winged figures of Fame in stucco blow long slender trumpets, while their disengaged hands support the papal arms, tiara and keys of the Chigi pontiff. The aisled and vaulted stairway is one of the world's great architectural triumphs over awkward siting. For although the space provided was not straight, nor wide, nor even of ascent, nor adequately lit, Bernini overcame each obstacle in turn and created by tricks of perspective a long, regular and impressive approach to the papal apartments.

The culminating offspring of the fruitful partnership of Bernini and Alexander VII is the Cattedra Petri, or Throne of Peter. This astonishing object designed as a receptacle for the greatest of all St Peter's treasures is found at the westernmost end of the basilica, in the tribune apse.

For centuries St Peter's chair had been on view, and probably in use in the old baptistry. It was believed to have been sat in by the Apostle in the house of Pudens where he lodged on first coming to Rome. But there is no written record of the chair's existence before the year 1217. It has four solid legs of yellow oak to which iron rings were attached at one time, doubtless in order to make it a portable chair. The panels between the legs and the arcaded back with pointed crest are of acacia wood, inlaid with ivory. The ivory ornament may have been applied in the ninth century. When last examined in 1867 the chair was found to be in a very decayed condition owing to bits and pieces having been cut off by relic hunters, not to mention the usual depredations made by worm. Alexander was determined that this precious treasure must be put in some inaccessible part of the church where it would be safe and yet could be venerated. In 1656 the Fabbrica agreed to it being removed to a place of honour in the apse. In the following year they approved Bernini's scheme to enshrine it.

The whole operation appealed to Bernini's strong devotional sense. As a boy, he had once accompanied Annibale Carracci into St Peter's. After their prayers, he is said to have told the older artist that his ambition was to raise a magnificent throne to the glory of God in the western apse. The opportunity was eventually granted to him.

From the number of Bernini's preparatory sketches, it is clear that he always intended the Cattedra Petri to be glimpsed through and framed by the baldacchino. In this way, the long approach up the nave was to be made all the more exciting by the partial vision. To the visitor finally skirting the baldacchino anticipation gives way to a burst of revealed glory. When he has passed between the great west piers of the dome, two porphyry steps, worn, dented, battered by the ages, and made out of the stairs which led to the raised tribune of the old basilica, bring him face to face with the cattedra. The extraordinary object is raised on a plinth of black and white Sicilian marble, mounted with the papal arms of Alexander VII in bronze. On the plinth is a platform of marble the colour of gooseberry fool. At the platform's two projecting ends stand the figures in gilt bronze of Saints Ambrose and Augustine wearing mitres. They are the two Fathers of the Latin Church (badly in need of dusting). Behind them less prominent and uncovered are Saints Athanasius and John Chrysostom, representing the Greek Church. The exquisitely emotional attitudes and the enraptured expressions of the Fathers set a fashion in ecclesiastical sculpture which was followed by innumerable Germanic rococo artists in the eighteenth century. The grouping was devised to symbolize the unity of Christianity, with a gentle reminder that the Eastern Church was subservient to the Western. When Bernini erected a temporary model of the cattedra wherefrom to judge the correct scale, he invited the painter Andrea Sacchi to give his opinion. After much cajolery Sacchi consented. Reluctantly the elderly painter left his studio and in cap and slippers struggled up the steps to the portico of the church. He would not advance an inch further than the central doorway. 'This is the spot from which your work must be viewed', he growled. 'Make those statues', indicating the Four Fathers, 'a foot higher', and he walked away. Bernini complied without demur.

With the utmost delicacy and nonchalance the two Latin Fathers hold, if 'hold' can be applied to an action of so little apparent effort, a loop attached to the front legs of the black and gilt bronze throne, which are deliberately splayed outwards in an exaggerated fashion suggesting levitation. Because the loops are not in the least taut an etheral movement is given to the throne, which in spite of its great bulk and weight seems literally to be floating off to the heavens. It is the receptacle of the wooden chair, which until the beginning of the last century could be seen inside by visitors climbing a ladder in the rear. Two angels, wingless and displaying from their flowing robes a generous length of leg, lean against the cushioned seat (Sacchi, who later was shown the drawings for the angels, pronounced them too small). On the back of the seat is a relief of Christ admonishing the kneeling Peter to 'feed my sheep'. Balanced on the crest a pair of *putti* brandish a key in one hand, and together raise the papal tiara with the other.

The actual enshrinement of the wooden throne was accompanied by a long drawn-out and solemn ceremony. At midnight of 16th January 1666 the ancient relic was reverently transported from its chapel in the old sacristy by means of shafts upon the shoulders of several clerics. It was then placed upon a brocade covering of the high altar between silver candlesticks, while the papal choir intoned the verses, *Exultent eum in ecclesia plebis*. When the final destination was reached the voices broke into a *Te Deum*. Next they sang the *Tu es Petrus*, and the chair was incensed three times. With every demonstration of piety the relic was fitted into its new resting place with the help of Bernini's brother, Luigi, who locked it up and presented the key to the canons present. Meanwhile in the piazza fireworks and mortars were let off, and the people danced and whooped with glee over the satisfactory conclusion of a highly important occasion.

Behind the throne rise golden clouds; and above the clouds in an oval explosion of rays angels point to a central vision in brown and yellow glass of the Holy Dove with outspread wings. This dramatic device is the origin of those still more elaborate *transparente* behind altars, of which the Spaniards became so enamoured in the eighteenth century.

Stendhal's complaint was that the Cattedra Petri was pretty rather than beautiful. Subsequent nineteenth-century critics have been less flattering in their observations. Murray's *Handbook to Rome* of 1899 dismisses it as 'an ineffective tasteless work'. Fraschetti[1] on the other hand said he lacked words to describe it. Wittkower's twentieth-century attitude towards it seems eminently just and wise.[2] It is useless, he advises, to approach the cattedra with religious or artistic bias. He describes it as a mystery given visual shape, 'and its comprehension rests on an act of emotional participation rather than on one of rational interpretation'. It is something which can hardly be judged by the unbeliever or the disdainful Protestant from the matter-of-fact north. He who looks at it must have a sympathy for, even if he may have no proper understanding of the world of saints and angels displayed before him, must have some inkling of what the preternatural communion means to the devout Catholic pilgrim. The Cattedra Petri could only have been created by an artist with implicit faith in the dogmas of the Roman Church. It is an extraordinary synthesis of Christian art, a symphony of that fervour which characterized the Church's attitude at a particular, triumphant moment of its history. It was the ultimate guaranty in this great basilica of the primacy of the Church of Rome, founded on the throne of Peter, from which emanates the only spiritual fodder for the lambs of Christ.

There is no doubt that Bernini intentionally vested all his works at St Peter's with a deep, devotional symbolism drawn from his upbringing by the Jesuits. No great artist has been more thoroughly grounded in the metaphysical teaching of that highly recondite Society, nor has interpreted it so consistently in his works. In consequence, much

---

[1] S. Fraschetti, *Il Bernini*, 1900.
[2] *op. cit.* page 23.

The explosion of rays surrounding the Holy Dove above the cattedra *left*. St Augustine at the foot
of the cattedra *right* (see also p. 266)

spiritual significance in Bernini's architecture and sculpture remains closed to the
exoteric majority. He deliberately set out to present in his various contributions to
St Peter's a sort of mystic way for the edification of the pious visitor. His son, Domenico,
tells us in words what the father clearly meant to express in his art. 'The piazza and the
cattedra', he says, 'are, as it were, the beginning and end of that great church, and the
eye is as much infatuated at the beginning on entering the piazza as at the end on seeing
the cattedra.'

Bernini, like Michelangelo, was fated to outlive a number of popes who had generously
befriended and patronized him. It was now his turn to erect a monument to Alexander VII.
The pope in his lifetime had made ample provision for his memorial on the customary
scale. His successor in commissioning Bernini to reconstruct the choir of S. Maria Maggiore
tried to transfer the monument there. But Clement IX only reigned for two years, and in
1670 plans were resumed for putting it in St Peter's. Even so, the site chosen was not a
good one, being over a closet entrance facing St Veronica's pier. Nevertheless, the

finished monument was one of the greatest of the baroque age. From drawings and documents in the Chigi archives, its complete history has been traced showing the manner in which Bernini's army of distinguished craftsmen was drilled for an undertaking of the sort.

Whereas Urban VIII's monument had in a sense to correspond with that of Paul III opposite it, here Bernini was under no obligation to take precedents into account. Moreover, he designed a less sublunary composition, one expressive not of temporal militancy, but of resignation to the divine will. Bernini was now older – he was seventy-three and less inclined than formerly to the terrible in art – and Alexander's character was entirely different to Urban's. This pope had not been autocratic and masterful, but moderate and melancholic. So the sculptor saw fit to convey in his monument not the picture of fame triumphing over death, but of spiritual humility ignoring the menaces of fate.

High up on a pedestal the pope in white marble is made to kneel on a cushion, his hands clasped meekly before him. His sensitive, patrician face shows in the puckered brow and uplifted eyes a soul concentrated on celestial things. Well below him in the foreground stand two of the most beautiful figures Bernini ever designed, namely Charity and Truth, specially chosen by Alexander. These exquisite creatures are only spoilt by the oversize child with a head like a mongol's in Charity's arms, and the metal tunic imposed upon Truth by Innocent XI (who evidently inherited from his Pamfili namesake the same prudery). The pair are made to control either end of a voluminous shroud of green veined marble, *diaspro di Sicilia*, in reality a veneer over travertine. This particular trapping of mortality is used here for the first time. Once again Bernini introduces the figure of Death, now winged. In horrid make-believe the skeleton flies from the door below, as it were out of the pope's tomb – in reality from a cupboard of brooms and mops. With his head he pushes aside the heavy folds of the shroud and in his right hand brandishes before the unheeding effigy on its knees an hour glass which has run out. The entire pyramidal monument is contained within a pair of vast Corinthian columns of crushed fig and cream.

Clement IX, Rospigliosi (1667–9), was sixty-seven years of age when elected pope. He was so generous to the poor and negligent of his own interests that the Romans, always extreme in their loves and hates, regarded him as a saint. He was a highly cultivated man and at once employed Bernini to beautify S. Maria Maggiore – it came to nothing – and to adorn the Ponte S. Angelo with statues. He was frail and sickly. When Louis XIV's double-dealing over the papal resistance to the Turks led to the downfall of Crete, Clement, whose nature was straightforward and trusting, was so shocked that he had a stroke and died.

Clement X, Altieri (1670–6), was even older. After a tussle to elect a pope lasting from December to April, the cardinals in despair chose this octogenarian. He lived, however, for six years. He had the stamina of an ox and the disposition of an angel. He attributed both these qualities to his rising two or three hours before dawn and retiring to bed at sundown. His reign, like that of his predecessor, was made hideous by the Turkish advances and the squabbles of the Catholic powers. In 1675 the French ambassador, D'Estrées, during a private audience rudely pressed Clement to create more French cardinals. An outspoken refusal did not prevent him from returning to the subject. The eighty-five year old pope tried to ring his bell and summon an attendant to

The monument of Alexander VII (see text p. 281)

dismiss the importunate visitor. But the ambassador had the audacity to push him back into his chair. With presence of mind the pope exclaimed, 'You are excommunicated!' and without uttering another word waited until D'Estrées withdrew of his own accord.

Clement X likewise patronized Bernini. Both master and artist were old. They did not conceive large-scale ventures but were content to put finishing touches to the basilica, now nearing completion. In this reign, Bernini began to reconstruct the fountain which Maderno had raised on the north side of the piazza. He designed the irreproachably classical stalls for the Choir Chapel, and fulfilled a long cherished scheme for the altar of the Blessed Sacrament Chapel opposite.

Bernini took immense pains over the tabernacle in which the Blessed Sacrament is reserved. Many sketches for it exist. At first the architect intended the tabernacle to be held in the air by four angels, an idea deriving from a plate in Domenico Fontana's book, *Della Trasportazione dell'Obelisco Vaticano*. Actually, two angels only were carried out in gilded bronze. They are made to kneel on the projecting ends of a marble platform in Sicilian jasper. One adores the tabernacle, the other looks down upon the faithful about to receive communion. There is inexpressible sweetness, not to say sublimity, in these figures which is usually lacking in the emotional fervour associated with the religious imagery of Bernini's middle years. The tabernacle itself, unveiled in 1675, is a slightly elaborated version of Bramante's classical tempietto design. Bernini enriched this beautiful object of gilded bronze with lapis-lazuli. He introduced a motif of keys and Altieri stars on the dome which is crowned by a figure carrying a long lance in his left hand. Behind the altar hangs, partly hidden, a canvas of the Trinity by Pietro da Cortona, which is sadly dirty.

The altar in the Blessed Sacrament Chapel is Bernini's last work for St Peter's. By the time that yet another pope, the Odeschalchi Innocent XI (1676–89), was on the throne of Peter, Bernini was a very old man. He was still at work on sculpture, but most of his days were spent contemplating the divine mysteries. On 28th November 1680 he died at the age of eighty-two. Henceforth, the tempo of work upon the basilica was to slacken considerably. There was in truth little more to be done. The Baroque, which was first introduced to the world in Rome, was almost spent there. Innocent XI did not follow in the tradition of the great baroque popes who had been lavish patrons of contemporary artists. The deplorable state of the papal finances would not allow it. Besides, Innocent's instincts were far from lavish. 'The father of the poor', as he was called by the Romans with a touch of asperity, was naturally parsimonious and ascetic. He lived like a hermit. He dressed in the last pope's garments which were far too short for him; and he wore them – his reign was long – until they were threadbare. Unlike his immediate predecessors, he detested ostentation and acclaim, prohibited entertainment and sternly set his face against women in low-necked dresses. Yet he was not a contemptible ruler. He was the sole European sovereign who dared stand up to Louis XIV. In order to counter that monarch's intrigues to ally Poland with the Turks against the emperor, invasion of the Spanish Netherlands, wars in Italy and Luxembourg and general promotion of Gallicanism and humiliation of the papacy, Innocent formed the Holy League against France. He admitted to his confidants that, however much he disapproved of Louis' diabolical conduct, he had a sneaking admiration for the effective form of absolutism the French king had evolved.

The Scala Regia (see text p. 278)

The figures of Charity *left* and Truth *right* that stand on either side of the monument to Alexander VII (see also p. 283)

For a time Innocent XI would not appoint an architect to succeed Bernini at St Peter's because, he affirmed, the basilican funds could not meet the salary. Soon, however, he was obliged to look for one owing to the first of several scares that the dome was unsafe. Laymen could never believe that Michelangelo's four piers were sufficiently robust to carry the weight of so enormous a dome. The smallest crack that showed itself in plaster or paving, even the unaccountable fracture of a pane of glass, provoked vehement jeremiads that the whole structure was on the point of collapsing. Now the Romans had got hold of the idea that Bernini in opening staircases up to the loggias within the four piers had seriously weakened them. No one dared go near the basilica for fear of a piece

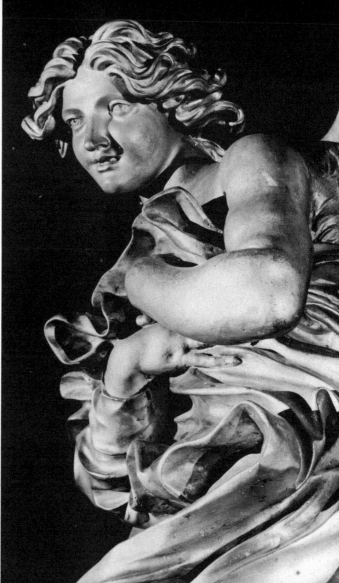

The stalls in the Choir Chapel *left*. One of the angels that kneel on either side of the tabernacle in the Blessed Sacrament Chapel *right* (see also pp. 255, 256)

of cornice or pilaster dropping on his head. Accordingly, Carlo Fontana was offered Bernini's vacant post. He at once investigated the condition of the dome and its foundations, and proved them both to be safe.

Carlo Fontana, great-nephew of Domenico and now a man of forty-six, had worked under several high baroque architects, among them Cortona, Rainaldi and last but foremost, Bernini. For a generation after the death of the last he was to be the undisputed leader on whose slender shoulders the mantle of the giants had fallen. And Fontana himself was not a giant. Nor was he as baroque as his greater predecessors and teachers. He was a graceful designer who reverted to the correct classical. Whereas the Baroque was now shifting to other parts of Italy, to be manifested in the novel buildings of Guarini, Juvara and Vittone, Fontana's style by comparison was almost academic. It was also uninspired.

Fontana was a genial, accommodating and industrious professional man. As such he commended himself to the cautious and frugal Innocent XI. The pope commissioned him to duplicate on the south side of the obelisk in St Peter's Piazza the Maderno-Bernini fountain on the north. The work is unexceptionable and Fontana cannot fairly be judged from a copy. Nevertheless, the south fountain is perceptibly coarser in workmanship than its prototype. At the same time, Fontana advocated an extension into the Borgo of Bernini's colonnade in two straight converging arcades, at the end of which there was to be a transverse gateway, or *propylon*. On this gateway, he wished to raise a clock tower. The scheme, however, like all previous ones relating to St Peter's towers, came to nothing.

The last pope of the seventeenth century, Innocent XII, Pignatelli (1691–1700), entertained a number of building schemes, including the foundation of the Curia Innocenziana. He was more liberal with commissions than his predecessor of the same name, if less ready with his payments. Fontana was frequently obliged to complain of the inadequacy of his salary. The pope wanted a memorial in St Peter's to Queen Christina of Sweden, in whose conversion he vainly foresaw a return of her country to the Faith and to whose contribution towards the culture of the city he looked back with gratitude. Fontana designed for the first pier of the right aisle a sepulchral memorial of unwonted

Fountains in the piazza. The Maderno-Bernini *left*; the Carlo Fontana *right* (see also pp. 94, 104–5)

Innocent XII *left* erected the monument to Queen Christina of Sweden *right*

importance for a royal personage. A white marble bas-relief shows the queen abjuring Protestantism at Innsbruck in 1655. Overhead, a large medallion frames a portrait of Christina in silhouette. It is an unromantic likeness, for she is given a double chin and a prominent nose with flaring nostrils. Both bas-relief and medallion were executed by G. B. Théodon, a French sculptor of talent whose last days were spent carving religious statues for the Palace of Versailles.

Innocent XII and Fontana's most notable contribution to St Peter's was the conversion of the first chapel of the south aisle into the baptistry. Since the reign of Nicholas V[1] (1447–55) baptisms had been performed in the sarcophagus of Probus,[2] fourth-century Prefect of Rome, which served as a font. The sarcophagus stood until 1694 in the chapel where the Pietà now rests. Fontana was extremely proud of his new baptistry, of which he published in 1694 a detailed *Description* in a sumptuously bound volume. The fact that he endured much tribulation through the pope criticizing his designs and complaining of his high charges probably accentuated the final achievement in his own estimation. The walls of the baptistry are lined with polychrome marbles against which are set little side tables of porphyry richly chased with bronze. The cynosure of this lavish chapel is

[1] Until Nicholas V's reign, Pope Damasus's primitive font had been used. It was then discarded because of wear.
[2] His temple, or mausoleum had been at the extreme west end of the old basilica.

of course the font and cover. For the first Fontana supplied the oval porphyry lid of the sarcophagus which once contained the remains of the Emperor Otto II buried in 983 in the atrium of Constantine's basilica. The lid may, before that, have served the same purpose for the remains of the Emperor Hadrian. It was taken by the architect from the crypt of the new basilica where it had been stored since the destruction of the medieval atrium. On removal, it was dropped and broken into ten pieces, but was so skilfully repaired that the fractures are scarcely visible. The beautiful gilded bronze cover surmounted by the Lamb of God and the enrichments of the font itself were to Fontana's design.

It may not be out of place here to take some stock of the liturgical significance of the new St Peter's. What in fact is this enormous building all about? It was certainly not intended as a mere exercise in monumental architecture. Nor was it raised primarily for day to day worship.[1] On the contrary, many people find its great size and emptiness chilling. Its lack of intimacy does not readily invite our prayers, as do many less impressive and more humble churches in Rome and elsewhere. Clearly, its creators had more specific views in mind than art and the celebrating of Masses, although, needless to say, these considerations were never overlooked. The renaissance St Peter's is indeed thoroughly different from the old church it replaced both in intention and in style. First of all, the idea of putting an empty altar in a conspicuous central position under the dome, where it could be viewed from all sides, was something new. The medieval idea had been to veil the holy of holies behind high screens and curtains, and to give it mystery. The relegation of the choir to a side chapel was also quite new. The medieval practice had been to place the choir for the monks in a chancel, secluded by screens it is true, but central enough for their voices to be distinctly heard by the congregation in all corners of the building. In the renaissance St Peter's even the Blessed Sacrament Chapel is situated rather unceremoniously off the north aisle. What is the significance of these changes? It is surely this. St Peter's is really a church built round an altar over a tomb, and everything in its design is subservient to the commemorative purpose. It is no less than a shrine which marks the spot where the first of the apostles was buried. Next, its practical purpose is for ceremonies and spectacles on the grandest and most magnificent scale – pontifical Masses, the opening of the Holy Door in Jubilee Years, canonizations, beatifications, the coronation and funeral of popes, public audiences and even ecumenical councils. As much room as possible was made to enable the Pope to be seen when he officiates at the high altar facing the nave; also room for the processions. These reasons account for the uninterrupted space provided in the nave and transepts.

Papal ceremonies are rare events; and we ordinary people are seldom privileged to witness them. Even a pontifical High Mass these days takes place seldom enough. But it is one of the most splendid ceremonies of the world. It lasts something like four hours from beginning to end, and is a tremendous ordeal for the chief participant. No wonder St Gregory the Great complained in a letter to the Patriarch of Alexandria that when it was over he suffered excruciating pain from the gout it caused him from so much standing.

The preparations and rehearsals are extremely elaborate and complicated. The high altar under the baldacchino reserved for the Pope's sole use is covered with embroidered

---

[1] Indeed, the daily office sung by the chapter has been discontinued since the Second World War.

A papal procession entering St Peter's; a water colour by Louis Haghe, 1864 (see also p. 179)

frontals. Seven candlesticks holding painted candles, a crucifix the work of Benvenuto Cellini and silver statuettes of Saints Peter and Paul are placed upon them. The pontifical throne is set in the apse in front of Bernini's cattedra against hangings of crimson velvet. Between the altar and the throne two rows of benches are ranged for the cardinals and prelates. In the south row near the altar is a smaller throne of crimson and gold, without a canopy, where the Pope will sit during the singing of Terce. It is set on a scarlet dais raised upon steps covered with an emerald green carpet. On various credences the sacred vessels and missals needed for the celebration are carefully disposed.

At last the long awaited procession enters the basilica from the portico led by procurators of the religious orders. A prelate swings a thurible, another carries the papal cross. Acolytes bear gleaming silver candlesticks. Friars in chasubles, abbots, bishops, archbishops and cardinals follow in close order of precedence; next, the Vice Steward of the Holy Roman Church, the Prince Assistant at the Throne (wearing a black velvet doublet, hose and cloak, a white ruff, sheathed sword and carrying a cap, for all the world like Titian's portrait of the young Philip II of Spain), the Quarter Master Major and the

Master of the Horse gorgeously caparisoned. The Cardinal Deacon precedes the Pontiff. The Holy Father is borne in the gilded *sedia gestatoria* (or portable throne) under an eight-poled canopy, and escorted by Swiss Guards, Palatine Guards and Noble Guards in all the splendour of their traditional uniforms. Behind walk the Dean of the Rota carrying the mitre, the Papal Physician and that strangely symbolic figure, the 'secret sweeper' (*lo scopatore segreto*) and other officials. On either side of the Pope are carried the nodding *flabelli*, or huge fans of ostrich feathers, those exquisite relics of the fourth century, then used for keeping off flies and insects from the oblations, and now a mere memory of the splendours of the Byzantine East.

Suddenly the silver trumpets in the Hall of the Benedictions over the portico sound a fanfare, and the choir bursts into the refrain, *Tu es Petrus*. The Pope, amid shouts of acclamation, the clapping of hands and the waving of handkerchiefs is borne slowly to the small side throne behind the high altar. The cardinals advance to kiss his hand, the bishops his knee and the abbots his foot.

The Hour of Terce is now sung and the Apostolic Subdeacon, wearing the humeral veil, brings to the throne the buskins and sandals which are put on the Pope by the *aiutante di camera*, or valet. His livery is possibly the most beautiful of them all. He wears a jacket, waistcoat and breeches of cut velvet in a pattern of the papal insignia upon brocade, the whole being of deep wine colour. Long strips hang from his shoulders and ribbons from his knees. His stockings are likewise of crimson silk and his black slippers have crimson tongues. After Terce the Pope's hands are washed and his cope is replaced by a girdle from which hangs a wide maniple with the Agnus Dei embroidered upon it. After vesting for Mass, the Pope puts incense in the thurible and blesses it. Then the procession is re-formed and approaches the high altar. On arrival, the three junior cardinals meet the Pope and receive from him the kiss of peace. In return they kiss his breast. Seven acolytes place their candles on one of the credence tables; the cross is inserted in the pedestal on the gospel side of the altar. And the Pope advances to say Mass.

The special rites of the pontifical Mass are just as complicated as the preliminaries and steeped in long traditional usage. They are also long drawn out. When, however, the celebration is over, the Pope from the great throne under the cattedra gives the final blessing and grants a plenary indulgence. He then resumes his seat in the *sedia gestatoria*, and the tiara is placed on his head. The Cardinal Archpriest in a last symbolic gesture presents him with a purse containing twenty-five jules with the words: 'Most Blessed Father, the Chapter and canons of the most holy basilica offer your Holiness the usual stipend for a Mass well sung.'

It is on occasions such as the one I have just described that St Peter's Basilica truly comes into its own, and that those of the faithful who are proud and jealous of the Church's traditions, bless those popes and architects whose art and unashamed extravagance created a setting of such unparalleled magnificence.

The arms of Pius VI on the floor of the sacristy (see text p. 310). *Overleaf* St Peter's piazza; a water colour by Louis Haghe, 1868 (see text p. 275)

9 The Last Centuries

The end of the seventeenth century virtually coincided with the end of the building of St Peter's. Virtually but not absolutely, because there were still two important additions to come during the last quarter of the eighteenth. They are the clock turrets and the sacristy, which I shall mention later. In all other respects, St Peter's fabric was complete and a comparison of contemporary photographs with eighteenth-century engravings of the basilica reveals only a few minor changes outside, and rather more, if we look for them, inside. In fact those eighteenth-century popes anxious to make a grandiose contribution which would immortalize their reign found precious little space available. All that the majority were able to do was to adorn altarpieces, and raise monuments, not to themselves, for that was no longer the fashion, but to their predecessors. Clement XI's long reign of twenty-one years (1700–21) opened with the century. It was punctuated by a series of misadventures. The War of the Spanish Succession embroiled him against his will with the chief contestants, the Archduke Charles of Hapsburg and Philip Duke of Anjou, each of whom shamelessly treated the pope's territories as though they were Tom Tiddler's ground to be fleeced of gold and silver. Clement was soon plunged into difficulties with the archduke's brother, the Emperor of Austria, which led to the imperial troops over-running Italy, the capture of Milan and Naples and, in 1707, the invasion of the Papal States. As if these vexations were not enough – for the pope was obliged to surrender on humiliating terms, which infuriated the French against him – he endured the treachery of Anjou, by now Philip V of Spain, who in professing to repel the Turkish advances in the Mediterranean merely annexed Sardinia to the Spanish dominions. The revival of Jansenism threatened a schism in the French Church (it occasioned Clement's courageous Bull of Condemnation, *Unigenitus*); and the Chinese converts, supported by the Jesuit missionaries, caused some embarrassment by their wish to retain the ritual honours traditionally paid to Confucius and to their ancestors.

The papacy as a European power may during Clement XI's reign have fallen into eclipse. The pope was not however a member of the cultivated Albani family for nothing. He was one of the Vatican Library's greatest patrons. His interest in archaeology and art was very positive. He founded the Vatican Museum and instituted art exhibitions which hitherto had been unknown in the capital. He was a true lover of historic buildings which he would conscientiously restore when they were in danger of collapse. This did not prevent him from drastically remodelling Pirro Ligorio's great niche (the exedra) and giving a new balustrade to Michelangelo's staircase in the Court of the Pine-Cone.

In St Peter's Basilica, Clement XI supervised the completion of Queen Christina's monument. He also had the domes of the chapels of the Presentation and Blessed Sacrament lined with mosaics, appropriate enough in story but dull as art. His most important contribution was the equestrian statue of Charlemagne, made to offset that of Constantine,

The sacristy, the last major addition to St Peter's (see text p. 309)

Two additions to the basilica commissioned by Clement XI. Cornacchini's statue of Charlemagne *left* stands at the south end of the portico. The monument of Gregory XIII by Rusconi *right*

beyond the southern extension of the portico. Cornacchini's effort is a sadly watered-down version of Bernini's masterpiece, with which it hardly merits comparison. That the pendant to Constantine should represent the second greatest monarch to champion the universal Church is at the same time fitting. It is a massive and conspicuous piece of statuary, which is the most that can be said for it. The poet Byron, standing one morning of 1817 in the portico, overheard an Englishman mistake the two equestrian statues for those of Saints Peter and Paul, and remark to a companion, 'I never knew that Paul rode a horse again after his dreadful accident.'

Clement XI was further responsible for the monument begun in 1719 to Gregory XIII who had died in 1585. Camillo Rusconi was the sculptor. Rusconi, who was very much influenced by Bernini, departed from the baroque master here in two particulars. In the first place, he made the whole monument of unrelieved white marble in contrast with Bernini's deliberate polychrome surfaces. Then he seated the pope's effigy directly on the lid of the sarcophagus, which is a slightly uncomfortable arrangement. On one side, Religion leans backwards the better to see the pope, whereas Science, wearing a martial helmet like Minerva's, lifts up the pall to disclose a bas-relief relating to Gregory's great achievement, the reform of the calendar.

Benedict XIII, Orsini (1724–30), was neither popular nor gay. He was an ascetic Dominican monk with a long mortified countenance and hooked nose. As pope, he inhabited a cell and turned his dark livid eyes well away from the vanities which make life endurable to most men. Puritanical, petty and rather silly, he gave away his beautiful furniture because he deemed it frivolous, and forbade the clergy to wear wigs because such personal adornments were distracting from inner piety. Yet this sombre man was responsible for one of the most joyous contributions to St Peter's in the pair of holy water stoups (*le acquasantiere*) upon the first two piers facing one another across the nave. Cornacchini made the overall design. A couple of winged *putti*, carved by Francesco Moderati, perch on the moulded base of each pier. They hold up a shell of *giallo antico* (yellow marble) which with the folded drapery of *bigio antico* (blue grey) that swathes it, is carved by Giuseppe Lirone. Only when one watches a child clambering up the drapery in a vain attempt to dip a small finger in the blessed water far out of reach, can one realize the colossal size of these seemingly normal stoups.

Clement XII, Corsini (1730–40), continued, after a break of several years, some of the works begun by Clement Albani. He was a munificent patron of art and learning. He began the most beloved of all Roman fountains, the Trevi, built the Palazzo Consultà

Benedict XIII *left* commissioned the holy water stoups *right* that are placed against the first piers on either side of the nave (see also p. 209)

and the monumental façade of St John's Lateran, adding to that basilica the Corsini Chapel. He founded the Museum of Antique Sculpture on the Capitol.

Clement XII's election was announced by a serious earthquake in Rome. It occasioned yet another scare – not perhaps unreasonable – about the safety of St Peter's dome. In 1703 a lesser earthquake had undoubtedly done some damage to the fabric of the basilica. The 1730 quake occurred during the day-time when people were inside the building. Fortunately no one suffered injury if we discount the death from heart failure of one of two Spanish monks who happened to be crouching in the ball over the cupola at the time. The news of this tragedy quickly spread, and caused consternation among the citizens.

For ten years, no action was taken to investigate the dome's condition. Then Benedict XIV (1740–58) was, after a six months' conclave, elected pope. Prospero Lambertini was not the man to allow the dome, which was the pride of Rome and the world, to collapse. He called upon leading architects, engineers and mathematicians to make the minutest examination of the cracks in the fabric. They inspected every pilaster, cornice and crevice. On four successive occasions, these experts were made to carry out researches and deliberate upon their findings. Again, the pronouncement was: Nothing to fear for the safety of the dome. Benedict, nevertheless, was still not reassured. A fifth time, he set up a commission of twenty-nine persons under the Professor of Mathematics at Padua University, Giovanni Poleni. Each of the twenty-nine members signed a report, none of which expressed alarm, but all of which made different suggestions how to take precautions. Some recommended substituting copper for lead on the dome, some filling up the spaces made for Bernini's staircases to the loggias within the four crossing piers, some strengthening the buttresses of the drum, and some removing the lantern. Poleni believed that the lateral pressure from the components crowning the dome was too concentrated. He advised that the worst cracks ought to be filled and the dome girdled with rings of iron. His recommendations prevailed.

Accordingly, Luigi Vanvitelli, one of the century's most distinguished architects and the builder of the Palace of Caserta for the King of Naples, was employed to carry out these precautionary measures. In 1743–4 he encircled the drum and dome with five stout chains. He put the first in the pedestal, the second above the cornice, the third on top of the attic just under the entablature of the drum, the fourth around the waist of the dome, and the fifth under the metal balustrade of the lantern.

Benedict XIV was one of the most popular popes to sit on St Peter's throne. He was magnanimous and honest; exceptionally good-natured and witty. The most approachable of men, he would walk casually about Rome cracking jokes with anyone he met. To the end of his life at eighty-three, witticisms flowed from his lips. On his deathbed he remarked to his doctor, whose name was Pontio: 'Our Lord died under Pilate: I shall die under Pontius.' This attractive and liberal-minded pontiff liked to treat others as he expected to be treated by them. Consequently he was criticized for pandering to the secular European monarchs whose returns of friendliness were usually far from disinterested. Benedict's chief failing was ductility. A too eager readiness to mediate sometimes led him to make concessions which exceeded the deserts of the recipients. His natural sociability did not conflict with his passion for learning. He was the greatest expert of the age on canon law. His happiest moments were spent in his library. Scholars from every country sent him their books; and Voltaire dedicated a couplet to him. His friendship for the agnostic sage of Ferney brought him a good deal of disapproval from those conservative cardinals to whom this most dangerous of the Encyclopedists was absolute anathema.

Benedict enriched the Vatican Library. He extended the Capitoline Museum and founded the Museum of Christian Antiquities. He saw the Trevi Fountain finished and witnessed the release of the first waters over that delicious cascade of sea horses, tritons and rockwork. His repair of churches and hospitals – not always happy, for he went a long way to ruin the Pantheon and S. Maria degli Angeli by over-restoration – often amounted to total rebuilding. He employed Fuga to add the colonnaded façade to S. Maria Maggiore, and Gregorini the elliptical atrium to S. Croce in Gerusalemme. He befriended the painter Pompeo Batoni, who is renowned for countless portraits of handsome and elegant young milords now hanging in English country houses. Life in the city under Benedict XIV was made ineffably sweet by the pope's tolerance, joy and gaiety. His reign witnessed the zenith and decline of the Roman Rococo depicted in the engravings of Vasi and Piranesi. The chief contributor to its ephemeral humanism and fragile beauty was the magnanimous, pleasure-enhancing Prospero Lambertini.

In St Peter's Benedict had to rest content with a series of minor embellishments. He got Vanvitelli to enrich with gilded stucco the vaulting of the three west apses. He had copies made in mosaic of paintings by the artists Pietro Bianchi and Pierre Subleyras for the altars of Saints Basil the Great and Chrysostom. These enormous propaganda subjects of the triumph of the Sacraments over heresy barely qualify as works of art. They are careful representations in a mechanical medium which has completely lost the subtle gradations of line and tone of medieval mosaic work. Later eighteenth-century popes continued the process of substituting vast framed altarpieces in mosaic for original baroque canvases, which were relegated to S. Maria degli Angeli and other churches about the city. Benedict presented a new bell, many gorgeous vestments, silver candlesticks, a cross and a gilt urn still used for laying before the confession at the blessing of the new pallia. He commissioned for several empty niches of the nave and transept statues by the sculptors Slodtz, Bracci, della Valle and Spinazzi. In 1746 Filippo della Valle's tomb for Innocent XII was carried out. Pope Innocent, represented as a frail old man, and not as the masterful champion of the regenerated Catholic Church, is seated between Charity and Justice. The composition is rococo, and the figures are calmer and more elegant than those of the more stalwart baroque age.

When Maria Clementina Sobieski, the wretched wife of that pious stick, the Old Pretender, died at the age of thirty-three, Benedict XIV, out of natural sympathy for the queen who had never reigned and the good woman who had never known happiness, raised a monument to her memory. Although jammed in a passage of the left aisle, its presence in the basilica at all was a signal honour. Just as Innocent XII had found a place for Queen Christina in order to encourage the Swedes to revert to Catholicism, so Benedict also meant the inclusion of the Pretender's wife to be an encouragement and a reproach to Protestant England. The monument, designed by Filippo Barigioni, was carved by Pietro Bracci in full baroque polychrome splendour at a time – 1745 – when the style was already out of date. The portrait of the queen in mosaic is held by a *putto* and the figure of Charity, who with her left arm thrusts towards the altar the burning heart of the devout and unhappy woman. A pink, gold-fringed drapery hangs in heavy folds over both sides of the door to the lift which whirls visitors up to the dome. Below the por-

The monuments of Innocent XII *left* and Benedict XIV *right*

phyry sarcophagus of this very noble monument, two little angels receive the crown which the queen never wore and the sceptre she never held.

Bracci was wholly responsible for the design and most of the carving of Benedict's own monument facing St Basil's altar. The cheerful pope is made in death to gaze for ever upon the grizzly remains of St Josophat, bishop and martyr, who died in 1623 and whose leathery skull protrudes from his vestments in a glass case at the foot of St Basil's altar. Benedict stands in magnificent hauteur, which he never assumed in his lifetime. He blesses the world with an ample gesture of the right hand. With the left he clutches the curly head of an angel. The Romans liked to pretend it was a box of snuff, to which their beloved pope was much addicted. The fingers of his right hand were, they declared, shaking off the remnants of the last pinch he had just taken. Below Benedict Wisdom and Disinterestedness lean on the head of a doorway. The first allegory honours the pope's unexcelled knowledge of canon law; the second his tolerance and complete lack of political ambition.

Even the reign of Benedict XIV had not been wholly carefree. What pope's reign ever has been? The Wars of the Austrian Succession brought ravages upon the Papal States. Spain and Austria, without having any direct quarrel with the Holy See, waged a series of senseless and bloody campaigns outside their own frontiers. Not for the first or last time in history Italy was made into a battleground over an issue with which she had little concern. The insidious propagandism of the moribund Jansenist heresy had, like the sting of a wasp after it has been swatted, aimed a parting thrust at the papal armoury. All over Christendom the Jesuits were being assailed. It is true that during the past few decades their unpopularity had been growing apace. The Society's missionaries in distant parts of the globe were long held by the imperial powers to be subversive of colonial government. Fear for the empire as much as hatred of priestly tyranny was Pombal's excuse for banishing all Jesuits from Portugal and the Portuguese dominions in 1759.

The reign of Clement XIII, Rezzonico (1758–69), was clouded by perpetual anxiety over the fate of the Jesuits. If the European statesmen came to identify the Jesuits with the enemies of secular rule, the popes knew that they were their standing force, their right arm against the increasing disbelief fostered by the French Encyclopedists' hatred of religion. It was clear to the papacy that the elimination of the Society was a means of destroying its chief resistance to atheism. A complex and dangerous situation was developing in which the Jesuits were the buffer between two extreme forms of absolutism, that of the popes and that of the dynastic sovereigns of Europe. The scales were weighted against the former by the great influence of the Encyclopedists who regarded the Church's absolutism as the worse evil and the Jesuits as the instruments of reaction.

Clement XIII was bald, corpulent, deeply pious, timid and sixty-five. Nevertheless, he had sufficient perspicacity to foresee the alarming trend of the papal fortunes. With unwonted courage he took action. He roundly denounced Pombal and broke off relations with Portugal. His action was a declaration of war against secular interference with the Church's authority. As a consequence, the Jesuits were driven from France in 1764. Undeterred, Clement issued a bull re-endorsing the Society's privileges. In 1767 the Jesuits were driven from Spain, Naples, Parma and Malta. The pope thereupon issued a *monitorium* nullifying all anti-clerical laws whatsoever. A League of Catholic Powers promptly formed against the Holy See and the Bourbon kings occupied the Papal States. The pope, pressed to dissolve the Society, refused. His distress was such that, being delicate, he suffered a heart attack and died. Heroic in defence of the Church's rights, Clement was the victim of concerted hostility from the European powers.

He did not therefore have much time to devote to learning and the arts. But he encouraged letters and was fully conscious of the stylistic evolution from the Rococo to the Neo-Classical, which coincided with his reign. His favourite painter was Raphael Mengs, and he preferred the engravings of the Roman revivalist Piranesi to those of his master, Vasi, who had been schooled in the rococo tradition. He appointed Winckelmann, the great apostle of Hellenism, his Commissioner of Antiquities. Clement's only tangible contributions to St Peter's and the Vatican Palace were the screen of the Choir Chapel and the fig-leaves of the nude statues in the sculpture galleries.

Canova's monument of Clement XIII. The pope *left*; the Spirit of Death *right*

If the design of Clement XIII's monument owes nothing to the subject – it was not begun until 1792 – it is so important a piece of sculpture in the developed neo-classical style, and so fitting a memorial to this sad and extremely benevolent pontiff that it deserves mention here. It is the work of Antonio Canova, then in his early thirties. Clement's effigy kneels above a sarcophagus. It faces the tribune. The hands are clasped in prayer. The attitude and expression denote intense spirituality. The lips appear to be murmuring. A pair of attendant virtues are by contrast so dehumanized as to be rather insipid. Religion stands indifferently handling a cross. Rays of light spring from her chaste forehead. The Spirit of Death, a naked winged youth, reclines against the sarcophagus. The beautiful figure is de-sexed to the extent of having no nipples on his flat breasts. A pair of couchant lions, one roaring, the other dozing, guard the entrance to the tomb. Although meant to symbolize Clement's strength in action and repose, these beasts – the artist went specially to the royal zoo in Naples to sketch them – approximate closer to nature than the virtues do. Canova in carving the figure of Religion injured himself with a drill. As a result, he suffered all his life from severe stomach pains, which eventually brought about his death.

The reign of the fourteenth Clement (1769–74) was more disastrous than that of the thirteenth. The election of 1769 was openly fought by the European powers over the

Jesuit issue. Lorenzo Ganganelli, a former Franciscan monk, was chosen because he was considered by the powers the least likely candidate to obstruct their determination to destroy the Society. Ganganelli lacked conviction and strength of purpose; yet he was good and devout, and tried to put the Church's interests before other considerations. In spite of his simple pleasures, bowls, bird-snaring and riding in a short white coat and red hat – he was frequently thrown to the consternation of his attendants – Clement was liked neither by cardinals nor nobles. After relentless pressure from all sides, he at last consented in 1773 totally to dissolve the Society of Jesus on the ill-founded belief that by this means he would make peace with the Catholic sovereigns. 'It is done', he said, as he laid down the pen with which he had signed the fateful brief of dissolution. 'It is necessary for the Church, but it will be the death of me.' The following year Benevento and Avignon were restored to the papacy. These acts of restitution however brought the pope no comfort. He never ceased to be remorseful for what he knew to have been an act of treachery and base surrender to the forces of irreligion and secular tyranny. He looked upon the two restored fiefs as though they were blood money. The wretched man's sufferings for the few months that remained to him were pitiable. Worry and depression induced herpes and pimples. Without entirely losing his reason, he became mentally unhinged. His mouth slavered and his eyes darted in their sockets as he shuffled from room to room, always keeping close to the wall in deadly fear of assassination by some member of the Society which he had betrayed.

The suppression of the Jesuits has eclipsed all other deeds of Clement XIV. His praise-worthy attempts to reduce taxes and alleviate the wretched condition of his subjects are overlooked. His was a gentle and even poetical nature. He patronized the neo-classical

The lions from the monument of Clement XIII

painters and he befriended Mozart. He increased the treasures, notably statuary, of the Vatican and founded the Museum of Antiquities, which now goes by the name of Museo Pio-Clementino. His architect, Michelangelo Simonetti, in making room for the new galleries, necessarily destroyed some notable frescoes by Pinturicchio and Mantegna in the old Belvedere of Innocent VIII. Simonetti furthermore cherished designs for converting one of the lateral chapel domes of the basilica into a bell tower. They were not carried out, and the long, vexed problem how to provide a belfry for St Peter's was to be resolved – not wholly satisfactorily, it must be admitted – by another architect under Clement XIV's successor.

Over the next half century, short of only two years, the throne of Peter was occupied by the two most tragic popes of modern times, Pius VI and Pius VII. For 265 days, the cardinals wrangled and the Catholic ambassadors intrigued before electing Angelo Braschi. Pope Pius VI (1775–99) was a patrician. His extreme dignity and beauty of person were enhanced by amiability and charm. Devout and of irreproachable conduct, this splendid person with his snow-white hair was, understandably, just a little vain. He courted admiration to which he attached more than face value. He was anxious both to love and to be loved.

His pontificate opened with promise of another golden age. Europe was more or less at peace and the great powers were gloating over their defeat of the Jesuits. That issue had been at least temporarily settled. Discreditable though the outcome was to the papacy, Pius VI could in no sense be held personally responsible. Healthy and hard-working, the pope set about all sorts of desirable improvements. He began draining the Pontine Marshes, making roads and building a cathedral in Subiaco. In Rome he put up the Egyptian obelisks at the Quirinal, Trinità dei Monti and Monte Citorio. He extended the Museum of Antiquities begun by Clement XIV, and added largely to the collection of sculpture, including six hundred pieces of antique statuary. He enabled his nephews to raise the monumental Palazzo Braschi in the Piazza S. Pantaleo, the last of the great papal palaces of Rome. He patronized the painters Mengs and David, and the sculptor Canova. Rome became the Mecca of aristocrats and artists from the north, who were drawn by the climate, the monuments, the licence and the free entry into all social circles. It was the city of the carnival and the stimulating intellectual exchanges described by Goethe in his journals. There can seldom, if ever, in history have been a cosmopolitan centre offering more beauty, tradition and agreeable living than Rome during the first half of Pius VI's reign.

These idyllic conditions were destined not to last. The clouds of popular discontent gathering in Austria and France, of disbelief and anti-clericalism in every quarter of the old and new world, were gradually drifting into Italy, until they could no longer be disregarded. Rome was about the last place where the eclipse of the old patrician civilization happened. In 1792 vindictive measures were taken in France against the Church. In the following year, the official de-christianization of the French nation was accompanied by organized massacres and *noyades* of the clergy, and by destruction of ecclesiastical property on a monstrous scale never experienced before in a land which had risen to greatness through the benefits of Christ's gospel. The French Revolution disturbed the whole of civilized Europe, and extinguished once and for all the lamps of the most carefree city of culture in the world.

The seizure of Avignon by the French Republic was tantamount to an act of warfare against the Papal States. Pius VI, in his efforts to maintain neutrality when the coalition of nations was formed against republican France, exercised the most commendable restraint without, however, hesitating to condemn the outrageous misdeeds of atheistic anarchy. And what were the consequences of his restraint? Napoleon Bonaparte was invited by the Directory to destroy Rome. In 1798 the city was occupied by General Berthier and declared a republic. The Swiss Guards were dispersed.[1] The fickle Romans, assembled in the piazza, indulged in orgies of 'brotherhood' and burnt the pope's effigy below his windows. Close to the obelisk an altar of freedom was set up before which a 'fraternization feast' was held. Rome was systematically looted by the French. Neither the Vatican Galleries nor the Pope's private apartments were spared. The Laocoon, the Apollo Belvedere, the Dying Gaul were removed from the plinths on which they had rested for centuries. The Raphael tapestries were stripped; the Madonna della Sedia and countless famous pictures were taken. On one day, five hundred horse-drawn wagons left the gates of Rome on their way to France. Jewels, silver, archives and treasure of all kinds were plundered and transported. In the city wanton damage was done to the collections and the villas of the noble families which contained them.

The eighty-year-old pope was as temporal ruler deposed. Already a very sick man, he was deported one February morning before dawn. On being commanded by a French general to surrender the two rings he was wearing, he replied sweetly: 'I can give you one because it is my own property. But the other', pointing to the Fisherman's Ring, 'must pass to my successor.' Pius's terrible journey through rain and snow to Siena, the privations he endured there, the final expulsion from Italy across the Alps when he was mortally ill and half paralysed, and his death at Valence after forgiving all his enemies need no describing in this text. His sufferings from the hands of the new rulers of the Most Christian Nation of Europe far surpassed those of any pope in modern times.

After much agitation by his sympathizers, permission was granted in 1802 by the French Consulate for the body of Pius VI to be taken back to Rome. Although the pope's wish to be buried as close as possible to St Peter's tomb was not carried out, his kneeling effigy by Canova was placed in the confession of the basilica. It was the ailing sculptor's last work. He carved the head and hands, leaving the rest to his pupil Adamo Tadolini. Pius is in the act of deeply concentrated prayer. The head is tilted, the eyes gaze upwards as it were beyond the confines of the dome into the distant heavens, and the mouth is half open. The face is wrapped in a holy fervour which is too melodramatic to be entirely agreeable.

More to our purpose are Pius VI's benefactions to the church of the Saint whose name he honoured above all others and to whose mediation he committed himself with the fortitude of an early Christian martyr, when he was expelled from Rome. Among his renovations had been new windows to the dome and the regilding of the nave ceiling on which the Braschi arms were substituted for those of Paul V; among his embellishments were the gift of mosaic frontals to twenty-five altars. His two innovations amounted to the pair of clocks on the façade, and the new sacristy.

The hopelessness of previous attempts to build a belfry has been described in a previous chapter. Ever since Bernini's abortive efforts, successive popes recognized that some

---

[1] In 1800 they returned to the Vatican.

sort of provision for bells and a clock ought to be made. Pius VI called upon Giuseppe Valadier to settle the problem for all time. Valadier, son of a Dutch father and Roman mother, had been appointed by the pope St Peter's Architect at the age of twenty-seven. He was to become the best known of Rome's neo-classical architects. In selecting the two ends of the church façade, in other words the bases of Maderno's intended towers, for a pair of clocks, Valadier had the taste, and the good manners, to design crests to accord with the style of the rest of the building. Two pairs of angels, of whom Bernini would not have felt ashamed, hold the mosaic clock faces which are crowned with the papal insignia of the Braschi. The southern face registers European mean time, the northern Italian actual time. One enormous bronze bell, founded by Luigi Valadier, the architect's father, and weighing 28,000 lbs, was hoisted into the opening of the attic immediately below the southern dial. The grave, sublime, melodious tone of *il campanone* echoes on solemn occasions across the piazza like a paternal call from distant Jehovah.

The new sacristy was an even greater undertaking. Its high cost, which aroused a good deal of criticism, is not altogether surprising when we consider that the building is the size of a very large parish church. Pius VI was undeterred by opposition. He was resolved to supply the one necessary appendage which the mother church of the Christian world had been lacking for centuries. Maderno at the beginning of the *seicento* had wished to build, and Carlo Fontana at the very end had actually designed, a sacristy. The first architect was thwarted by lack of funds and the second by the then pope's reluctance to destroy the existing ancient structure on the only site available. This was the circular Roman tomb of the Emperor Theodosius, the survivor of the two rotundas attached like loose beads to the south transeptal arm of Constantine's basilica. It had undergone various transformations and uses since Roman times. Early in the sixth century, Pope Symmachus remodelled it in the shape it retained until the eighteenth century. In the Middle Ages it became the Church of S. Maria della Febre (Our Lady Protectress against Plague). In the mid-fifteenth century, Pius II deposited in it the head of St Andrew brought to Rome from the Peloponnese. Thereafter, it became known as the Cappella di S. Andrea. The venerable building, the last link with the old basilica, had for a long time served, inadequately it is true, as the sacristy to the renaissance St Peter's. It was regarded by many Romans as a valuable piece of antiquity, and accordingly reverenced. But not by Pope Pius VI. He had no scruples whatever in having it replaced with a more commodious structure capable of accommodating, as well as a sacristy, a treasury, canonry and chapter house, where cardinals and dignitaries might assemble for important functions.

In 1776 Pius chose from several projects submitted by contributors one by Carlo Marchionni, architect of the Villa Albani. Without delay, orders were given for the ancient rotunda to be pulled down. But this last vestige of Constantine's basilica was so soundly built that a squad of demolition workers took months to remove it. At last the site was cleared and completely flattened. On 1st October the Romans watched the strange spectacle of the pope driving triumphantly in a carriage over the open ground. In 1784 the new sacristy was finished and in the presence of a large assembly consecrated by the pope with tears of joy coursing down his cheeks.

The sacristy stands midway to the south of the basilica to which it is attached by two corridors, enclosing the small Piazza Braschi. The roadway to the Vatican precincts passes through the piazza and under the corridors. The sacristy is approached by the

The north clock of the façade

public through a doorway leading to the western corridor under Pius VIII's monument. Marchionni, like Valadier with his clock turrets, subordinated the style of his own generation to that of the great basilica dominating the site. Michelangelo's south elevation had to be respected. The best tribute that can be paid to Marchionni is gratitude for leaving the great south transeptal apse free and undisturbed, and for designing the new sacristy in the mannerist style which he found around him. Creative architects are not conspicuous for humility. They seldom show respect for an outmoded style, even if it be that of a great genius. Marchionni was an honourable exception. He deliberately crammed the windows of his sacristy between pilasters, set them at irregular intervals and heights, and thrust the pediments of the upper into entablatures in that outrageous manner first introduced by Michelangelo and soon widely copied by his contemporaries.

The central apartment of the sacristy, called the Sagrestia Commune, is octagonal. Yellow Siena pilasters support a dome. The four entrances are carried by fluted Ionic columns of grey marble. These had been brought from Hadrian's Villa and used by Bernini for the lower stage of his ill-fated belfry. In the middle of the marble pavement are displayed the arms of the Braschi pope – under three stars a child's head or zephyr blowing at a bunch of lilies.

With the sacristy, the new basilica was definitely finished. Nearly two hundred years had elapsed since Sixtus V built the dome; two hundred and thirty-eight since Paul III summoned Michelangelo to make a start on the great piers that support it; and three hundred and thirty-eight since Nicholas V, having decided that the ancient basilica of Constantine must be replaced, called upon Alberti to advise how this could best be done in a style worthy of the age of humanism, of which this pope's reign was witnessing the first streaks of dawn.

St Peter's today *below*. The Stuart monument *right*

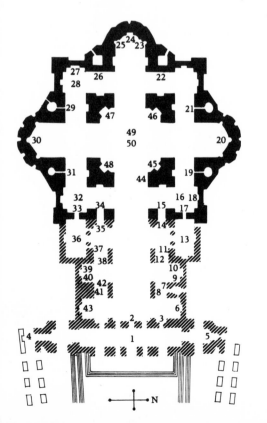

1 Portico	26 Monument to Alexander VIII
2 Filarete Door	27 Altar of St Leo the Great
3 Holy Door	28 Chapel of the Column
4 Statue of Charlemagne	29 Monument to Alexander VII
5 Statue of Constantine	30 Altar of SS Simon and Jude
6 Pietà	31 Monument to Pius VIII
7 Monument to Leo XII	32 Clementine Chapel
8 Monument to Christina of Sweden	33 Monument to Pius VII
9 Monument to Pius XI	34 Monument to Leo XI
10 Monument to Pius XII	35 Monument to Innocent XI
11 Monument to Innocent XII	36 Choir Chapel
12 Monument to Countess Matilda of Tuscany	37 Monument to Pius X
13 Blessed Sacrament Chapel	38 Monument to Innocent VIII
14 Monument to Gregory XIII	39 Altar of St Pius X
15 Tomb of Gregory XIV	40 Monument to Benedict XV
16 Gregorian Chapel	41 Monument to Maria Clementina Sobie
17 Monument to Gregory XVI	42 The Stuart Monument
18 Altar of the Madonna of Succour	43 Baptistry
19 Monument to Benedict XIV	44 Statue of St Peter
20 Altar of SS Processus and Martinian	45 Statue of St Longinus
21 Monument to Clement XIII	46 Statue of St Helena
22 Monument to Clement X	47 Statue of St Veronica
23 Monument to Urban VIII	48 Statue of St Andrew
24 Cattedra	49 Papal altar under Baldacchino
25 Monument to Paul III	50 Confession of St Peter

Additions by Maderno shown thus   ▨

Additions by Bernini shown thus   ▭

IACOBO·III
IACOBI·II·MAGNAE·BRIT·REGIS·FILIO
KAROLO·EDVARDO
ET·HENRICO·DECANO·PATRVM·CARDINALIVM
IACOBI·III·FILIIS
REGIAE·STIRPIS·STVARDIAE·POSTREMIS
ANNO·M·DCCC·XIX

BEATI·MORTVI
QVI·IN·DOMINO·MORIVNTVR

Pius VI, the monument by Canova *left*. The monument of Pius VII *right*

There is little more to be told. This book is neither a history of the Catholic Church nor of the papacy. Individual popes have been introduced in so far as they personally, or events in their reign, have had some bearing upon the fortunes of St Peter's. Since Pius VI's reign, few alterations to the fabric have taken place; and the chief additions have been papal monuments, in their style, taste and cost the most telling records of their period. Some of them have been good, some downright bad, and many more indifferent.

Pius VII, Chiaramonti (1800–23), was a scarcely less tragic figure than his uncle Pius VI. Benevolent and generous to a fault, he was one of the sweetest and mildest of men. Yet he was treated as the shuttlecock of Europe, knocked hither and thither by those battle-dores, Consalvi, his active Secretary of State, a diplomatist of the highest skill, and Napoleon Bonaparte. Yet Pius VII was not a mere featherweight. Although humiliated and bullied by the emperor and grossly maltreated during his captivity in Savona – to which town in 1810 he was whirled away from Rome in a carriage without a single attendant, a change of linen or even his spectacles – his extreme goodness gave him a strength of resistance almost divine. He survived to lament the death of his old enemy, towards whom he always felt more compassionate than resentful and for whose health during the banishment in St Helena he was touchingly concerned.

Pius VII during the years when he was not in exile was a generous friend to artists. In his patronage of the arts, as in all his interests, he was encouraged and guided by Consalvi. While still a cardinal, he had befriended the composer, Cimarosa. While pope he patronized Canova and Thorwaldsen. The Secretary of State was chiefly responsible for the Stuart memorial by the first and the tomb of his master by the second sculptor.

Consalvi never forgot that he owed his rise to greatness to Henry Stuart, Cardinal of York. On the death of the cardinal and titular King of England, he persuaded Pius to commission a monument to the last three Stuarts. He was also astute enough to persuade the Prince Regent of England to pay for it. The project appealed to the pope who liked to recall the loyalty to the Catholic Church of the Pretenders, and to the Regent who was both romantic and generous. In 1819 Canova set up the beautiful memorial against the first pier in the left aisle. It is perhaps the most successful neo-classical monument in the world. Of the utmost simplicity, it takes the form of a Greek funerary *stele*. A bust in relief of each of the three crownless kings appears above an inscription. Alas, that the head of Bonny Prince Charlie resembles a prosperous butcher's with double chin! On either side of the closed door of the tomb, symbolizing the exit of the old and unfortunate dynasty, stand a pair of mourning angels. These partly draped figures, with wings folded, heads bowed, and arms leaning upon extinguished torches, revive the very spirit of ancient Hellas. Stendhal was so enamoured of the mourners that again and again he returned to visit them at dusk when he said they assumed a celestial beauty. He advised tourists on their first visit to Rome to rush to the Stuart tomb in order to gauge whether or not they had a heart capable of appreciating sculpture. The beauty of the mourners is undeniable. But it is a classical and impersonal beauty. I find it difficult to understand Roger Peyrfitte's insinuation that what the guide books describe as 'l'indicibile soavità della morbida patina' of the marble thighs of these sexless ephebes is caused by the libidinous fingers of passers-by.

Pius VII's monument in the Cappella Clementina is a greater tribute to the devotion of the faithful Consalvi than to the art of the Danish sculptor, Thorwaldsen, who was Canova's pupil. Geometrical and frigid in composition, the monument does not merit detailed attention. There is something stiffly incongruous in the attitude of the seated pope within a renaissance tabernacle. The studious and handsome face, however, shows plenty of character. The eyes gaze under beetling brows. The mouth is half quizzical, half disdainful. The expression does not accord with what we know of Pius VII's guileless nature, which is more faithfully interpreted in the splendidly sympathetic portrait by Sir Thomas Lawrence.

The monuments of the next three popes, Leo XII (1823–9), Pius VIII (1829–30) and Gregory XVI (1831–46), are still in the neo-classical, sub-Canova style. Leo's effigy resembles an opera singer of the 1830s. It stands stiffly over the doorway to a little oval chapel which now contains the lift to the Pope's apartments and the *sedia gestatoria* under a dustsheet. Pius VIII kneels below a seated figure of Christ, larger in scale than the pope's, and over the sacristy entrance. It is a colossal and static composition, given faint praise by the official guide book for 'a classicism less frigid than usual'. Gregory XVI's monument is, like the man it commemorates, overbearing and insensitive. Reigning at a time when Europe was in the throes of democratic claims and Italy undergoing a succession of revolutions, Gregory did much harm to the papal prestige by identifying himself with the forces of reaction. He inveighed against secret societies, the liberty of conscience and the press, and refused all civil reforms. Modern inventions were to him anathema. 'Chemin de fer, chemin d'enfer!' he is reputed to have said. He did not make himself less unpopular by the equivocal favouritism of Gaetano Moroni, a former baker's apprentice, from whom he was inseparable. Yet Gregory XVI loved the arts, and patronized the Protestant sculptor Thorwaldsen and the painter Albert Küchler. He established the Museums of Egyptian and Etruscan Antiquities in the Vatican Palace.

Gregory XVI knew that he was walking round a volcano and hoped that the eruption might be reserved for his successor. It was. The reign of Pius IX (1846–78) was the longest of any pope on record. It was also the most significant within modern times in that it witnessed the end of the temporal power of the papacy. This end was inevitable. The wonder is that it did not come sooner. Anticipated by the Church with terror ever since medieval times, it was finally provoked by the retrogressive policy of Gregory XVI and brought about by the intransigence of Pius IX. The grant of temporal power to Pope Stephen III by Pepin in the eighth century had been the greatest disservice ever done to the papacy. That the successors of St Peter should wield the sceptre over the nations of the earth as well as the keys to the kingdom of heaven was an anachronism disastrous to Christendom. It involved the popes in disputes over frontiers with the sovereigns of Europe in which they invariably came out worst, disputes in which they should have been above playing any part at all. It depreciated their spirituality in the eyes of Catholics, and debased their moral authority in those of heretics. Not the least unfortunate sequel was the popes' utter incapacity, because of their sacred office, to wage wars and govern laymen efficiently by profane means.

Pius IX had a strong personality but certain weaknesses of character. He was a man of commanding presence, bewitching charm and angelic beauty. His voice was dulcet and persuasive. His one consistency was his priestly duty which made him blind to all shades of opinion, except those which he was convinced were right. He was a sentimental man who welcomed adulation, which at the opening of his reign he received. For he began by being extremely tolerant, determined on much needed reforms of papal government. Mischievous opposition to his liberalism by Austria and dissatisfaction with the speed of his improvements among Italian republicans, which led to the invasion of Ferrara by the emperor in 1847 and the assault on the Quirinal Palace by the Roman mob in 1848, quickly disillusioned the pope. In spite of great courage and gallantry, the Swiss Guards were overcome in the fighting that broke out. Pius, who was obliged to flee from the capital in disguise, felt profoundly injured and humiliated. After that event, he completely changed from the indulgent father figure to the harsh autocrat who had

The monuments of Leo XII *left* and Gregory XVI *right*

learned from bitter experience that lenity was an ineffective means of guiding his unruly children. But it was now too late to adopt this rôle. The advance of democracy in nineteenth-century Italy could no longer be stemmed by pontifical excommunications. Pius was, however, buoyed by the support of the Emperor Napoleon III, whose approval of the pope maintaining his temporal power was clearly actuated by a desire to hinder Italian unity. In vain, as it turned out, for in 1861 Victor Emanuel of Savoy was proclaimed King of Italy. As though to counter this unpalatable circumstance, the pope summoned the ecumenical council, known as the Vatican Council of 1869–70, the first since that of Trent held over three hundred years before.

The council assembled in the north transeptal arm of St Peter's which was walled off from the rest of the church with what looked like a massive partition of solid marble in

During the First Vatican Council a temporary partition, simulating a marble wall, sealed off the north transept *left*. The scene inside the transept *right*

many colours, entered through a pair of bronze doors. In fact the whole counterfeit thing was made to fold up like a screen. Reading-rooms, drawing-rooms and cloak-rooms were fitted up in an ingenious way. Six hundred prelates sat on benches of eight tiers on either side of the transept. The opening session saw them resplendent in their silver copes and linen mitres. Royal visitors in ribbons and jewelled decorations were ensconced in tribunes to watch the proceedings as at an opera. Eyewitnesses have left lively accounts of the council's proceedings and the conditions in which they were conducted – the appalling acoustics which prevented all but the younger prelates hearing the speeches delivered in halting Church Latin from the temporary pulpits; the incessant shouts of *placet* which echoed down the nave like the sharp rattle of rifle fire, as the bishops gave assent to the barely audible motions put by the chairmen. And the final session which opened in teeming rain on 18th July 1870. The transept was filled to the utmost with cardinals and bishops soaked to the skin and sweating in the heavy heat. From their steaming vestments, a veil of mist hovered over the nodding mitres. The floor between the benches was a river bed of slush. Then the storm broke again. Lightning flashed upon the baldacchino and thunder echoed round the dome while the pope, supremely unconcerned, delivered in musical accents his culminating speech. The outcome of the Vatican Council was a triumph for ultramontanism, but a pyrrhic victory for temporalism. The doctrine of Infallibility was indeed passed in spite of a few dissident prelates who voted against acceptance and a larger number who, out of loyalty to the Holy See, absented themselves. Henceforth, papal pronouncements made *ex cathedra* were to be regarded as divinely protected from error. In a spiritual sense the papacy was immensely strengthened. In a temporal sense it was doomed.

On the following 20th September, the Italian troops of Victor Emanuel entered Rome. In the plebiscite held on 2nd October, an overwhelming vote was cast for union with the Kingdom of Italy. By this means, the Papal States ceased to exist, and the Pope was deprived of his territorial sovereignty. Pius's ineffectual protests were accompanied by a resolve never to leave the Vatican until his rights were recognized by the State. His successors continued to observe a self-imposed imprisonment until the papal sovereignty was restored to Pius XI in a strictly modified form under the Lateran Treaty of 1929.

Pius IX never recovered from the shattering blow. His humiliation was made all the more bitter by King Victor Emanuel's lack of tact, ostentatious self-congratulation and shameless confiscation of Church property. The pope in public audiences was provoked to refer to Victor Emanuel and his party as thieves, hypocrites, children of Satan and monsters of hell.

Pius IX's love of St Peter's never wavered. In 1838 he erected two vast and mediocre statues of Peter and Paul on either side of the steps leading to the portico, which they guard like mute and stupid sentinels. He agreed to a suggestion of Antonio Sarti to place around the obelisk four bronze candelabra with branched arms, crowned and dated 1861. Only within the ring formed by them and the fat granite bollards, embossed with the Borghese eagle of Paul V, is the spectator safe today from the motors and charabancs swirling around the piazza. Pius also paved the piazza with square cobbles. He laid the wide steps to the portico and fashioned the central ramp in the likeness of a flood

Pius IX, by G. P. A. Healey *left*, installed four bronze candelabra around the obelisk in the centre of the piazza *right*

The body of St Pius X lies enshrined below his altar

of petrified lava. Inside the basilica he substituted Carrara marble for the travertine bases of thirty-six pilasters of the transept. Michelangelo had intended the whole interior to be of naked stone, but the later baroque process of clothing the walls with marble had made a contrast with the pilasters of austere stucco too strident to be tolerated any longer. Pius also marked the proclamation of the dogma of the Immaculate Conception of the Blessed Virgin Mary, in 1854, by solemnly crowning her image in the mosaic of the altar in the Choir Chapel.

Pio Nono was not buried in the basilica which he so deeply revered, nor has he a sepulchral monument there. His memorial is associated with the famous enthroned figure of St Peter against the last pier (St Longinus's) of the nave. It is an appropriate one. Pius held St Peter in greater affection than any pope had done within modern times. In 1857 he granted by brief an indulgence of fifty days to whomsoever kissed the Prince of the Apostles' bronze toe. From the first, he had regarded the Apostle as a sort of friendly rival. When on his election the customary words, 'Thou wilt not see Peter's years', were read to him, the new pope, much to the bystanders' surprise, retorted, 'This is no article of faith.' Peter, the first Vicar of Christ on earth, was reputed to have been bishop of Rome for a quarter of a century. It was a remarkable fact that up to date no successor had exceeded this span of years. Pius IX was the first pope to do so. His Jubilee in 1871 was celebrated, in defiance of the recent terrible reverses to the papacy, with much acclaim and no little awe. Characteristically, the pope took care to record the achievement for all time. And he chose the environment of the Apostle's venerable statue upon which to emblazon it. Henceforth, every pious pilgrim after making obeisance at Peter's foot, and so benefiting from Pius's indulgence, must, on stepping back and raising his head, see the mosaic portrait of the pope and the inscription announcing how he surpassed the years of the Apostle's bishopric. Pius had the background to the statue lined with a shiny marble imitating Genoese velvet and the rather flimsy canopy and lamp suspended overhead.

Without reaching the thirty-two years of Pius IX, his successor Leo XIII (1878–1903) also exceeded a quarter century's reign, dying at the age of ninety-three. This kind, open-minded pope who welcomed railways and all modern technical improvements, was a complete contrast to Pius IX. 'Away from narrowness!' was his constant cry. A prisoner in the Vatican and seldom seen, he nevertheless made his conciliatory authority felt in world affairs. He left little mark upon St Peter's beyond re-laying Bernini's pavement in the portico. The sainted Pius X (1903–14) was a different character again. This son of a postman and a seamstress radiated a holiness which deeply impressed those who came in contact with him. The ordinary Italian people hailed him as a saint – a verdict that was confirmed by the Church forty years after his death. As a spiritual leader, Pius was notable for his encouragement of frequent communion, a practice that has transformed the lives of the faithful throughout the world. His agglutinate effigy stands in a niche of the left aisle. The pope, with outstretched arms and head bowed under the weight of an outsize triple tiara, is wrapped as it were in a blanket of white flour. He is shown in the act of supplicating the Almighty for the deliverance of mankind from the First World War, the declaration of which broke his compassionate heart. On either side of the cupboard door below him are bronze reliefs representing the grant of Holy Communion to children and the homage of intellectuals to the Faith. St Pius X's embalmed remains, with copper mask and hands exposed, lie behind glass in the altar of the adjoining Chapel of the Presentation.

The election of Benedict XV (1914–22) coincided with a terrible moment in history. The pope was unhesitating in his condemnation of the First World War, against which he courageously made eight pronouncements and which he declared to be 'degrading' mankind. He demanded a league of all nations, and disarmament. When these were not forthcoming, he organized relief work on a wide scale. He denounced the Versailles peace terms as a 'consecration of hatred'. His monument by Pietro Canonica depicts him kneeling in prayer for divine propitiation against the horrors of war. It is by far the least banal of this sculptor's several statues in St Peter's.

The monuments of Pius X *left* and Benedict XV *right*

The Borgo, before *above* and after *below* the construction of the Via della Conciliazione (see also pp. 103, 106)

Pius XI (1922–39) was the first pope since the voluntary imprisonment of Pius IX within the Vatican to appear in public. This was a consequence of the Lateran Treaty of 1929 which settled the Roman question, in the words of those who drafted it – 'once and for all'. The Vatican City was officially recognized as a sovereign state by the Italian government, which in return was acknowledged by the Holy See. Attached to the treaty was a concordat providing for Catholic religious instruction in the state schools, and the freedom of Catholic Action, that proselytizing but non-political organization for pastors and laymen founded by the pope on the words of St Peter's first Epistle: 'Ye are a chosen generation, a royal priesthood, an holy nation, a peculiar people, that ye should shew forth the praises of him, who hath called you out of darkness into his marvellous light.' The ratifications were immediately followed by a Fascist campaign of confiscations of Church property and penalties against Catholic youth organizations. The pope denounced these unwarranted reprisals. He fearlessly rebutted the aggressive nationalism taught by Mussolini, and called his policy of anti-semitism 'a repulsive movement'.

There are no reasons for supposing that Pius XI was a man of taste. He is not known to have expressed an opinion favourable or unfavourable upon Mussolini's mutilation of the Borgo and opening of the straight, axial Via della Conciliazione in 1937. The operation took place outside the Vatican City on territory over which he had no jurisdiction.

The demolition of the *spina*, or spine of the Borgo, which consisted of a conglomeration of old and picturesque buildings, pierced by three very narrow streets running more or less parallel from the S. Angelo Bridge to St Peter's, has provoked hostile criticism. The main objections are that the most remote and mysterious quarter of Rome has been sacrificed to form a pompous and boring boulevard, and that the straight wide vista formed has totally deprived the first view of the church of that surprise and contrast which were formerly so striking. Augustus Hare wrote in 1892 that 'the whole external effect of St Peter's depends upon the sudden entrance into the sunlit piazza from the gloomy street'. That effect has certainly gone for ever.[1]

On the other hand, the architects[2] of the new Via della Conciliazione have defended themselves on practical as well as historic grounds. Firstly, they declared that had the narrow streets been left as they were, the flow of traffic to and from the Vatican City would long ago have come to a standstill. This is an argument of unimaginative town planners to which we have become only too well accustomed. There are usually alternative solutions to destruction of what is traditional and beautiful. And in the Vatican environment there were other approaches, even underground ones, which could have been explored and probably made available. Secondly, the architects referred to the fact that Bramante, Bernini and Carlo Fontana wished to carve some sort of processional approach to St Peter's, and were only prevented by lack of funds. This argument is, I concede, irrefutable. No renaissance or baroque creator of a monumental building would

---

[1] Certainly for the vast majority who approach St Peter's by the Via della Conciliazione. Those who walk up the Borgo Santo Spirito may get an oblique glimpse of the south clock turret and then, at the bend by the eponymous church a tantalizing view only of the grey dome and top stage of the façade, cushioned, as they seem, upon Bernini's colonnade. A vague idea may thus be got, first of a partial and then of the full revelation of St Peter's previously granted to the traveller on his emerging from the old Borgo streets now destroyed.

[2] Marcello Piacentini and Attilio Spaccarelli.

have preferred it to be cluttered up to the entrance with small houses of little architectural value, however picturesque these might be. When allowed a free hand, one and all gave their monuments as exposed and generous a setting as possible. Nonetheless, the 1937 destruction of the Borgo *spina* and the making of the boulevard have proved to be a mistake for the following reasons. The approach to St Peter's is up a hill. You come to it not from a level, but from below. In consequence, your upward vision is restricted, to start with. Then Maderno's prolongation of the basilica towards the piazza is an additional cause of the drum and dome being hidden from the eye at close quarters. Before you have walked or driven halfway along the processional road the drum begins to disappear, and when you are at the obelisk the dome has gone altogether. By the time you have climbed to the inert façade you experience anti-climax. It is true of course that when the Borgo existed, and you emerged from the narrow arteries into the piazza, there were still no complete drum and dome. But you had not been led to expect them. Instead you marvelled, not at the vertical, but the sudden horizontal effect around you, at the wonderful expanse offered by those outspread welcoming colonnades. In 1937 this instantaneous effect was taken away. But in 1950 the authorities, as though to make some amends for the regrettable deprivation, built two projecting arms at the west end of the boulevard. To a slight extent, the arms have corrected the trouble by narrowing the entrance to the piazza, and restoring to the visitor who emerges upon it a faint illusion of surprise.

In fairness to the authors of the 1937 scheme, the minor merits of the Via della Conciliazione ought to be pointed out. The sky-level, set by the old buildings which are left, has been maintained by the new street. The Bramantesque Palazzo Giraud, the Hotel Columbus and S. Maria in Traspontina have mercifully been spared. The new intervening blocks may be uninspired, but they are good-mannered, made of Roman brick scantling in traditional tones of yellow, brown and pink. The long serried row of obelisks bearing lanterns on either side of the boulevard are perhaps a trifle absurd. Certainly the sight of the whole twenty-eight popping up within a fortnight provoked mirth in those tourists used to the leisurely methods of British builders. But then the lovers of architecture in Great Britain have nothing there to be mirthful about. They are perpetually in tears. When they consider how the post-war opportunities of improving the precincts of St Paul's in London have been bungled, they have cause to weep. Have the English then any right to criticize what is at least a serious, if on the whole misguided, attempt made by the Italians to improve the approach to St Peter's?

Pius XI had the misery of seeing the unavoidable approach of the Second World War. He died in February 1939 when the horizon was black indeed. His monument in the Chapel of St Sebastian by Canonica was about the worst in the basilica. No observer would have guessed that the cloddish figure represented was of a man who had been a lithe mountaineer. A couple of years ago it was replaced by a new monument by Francesco Nagni. A seated, bronze figure of the pope, holding an open book on his lap, is raised against a background panel of highly polished porphyry.

Pius XI's monument confronts the effigy of his successor, Pius XII, which is by Francesco Messina and was erected in 1964. This is the best papal monument to appear since Canova's to Pius VI. The great bronze mitred figure with sloping shoulders, sharp bespectacled features and infinitely beautiful hands, gives an excellent impression of the delicate, patrician pope, whose mystical spirit, wilfully misrepresented in certain quarters today, left on those encountering it an indelible memory of benignity and grace.

The reign of Pius XII (1939–58), although covering a period of world cataclysm, saw much repair work done to the fabric of St Peter's. In 1933 extensive reinforcements of the dome found necessary by his predecessor had been completed. Pius XII was nevertheless obliged to have metal substituted for wooden frames in the large windows of the drum. Then he had every window in the building fortified by a complete armour. The pope also continued the task, begun by Pius IX and resumed by Pius X in 1914, of encasing the pilasters of the apse in marble. In preparation for the Holy Year of 1950, Pius XII held a competition for three new bronze doors to lead from the portico to the basilica. Of the winners, the most distinguished artist was Giacomo Manzù. His door has large modelled panels of the Crucifixion and Annunciation, and lesser panels of prophets, apostles and saints. The designs are linear and economical. Venanzo Crocetti has recently been responsible for a second door. The third is still awaited.

Pius XII's most remarkable achievement at St Peter's was undoubtedly the excavations below the pavement level of Constantine's basilica. What these excavations have revealed was described in chapter 3. The process called from the pope the greatest courage and enthusiasm. Leo XIII had allowed Father Hartmann Grisar to begin certain tentative researches, which were inconclusive. Benedict XV gave reluctant permission for digging below the confession, permission which he afterwards withdrew. When at the beginning of the last war Pius XII was erecting the tomb of his predecessor in the crypt, some eighteen inches of floor were removed for installing the base. The work brought to light signs of a Roman burial ground which had not previously been suspected. Pius was deeply interested, and gave funds and encouragement to an extremely distinguished team of archaeologists. Their systematic excavations lasted for more than a decade.

A memorial of the beloved Pope John XXIII (1958–63) is being installed in the Chapel of the Presentation. It is a huge bronze relief of the pope by the sculptor Emilio Greco. Meanwhile, the opening of the ecumenical council in 1962 is commemorated in the more or less rectangular marble escutcheon in the centre of the portico pavement. It is designed by Manzù. The edges of the shield are curiously, but, I presume, consciously irregular to make us suppose that the mason could not cut straight. The lion of St Mark emblazoned on the shield is of semi-modernistic design. This memorial may be considered interesting by posterity as indicative of a rough and ready interlude in the long annals of the fine arts which have been lavished upon St Peter's.

It is too early to judge the effects of the Second Vatican Council which met in four sessions from 1962 to 1965. Like the first, it was held in St Peter's Basilica – but not in the transept. The vast attendance could only be accommodated in the nave which was entirely separated from the aisles by high walls of red damask. Rows of red damask seats were raised against them in two opposing tiers. Of the two thousand eight hundred and sixteen bishops who participated, forty per cent came from Europe, thirty from North and South America, ten from Asia, ten from Africa and ten from the Eastern Rites. For the first time in history observers from almost all the non-Roman Catholic Churches were present. In an astonishing atmosphere of good will and understanding innumerable speeches were made in Latin.

To many a layman the conclusions of the council may appear negative. No new dogmas were promulgated, and no old ones dissolved. No heresies were condemned, and no

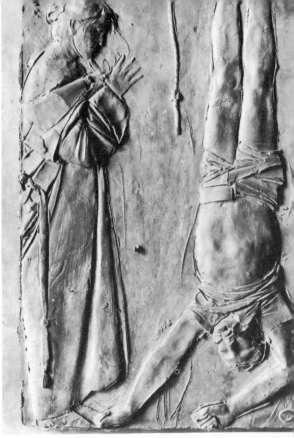

Detail from the monument of Pius XII *above left*. The doors by Manzù *below left*. Detail of the martyrdom of St Peter from the Manzù doors *above right*. Detail from the monument of John XXIII *below right*

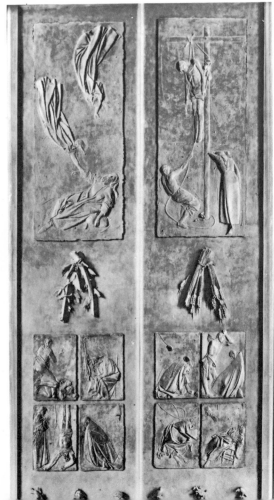

fundamental differences between Churches done away with. Many world problems, such as peace and matrimony, were discussed, but not settled. The two major positive results were to make permissive use of the vernacular in parts of the Mass, and to establish a Senate of Bishops to assist the Pope in Church government. In addition, declarations of religious liberty and of tolerance of beliefs by non-Catholics were made in deep earnestness. Probably the most important outcome of all was the council's absolute determination that in the immediate future the Church should work by all possible means for Christian unity. The Second Vatican Council has been called a process rather than an event. It certainly witnessed an astonishing development within the body of the Church, a change from a defensive inward look to a more sympathetic outlook upon the non-Catholic world.

In attempting a final assessment of St Peter's Basilica, what conclusions do we arrive at? If we can first decide by what procedure our assessment should be guided, I believe the conclusions will eventually emerge of their own accord. To begin with, we should not look upon the building as a single, concerted work of art. If we do, then we are bound to call it a gigantic failure. For it is no coordinated entity like Wren's St Paul's Cathedral, designed and carried out by one master mind. Over a period of several hundred years, nearly every great architect of his generation had a 'go' at St Peter's. One by one they dropped off the stage, thwarted, disillusioned, disappointed, their schemes either rejected or incomplete, to be altered by a successor. How then can the finished thing, made up of so many men's conflicting and only partially fulfilled ideas be called an architectural success? Strictly speaking, it is nothing of the kind. The mixed-up children of frustrated geniuses do not always marry well. If we relate one to another, we become sadly aware of their incongruities. In the aesthetic context Michelangelo's elevations seem cramped and grotesque. Maderno's façade is squat and lumpish. Della Porta's lantern is too small for the dome, which is only visible from a distance. On the other hand, the single quality which every feature of the church has in common is immensity. To maintain this all the artists who worked at St Peter's were in agreement, at considerable trouble to themselves. Each had to observe an abnormal scale in making his particular contribution.

St Peter's is certainly a hotchpotch of great warring components. Byron, who had little understanding of art, and was inclined to be sentimental about St Peter's, nevertheless grasped this fact:

'Thou see'st not all – but piecemeal thou must break
To separate contemplation, the great whole;'

is what he advised the spectator in *Childe Harold*.[1]

In walking into the church our first amazed impression of 'the great whole' is a soft, dove-grey fluttering of pavement, pillar and arch which is very sympathetic. But on close scrutiny we find that a good deal of the interior offends us just as much as that of the exterior. Having discountenanced the heavy mustard ceilings, the flashy mosaic copies of pious paintings by mannerist artists, the hackneyed evangelists under the

[1] *Childe Harold*, IV, line 157.

dome, the excessive polychrome marble of the walls, and the sickly stucco saints, what are we left with? An impressive temple of stupendous proportions filled with an almost infinite number of works of art. There is no need to recapitulate by way of apologetic the masterpieces, which have already been described at some length in these pages.

But immensity and works of art are by no means St Peter's only title to our veneration. We have surely to take into account the purposes for which the place was built. The first was practical. Twenty thousand people must be accommodated in the nave and transept. The second was proselytistic. The enormous basilica was meant to demonstrate the Church's triumph over schism, heresy, the abnegation of her Sacraments and interference in her affairs by emperors, kings and councils. It was to be a concrete testimony to her powers of withstanding the tempests of a hostile world. It was the loud proclamation of papal supremacy over the universal Christian Church. Nearly every component of St Peter's is symbolic of this great boast. The marble relief of Bonvicino over the central door to the portico pictures Christ handing the keys to Peter. This is the initial reminder to those about to enter that divine authority has been committed to the papacy. Lest the visitor should be in any doubts, the relief by Bernini over the central door into the church itself next brings to his eyes and understanding the doctrinal incident, 'Feed my Sheep.' It lays emphasis upon the spiritual leadership given by God to Peter and his successors. The basilica was meant then to be not only a colossal token of victory but an instrument of propaganda.

> 'What could be,' Byron declaims again,
> 'Of earthly structures, in His honour piled,
> Of a sublimer aspect? Majesty –
> Power – Glory – Strength – and,' he concludes,
>   'Beauty, all are aisled
> In this eternal Ark of worship undefiled.'

And, indeed, beauty. St Peter's primary beauty is to be looked for in its historical context. It is surely found in the living continuity of Christian worship on this site, the sublimity of symbolism, and the everlasting thanksgiving it renders to the Prince of the Apostles, the uncouth fisherman from Galilee, one of the most human mortals who has ever walked the earth.

Catholics are no freer from frailties than the rest of mankind. No wonder they like to petition Peter to intercede with the Almighty on their behalf and that of their friends in the great community of the faithful. They have done so since time immemorial. 'Petrus roga Christus Iesus pro sanctis hominibus Chrestianis ad corpus tuum' – Peter, pray Christ Jesus for the holy Christian men buried near your body. This prayer was found by Pope Pius XII's excavators scratched beside the Apostle's shrine by a barely literate pilgrim, at some unknown date before the first stone of Constantine's basilica was even laid.

The Second Vatican Council in session

Selected Bibliography

Ackermann, J. S., *The Architecture of Michelangelo*, 1961

Alferano, Tiberio, *De Basilicae Vaticanae antiquissima, et nova structura*, written in the 1570s, ed. M. Cerrati, 'Studi e Testi', no. 26, 1914

Barnes, A. S., *St Peter in Rome and His Tomb on the Vatican Hill*, 1900

Bonanni, Philippo, *Numismata Summorum Pontificum Templi Vaticani Fabricam*, 1696

Carrington, P., *The Early Christian Church*, 2 vols, 1957

Cullmann, O., *Peter, Disciple, Apostle, Martyr*, trs. F. V. Filson, 1953

Duchesne, Louis, *Le Liber Pontificalis, Texte, Introduction et Commentaire*, 2 vols, 1886

Egger, H., *Römische Veduten*, 2 vols, 1931–2

Fontana, Carlo, *Templum Vaticanum*, 1694

Fontana, Domenico, *Della Trasportazione dell'Obelisco Vaticano*, 1590

Geymüller, H. von, *Les Projets primitifs pour la Basilique de St Pierre de Rome*, 1875

Grisar, Hartmann, *History of Rome and the Popes in the Middle Ages*, 3 vols, 1911

Guarducci, Margherita, *Le Reliquie di S. Pietro*, 1965

Hülsen, Christian und Egger, Hermann, eds, *Die Römischen Skizzenbücher von M. Heemskerck*, vols 1 and 2, 1913–16

John, Eric, ed., *The Popes, A Concise Biographical History*, 1964

Kirschbaum, Engelbert, S. J., *The Tombs of St Peter and St Paul*, 1957, trs. 1959

Letarouilly, Paul, *La Basilique de Saint-Pierre*, 1882, trs. with preface by A. E. Richardson, 1953

Mann, H. K., *Lives of the Popes in the Early Middle Ages*, 590–1304, 18 vols, 1902–32

Milman, H. H., *History of Latin Christianity*, 9 vols, 1854–64

Mortier, D. A., *Saint Pierre de Rome*, 1900

Muñoz, A., *Domenico Fontana, Architetto*, 1944

Nielsen, Fredrik, *History of the Papacy in the 19th Century*, 2 vols, 1906

Paluzzi, C. Galassi, *San Pietro in Vaticano*, 2 vols, 1963

Pastor, Ludwig, *History of the Popes from the Middle Ages*, 1305–1800, 40 vols, 1906–53

Toynbee, J. and Perkins, J. W., *The Shrine of Saint Peter*, 1956

Wittkower, R., *Gian Lorenzo Bernini*, 1955

Acknowledgments

The producers wish to express their thanks to the libraries, galleries, museums and individuals who have allowed objects from their collections to be reproduced in this book, and to the photographers who have supplied illustrations, as listed below.

All the colour photographs are by Mario Carrieri, except for the plates on pages 134, 179, 182 and 294–5, which are in the Bethnal Green Museum and are reproduced by courtesy of the Victoria and Albert Museum, and the plate on pages 180–1, which is reproduced by courtesy of the National Gallery, London, photos by Derrick Witty.

The plans of the excavations under St Peter's, and related subjects, are adapted from those in *Esplorazioni sotto la Confessione di San Pietro in Vaticano*, 1951, by permission of the Sacra Congregazione della Reverenda Fabbrica di S. Pietro. The various renaissance plans for the basilica are reproduced from Paul Letarouilly, *La Basilique de Saint-Pierre*, 1882.

Page 12 Photo Carrieri

Page 14 Catacomb of SS Peter and Marcellinus. Photo Pont. Comm. di Arch. Sacra

Page 15 *Top left* Hypogeum of the Aurelians. Photo Clarendon Press, Oxford. *Top right* S. Apollinare Nuovo, Ravenna. Photo Mansell Alinari. *Bottom left* R. Bosch Collection, Barcelona. Photo Mas. *Bottom right* Bowes Museum, Barnard Castle, Co. Durham

Page 16 *Above* Lateran Museum. Photo Mansell Anderson. *Below* Shugborough, Staffordshire. Photo Courtauld Institute

Page 19 Photo Carrieri

Page 22 *Left* British Museum. *Right* Photo Carrieri

Page 23 *Left* Museo Capitolino. *Right* Photo Carrieri

Page 24 Photo Mansell Alinari

Page 25 *Left* Cappella Palatina, Palermo. *Right* Photo Carrieri

Page 33 Victoria and Albert Museum

Page 34 Detail from tympanum, Door of Gallus, Basle Cathedral. Photo Peter Heman

Page 36 Victoria and Albert Museum

Page 43 *Left* Vatican Library. *Top right* British Museum. *Bottom right* John Rylands Library, Manchester

Page 44 *Left* Marcus Aurelius offering sacrifice. Museo Capitolino. Photo Mansell Anderson. *Right* Vatican Museum. Photo Mansell Alinari

Page 47 *Above* Arch of Titus. Photo Mansell Alinari. *Below left* Museo Capitolino. Photo Mansell Anderson. *Below right* British Museum

Page 48 *Left* Piazza del Campidoglio. Photo Mansell Anderson. *Right* Museo dei Conservatori. Photo Mansell Alinari

Page 49 *Left* British Museum. *Right* Museo Nazionale, Naples. Photo Mansell Alinari

Page 50 *Left* Museo Nazionale, Rome. Photo Mansell Anderson. *Right* Museo Capitolino. Photo Mansell Alinari

Page 52 *Left and right* Photos Pont. Comm. di Arch. Sacra

Page 53 *Top and bottom* Photos Courtauld Institute

Page 55 Cappella Palatina, Palermo. Photo Mansell Anderson

Page 60 *Homélies de St Grégoire de Nazianze*. Bibliothèque Nationale, Paris

Page 61 SS Quattro Coronati. Photo Mansell Alinari

Page 62 Metropolitan Museum, New York. Photo Mansell Alinari

Page 65 *Left* Museo Nazionale, Naples. Photo Mansell Anderson. *Right* Based on the reconstruction in *Roma Antica* by Giuseppe Lugli and Italo Gismondi, Istituto Geografico De Agostini di Novara, 1949

Page 66 Museo della Civiltà Romana

Page 68 *Left* Photo Rev. Fabbrica di S. Pietro. *Right* Photo Carrieri

Page 69 *Left and right* Photos Rev. Fabbrica di S. Pietro

Page 78 *Left* Photo Carrieri. *Right* Reconstruction by John Platford

Page 79 *Right* Photo Mansell Anderson

Page 81 *Right* Reconstruction by Heinrich Wüscher-Becchi (1900) from a description of about 870, of a portrait in S. Andrea which has since disappeared

Pages 84-5 A. S. Barnes, *St Peter in Rome*, 1900

Page 86 By Taddeo di Bartolo. Palazzo Comunale, Siena

Page 87 *Top* Schledel, *Nuremberg Chronicle*. British Museum. Photo John Freeman. *Bottom* Padredio and Falda, *Descrizione della Chiesa di S. Pietro*, 1646. British Museum.

Photo John Freeman

Page 88 *Top and bottom* Padredio and Falda (as for 87)

Page 89 Photo Mansell Alinari

Page 91 *Top left* S. Martino ai Monti. Photo Mansell Alinari. *Top right* St Peter's crypt. Photo Mansell Alinari. *Bottom Vedute di Roma*, 1770. Victoria and Albert Museum. Photo John Freeman

Page 96 *Left* Victoria and Albert Museum. *Right* From Josephus, *Jewish Antiquities*, Bibliothèque Nationale. Photo Giraudon

Page 97 *Left* Photo A. F. Kersting. *Right* Victoria and Albert Museum

Page 99 Photo Mansell Anderson

Page 100 *Left* Photo Mansell Anderson

Page 101 *Left* Musée de Saint Germaine en Laye. *Right* Landesmuseum, Halle

Page 108 *Top* Codex Albendense. Il Escorial, Madrid. Photo Mas. *Bottom* Bibliothèque Nationale

Page 109 *Above* Mosaic from Carthage *c.* 400. British Museum. *Left* By Certosa di Pavia. Photo Mansell Brogi. *Below* Antikvarisk Topografiska Arkivet, Stockholm

Page 110 *Grands Chroniques de France.* Musée Goya. Photo Giraudon

Page 111 Louvre. Photo Mansell Giraudon

Page 112 *Left* Cavalieri, *Pontificum Romanorum Effigies*, 1580. *Right* Fresco, Umayyad period. Syrian National Museum, Damascus. Photo Larousse

Page 118 *Right* S. Clemente. Photo Mansell Alinari

Page 119 After Anthony van den Wyngaerde, 1550. Ashmolean Museum, Oxford

Page 120 Photo Mansell Anderson

Page 121 Albertina, Vienna

Page 122 Padredio and Falda (as for 87)

Page 126 *Left* Germanisches National-Museum, Nuremberg

Page 127 Chatsworth Collection. Photo Courtauld Institute

Page 129 *Left* By B. Bellano. Palazzo di Venezia. Photo Mansell Alinari. *Right* By Piero di Cosimo. Photo Radio Times Hulton Picture Library

Page 130 Photo Mansell Alinari

Page 131 *Left* Photo Mansell Alinari. *Right* Borgia Apartments, Vatican. Photo Mansell Alinari

Page 137 *Left* Uffizi, Florence. Photo Mansell Alinari. *Right* Vatican Gallery

Page 140 British Museum, Dept of Prints. Photo John Freeman

Page 141 British Museum, Dept of Prints. Photo John Freeman

Page 142 Soane Museum. Photo Courtauld Institute

Page 144 Photo Mansell Anderson

Page 145 *Left* Photo Mansell Anderson. *Right* British Museum. Photo John Freeman

Page 148 *Left* Pitti, Florence. Photo Mansell Anderson. *Right* Photo Radio Times Hulton Picture Library

Page 154 *Above left* Ashmolean Museum, Oxford

Page 155 Palazzo Vecchio, Florence. Photo Mansell Brogi

Page 156 Photo Mella

Page 157 *Left* By Sebastiano del Piombo. Pinacoteca, Parma. Photo Mansell Alinari. *Right* Etching by L. Faure-Dujarric, 1866. Victoria and Albert Museum. Photo John Freeman

Page 158 Kupferstichkabinett, Berlin

Page 159 Kupferstichkabinett, Berlin

Page 160 Palazzo della Cancelleria. Photo Mansell Alinari

Page 162 *Below* Vatican Museum. Photo Mansell Alinari

Page 164 British Museum, Dept of Prints. Photo John Freeman

Page 166 Photo Radio Times Hulton Picture Library

Page 172 *Left* Museo Nazionale, Naples. Photo Mansell Anderson. *Right* Louvre. Photo Mansell Alinari

Page 173 Photo Carrieri

Page 174 Photo Mansell Anderson

Page 177 Photo Mansell Anderson

Page 184 Photo Mansell Alinari

Page 185 Photo Mansell Anderson

Page 186 *Right* Galleria Buonarroti, Florence. Photo Mansell Brogi

Page 188 *Left* Philippo Bonanni, *Numismata Templi Vaticani*, 1696. British Museum. Photo John Freeman. *Right* British Museum. Photo John Freeman

Page 189 *Left* Victoria and Albert Museum. *Right* Photo Mansell

Page 194 *Top left* By Anonymus Fabricy. Staatsgalerie, Stuttgart. *Top right* By B. Ammanati. Kunsthalle, Hamburg. *Bottom left* Photo Carrieri

Page 195 *Top left* Photo Mansell Anderson. *Top right* Photo Carrieri. *Bottom* British Museum, Dept of Prints. Photo John Freeman

Page 197 Photo Carrieri

Page 198 *Top left* Vatican Museum. Photo Mansell Alinari. *Bottom left* The Rector, Stonyhurst College. *Top right* Victoria and Albert Museum. Photo John Freeman

Page 200 *Left* Victoria and Albert Museum. *Right* British Museum, Dept of Prints. Photos John Freeman

Page 202 British Museum, Dept of Prints. Photo John Freeman

Page 203 Photo Christie's

Page 204 *Left* Museo Civico, Bologna. Photo Mansell Alinari. *Right* Photo Carrieri

Page 205 Photo Carrieri

Page 206 After Van Aelst. British Museum, Dept of Prints. Photo John Freeman

Page 212 *Above left* By Bactiano Torrigiano. Victoria and Albert Museum. *Above right* Photo Radio Times Hulton Picture Library. *Below* Engraving by E. Dupérac, 1569. British Museum, Dept of Prints. Photo John Freeman

Page 213 Photo Carrieri

Page 214 *Above* Municipal Gallery of Modern Art, Dublin. *Below Vedute di Roma* (as for 91)

Page 216 Kupferstichkabinett, Berlin

Page 218 *Left* Domenico Fontana, *Della Trasportatione*

dell'Obelisco Vaticana, 1590. *Right* Carlo Fontana, *Il Templo Vaticano*, 1694. Photo John Freeman

Page 219 *Left and right* Carlo Fontana, *Il Templo Vaticano* (as for 218)

Page 220 (as for 219)

Page 221 Seventeenth-century fresco in the Sala Sistina of the Vatican Library. Photo Mansell Alinari

Page 223 Photo Carrieri

Page 224 Photo Carrieri

Page 230 *Left* S. Maria Maggiore. Photo Mansell Alinari. *Right* From a sketch by E. F. Payne in *Rome and its Scenery*

Page 233 Collection F. Lugt, Institut Neerlandais, Paris

Page 237 Engraving by de Rossi, 1703. British Museum, Dept of Prints. Photo John Freeman

Page 238 Collection J. Lees-Milne. Photo Courtauld Institute

Page 240 *Above* British Museum. Photo John Freeman. *Below* Photo A. F. Kersting

Page 241 *Left* Philippo Bonanni, *Numismata* . . . (as for 188). *Right* Lord Methuen, Corsham Collection

Page 242 Bethnal Green Museum, by courtesy of the Victoria and Albert Museum. Photo Derrick Witty

Page 243 *Below* Bethnal Green Museum (as for 242). *Above left and right* Photos Carrieri

Page 249 *Left* By Giovanni Giavanni Giannelli. Palazzo Barberini. Photo Mansell Alinari. *Right* Self portrait. Galleria Borghese. Photo Mansell Anderson

Page 252 *Left* British Museum. Photo John Freeman. *Right* Photo Carrieri

Page 253 *Left and right* Photos Mansell Alinari

Page 258 *Left and right* Photos Carrieri

Page 259 *Left and right* Carlo Fontana (as for 218)

Page 260 *Left* Photo Mansell Brogi. *Right* Photo Mansell Alinari

Page 262 *Left* Palazzo Doria. Photo Mansell Alinari. *Right* Photo Mansell Alinari

Page 263 *Left* Photo Mansell Alinari. *Right* Photo Carrieri

Page 268 *Left and right* Photos Carrieri

Page 269 *Left* Photo Mansell Alinari. *Right* Philippo Bonanni, *Numismata* . . . (as for 188)

Page 270 *Left Chronologia Summorum Romanorum Pontificum*, 1831. Victoria and Albert Museum. Photo John Freeman. *Above* British Museum. Photo John Freeman

Page 271 Photo Carrieri

Page 272 *Vedute di Roma* (as for 91)

Page 273 Photo Carrieri

Page 274 *Left and right* Photos Carrieri

Page 275 Photo Carrieri

Page 276 *Left and right* Photos Carrieri

Page 277 British Museum, Dept of Prints. Photo John Freeman

Page 278 *Left* A. S. Barnes (as for 84–5). *Right* Photo Mansell Alinari

Page 281 *Left* Photo Carrieri. *Right* Photo Mansell Alinari

Page 286 *Left and right* Photos Carrieri

Page 287 *Left* Photo Mansell Anderson. *Right* Photo Carrieri

Page 288 *Left and right* Photos Carrieri

Page 289 *Left Chronologia* . . . (as for 270). *Right* Photo Mansell Alinari

Page 291 Bethnal Green Museum (as for 242)

Page 298 *Left* Photo Carrieri. *Right* Photo Mansell Alinari

Page 299 *Left Chronologia* . . . (as for 270). *Right* Photo Carrieri

Page 302 *Left and right* Photos Mansell Alinari

Page 304 *Left and right* Photos Carrieri

Page 305 *Left and right* Photos Carrieri

Page 308 Photo Carrieri

Page 311 Photo Carrieri

Page 312 *Left and right* Photos Mansell Anderson

Page 315 *Left and right* Photos Mansell Alinari

Page 316 *Left and right The Illustrated London News*, December 1869. Photos Mansell

Page 317 *Left* Casa Mastai, Senigallia. Photo Mansell Alinari. *Right* Photo Carrieri

Page 318 Photo Carrieri

Page 319 *Left* Photo Mansell Anderson. *Right* Photo Carrieri

Page 320 *Above* Photo Mansell Alinari. *Below* Photo A. F. Kersting

Page 324 *Above left* Photo Carrieri. *Below left* Photo A. Cartoni. *Above right* Photo Carrieri. *Below right* Photo Associated Press

Page 326 Photo Associated Press

Endpapers Engraving by Giuseppe Vasi, 1774. British Museum, Dept of Prints. Photo John Freeman

Index

This index covers the architectural aspects of St Peter's and ancillary subjects. 'St Peter's' is not used as a heading except for the plan of the building as it is today; there are separate headings for the different parts of the basilica. References to illustrations are indicated by *italic* numerals.